We've Come This Far
By Faith

Carrie Ayers Haynes

Published by
Three S Management Publications
1205 W. 80th Street
Los Angeles, California 90044
1-213-752-0663

Printed in the U.S.A

First Printing, 1975
Second Printing Extended Edition, 1986

Library of Congress Cataloging in Publication Data

Foreword

Large numbers of educators have struggled and failed to achieve excellent educational outcomes for Black, inner-city youth in America's public schools. Test scores for Black students while showing some recent improvements, still lag significantly behind the scores of their White contemporaries. One option is to look at these schools and join the chorus of doom and gloomers, while a second option is to read about the success like that described in Good News On Grape Street.

Grape Street Elementary School was, when Carrie Haynes arrived a prototype inner-city elementary with all of the negative influences in the environment that one can imagine. What happened at Grape Street School is nothing short of a miracle. A committed , caring and dedicated leader, used all of her talents and skills to convince a school staff to buy her dream of helping the students at Grape Street to achieve academic success.

Carrie Ayers Haynes, as Grape Street's principal, served as the consummate instructional leader, community organizer, counselor aide and any other role that would help the youngers, in her care, to want to learn. She drove hereself very hard on behalf of her students and demanded that all others in her environment do the same. Her simple philosophy, was that all children can learn if they are taught by caring teachers. She believed and demonstrated that high expectations and skilled, motivated teachers produce results.

While Ms. Haynes cared about her students, she knew that love alone was not enough. She combined the perfect blend of affective and cognitive techniques to ensure that students were respected, respectful and educated. Her educational processes included the members of her staff as constant learners, also. The weekly staff development activities were designed to build leadership skills and foster collaboration. The efforts of this outstanding principal to develop an excellent school staff, build an effective parent and community network and infect students with a desire to learn, truly serve to make for Good News On Grape Street School. Most importantly what happened at Grape Street stands as testimony to what can and should be continuously replicated in inner-city schools all over this country.

Raymond Terrell, Ph.D.
Dean of the School of Education
California State University of Los Angeles
June 1, 1986

I

About This Extended Edition

FROM THE AUTHOR

This is a book describing how deeply concerned teachers can be highly successful with all types of Black and other similarly-situated minority students. The first edition of GOOD NEWS ON GRAPE STREET: The Transformation of a Ghetto School was published by Citation Press, New York, 1975. Publicity and book reviews acclaimed the inner city school's success in *Newsweek, Christian Science Monitor, The Booklist,* (American Library Association), *Learning, The National BLACK MONITOR, Educational Leadership, Los Angeles Times,* syndicated newspapers across the country, PBS, national and local television and other national and local media. University and college classes studying conditions in inner city schools have used it as a text as well as for research and reference.

Because many relevant points which have significance to what is occurring on the educational scene today happened after the book ended, I have chosen to write an Extended Edition. This updated version, including the appendices, bring the dramatic narrative through my remaining years at Grape Street and beyond. The three years I spent as Administrative Consultant in the Area B office, my retirement in 1980, my service as Management Consultant for the Council of Black Administrators and my almost total involvement in the national Assault On Illiteracy Program (AOIP) are covered.

It is my very good fortune to have many friends, to whom I trust I am giving proper credit. These are those who introduced, commented, summarized and validated the story, the concepts, the principles and the need to choose from the proven-to-be successful approach those items which could be adapted for their own use and the replication by others.

The statistics about the ever-increasing number (particularly in our Black population) who can be identified as "functionally illiterate" is appalling. It is this actuality that has brought together nearly 90 Black-led national organizations into a networking coalition called the Assault On Illiteracy Program (AOIP). The national co-chairs are Faye Bryant, Supreme Basileus, Alpha Kappa Alpha Sorority, Inc. and Earl Gray, Imperial Potentate of the Ancient Egyptian Arabic Order Nobles Mystic Shrine (Shriners) of Prince Hall affiliation.

A major tribute was made to the efficacy and proven-to-be successful ego-strengthening approach described in this book when AOIP both developed all of the materials based on these community-building (or "affective-oriented") concepts and named this writer the "Mother of AOIP." One of these weekly fun-to-learn instruments is the *Who Am I*

Guide To Learning, which is designed to assist teachers and/or tutors with total non-readers. Another is *The ADVANCER* which is for persons reading below the 5th grade level. Most important about both of these tools is that any person reading at fifth grade level or above can both tutor and enhance their own reading skills.

This Extended Edition acquaints you with that extremely productive and continuing involvement in AOIP. It also invites you to join in with AOIP in enabling the success-producing lessons learned from GOOD NEWS ON GRAPE STREET to be spread throughout the land.

The Council of Black Administrators, the Advisory Council on Black Affairs to California State School Superintendent Bill Honig, the National Association of University Women, Delta Sigma Theta Sorority, Inc., The National Sorority of Phi Delta Kappa, Inc., and all the other national and local organizations to which I belong are making a broad based statement of assurance to you and all others concerned about the literacy-enhancement of *all* Americans by their becoming actively involved in the business of the Assault On Illiteracy Programs (AOIP) which is focused on the unique and....until now....unmet needs of many of our minorities.

ACKNOWLEDGMENTS — 1975

For the success Grape Street School has had or is attaining, recognition must be given and appreciation expressed to the following Los Angeles City School personnel who, each with his or her own enormnous responsibilities, has provided me patient understanding, unwavering faith and unequivocal support:

Dr. Robert L. Doctor, Board Member, Los Angeles City Schools
Dr. William J. Johnston, Superintendent, Los Angeles City Schools
James B. Taylor, Deputy Superintendent, Los Angeles City Schools
John F. Leon, Associate Deputy Superintendent, Los Angeles City Schools
Dr. Josie G. Bain, Superintendent, Area D
Mildred Naslund, Superintendent, Area A
Richard H. Lawrence, Superintendent, Area J
Dr. Sidney Brickman, Superintendent, Area B
Dr. George T. Edmiston, Deputy Superintendent, Area B

For loyalty, friendship, and typing the first draft of the manuscript:
Naomi Gilbert, Office Manager, Grape Street School

For sustained support of Grape Street School and its program, I am grateful to the following School-Community Advisory charter members who have been active and attended regularly throughout my first five years as principal:
Rev. W. J. Broussard, 1969-1973, Past Chairperson
Rev. P. J. Jones, 1969-1973, First Vice-President
Rev. Milton Marshall, 1969-1973, Second Vice-President
Mary Baker, 1969-1973, Recording Secretary
Luella Burton, 1969-1973, Corresponding Secretary
Addalyne Benford, 1973-1975, Chairperson
Willia Moore, 1969-1973, Hostess
Lillie Smith, 1969-1973, Hostess
Davetta Austin, 1969-1974, Member
Mollie Ashton, 1969-1974, Member
Alecia Jackson, 1969-1974, Member
Inez Henderson, 1971-1972, Past PTA President
Thelmarie Gray, 1972-1973, Past PTA President
Helen Teate, 1973-1975, Past PTA President

In loving memory of a great, dedicated, and devoted lady who bequeathed to us the spirit she portrayed and acclaimed, "Grape is Great!" --Margarette Broussard, 1969-1971, Past PTA President and School Mother.   *C.A.H.*

ACKNOWLEDGMENTS — 1986

To those leaders in the Los Angeles Unified School District who relate to or are members of the Council of Black Administrators who continue striving to bring about positive change, particularly for Black children:

Mrs. Rita Walters, President, Board of Education, LAUSD
Dr. Harry Handler, Superintendent, LAUSD
Dr. Sidney Thompson, Deputy Superintendent, School Operations, LAUSD
Dr. Theodore Alexander, Assistant Superintendent, Student Integration Options, LAUSD
Dr. Floraline Stevens, Director Research and Evaluation, LAUSD
Mrs. Pauline Hooper, Associate Superintendent, Office of Compliance, LAUSD
Dr. Robert Martin, Assistant Superintendent, Region C, LAUSD
Dr. Alfred Moore, Assistant Superintendent, Region D, LAUSD
Dr. Owen Knox, Assistant Superintendent, Personnel Review, LAUSD
Dr. Harriette Williams, Administrator, Operations Sr. High Schools Director, LAUSD
Mr. George McKenna III, President, Council of Black Administrators Principal, Washington Preparatory High School, LAUSD
U.S. Congressman Augustus Hawkins, Chair, House Education and Labor Committee
Mr. John Smith, Special Assistant to Congressman Hawkins

A very special and deep appreciation goes to those who have conceived, given leadership, promotion and support to the Assault On Illiteracy Program, nationally and locally:

Dr. Benjamin H. Wright, Volunteer Executive Director, AOIP
Dr. Calvin Rolark, Chairman, The BMI Cooperative
Ms. Emille Smith, National Coordinator, AOIP
Ms. Jeanne Jason, Executive Editor, National BLACK MONITOR
Dr. Betty Mansfield, Project Director, The ADVANCER
Mrs. Winnie Palmer and The National Sorority of Phi Delta Kappa, Professional Education Committee Co-chair

Mrs. Hortense Canady, National President, Delta Sigma Theta Sorority, Inc.
Dr. Carolyn Minor, Chair, West Region, Interorganizational Liaison Committee, AOIP
Mrs. Marguerite La Motte, President Los Angeles County Division, AOIP
Mr. Freddie St. Cyr, Vice-President, Los Angeles County Division, AOIP
Mrs. Lucille Bland, Co-Chair, War Chest Committee, LCD, AOIP
All of the other 90 national presidents, their members and the BMI Cooperative Newspapers.

C.A.H.

The second writing of this book is dedicated to the members of my family who have provided me love, support, friendship and encouragement to continue to carry on the giving of vitally needed services to humanity.

Sallye Chapple - No. 1 Daughter
Carolyn Minor, Ed.D - No. 2 Daughter
Thelma Minor - No. 3 Daughter
David Minor - No. 1 and Only Son
Lucious Minor - (Deceased Husband)

Theodore Haynes-Husband
Gus Chapple-Son-in-Law
Phyllis Minor-Daughter-in-Law

April Chapple - No. 1 Granddaughter
Michael Minor - No. 1 Grandson
Daniel Chapple - No. 2 Grandson
Rachel Chapple - No. 2 Granddaughter
Melody Minor - No. 3 Granddaughter
Lorene Davis - Very Best Friend

DAVID AYERS and CARRIE BRATTON AYERS

In Loving Memory
Of
My Father and Mother
The Roots Of It All

In deep appreciation to my sister, Thelma Ayers Hardiman and her usband, Dr. Winton J. Hardiman who gave me this picture for my Christmas present. With love to my brothers, David Ayers, Lawrence E. Ayers, my nephew, Lawrence Ayers, II, my nieces, Catherine Ayers, Joye Hardiman nd to our martriarch Aunt Leona Bratton Donald, who was 92, July 19, 986.

COMMENTARY

How You Can Be Helped In Specific Ways

A Personal View

by
Ben L. Gieringer
President Synergistic Educational Systems, Inc.

In the past seven years Carrie Haynes and I have conducted thousands of training sessions with administrators, teachers and parents. We have worked side by side and, as a result I have seen her live and manage herself by the ideas and strategies contained in this book.

Good News on Grape Street, "The Transformation of a Ghetto School" is a story that dramatically depicts the change within a school that seemed somewhat unbelievable but actually happened. And this transformation is brought to you through the eyes and perspective of the person who was responsible for providing the leadership which produced the ultimate student academic success at Grape Street School. The school which is located in the heart of Watts, was a most unlikely place in the early 1970's for a transformation like this to happen.

The question one might ask is why and how did this happen. It is my purpose in this commentary to help you to see the why and the how.

Carrie in writing this book wrote a novel, a drama that you can almost live through with her. The essence of what Carrie did may not be revealed to you unless you reread and reflect upon what she is communicating. It is my intent to summarize some of the key concepts and strategies Carrie used to produce the ultimate academic success at Grape Street School.

By keeping these concepts and strategies in mind as you read, you will be able to see how this educator made practical application of these in her leadership as she confronted the situations and obstacles in her path.

While reading this event-filled narrative wherein this school principal faced so many obstacles, some may be inclined to say that only Carrie Haynes could bring about this kind of success. I know this not to be true, because many educators...perhaps on a smaller scale than that of Grape Street...have had success. Thus as you read, it is instructive to look at Carrie simply as a model and symbol of many other like-minded and equally successful educators, from whom others may learn..and who in their own unique ways, may put into practice the key concepts and processes she, also, used at *Grape Street* on a large and highly visible scale.

What Carrie did at Grape can be replicated by others who will extract the essence of what she did and then build this into their leadership and management modus operandus.

CARRIE HAYNES: PERSONAL LEADERSHIP AND SELF—GOVERNMENT

Do you want to be a person who makes a difference, who leads and influences others positively, who works with others to make things happen? If you will study the contents of this book for its meanings and applications, you will discover ways to put into practice the principles and processes found through the use of your own uniqueness, talents and leadership.

Success in any endeavor or enterprise is based upon one's own leadership and self-management. As you read you will see Carrie's character and leadership in action. There are several characteristics and attitudes she displayed that were essential to her leadership success at Grape Street School. Among these are (1) clarity and fixity of purposes and goals - Carrie knew what she wanted to have happen. (2) an inner determination to succeed no matter what the obstacles or roadblocks, no matter what negative attitudes or roadblocks were placed by others in her path. (3) a deep commitment to the purposes and goals she had established at Grape Street School - the success of each student at Grape. (4) a confidence and belief in her ability to lead and succeed. (5) A persistence, a never-say-die attitude, that kept her going when things looked impossible, a habit and an attitude that kept her on track when others were trying to deter her. (6) Carrie kept a perspective on the current situation or problems because she knew her goals and worked through these predicaments to move in the direction she wanted to go and did not allow herself to become discou—raged. She knew that through her persistence and sense of right timing she would ultimately succeed. And, (7) this is one that may not be so obvious to you from your reading, but it is the motivation and foundation to Carrie's leadership. This is her deep biblical faith, her belief in God and the habit of prayer which is the source of the strength which governs and directs her life.

Leadership requires character and self-government which Carrie demonstrated throughout the transformation of Grape Street School.

PRINCIPLES, CONCEPTS AND STRATEGIES CARRIE HAYNES USED AT GRAPE STREET SCHOOL

The following ideas and comments are drawn from the content of this book to see how Carrie applied these leadership principles and strategies to particular situations to obtain the success she accomplished at Grape Street School.

1. She gained direct and personal knowledge of the way things were in the classroom of some schools in contrast to what was claimed by some. She became known as "the walking principal." She learned each of her teacher's habits, methods, strengths and weaknesses. This provided her with the knowledge she needed in order to begin to work with the teachers individually and as a faculty.

2. She recognized the present internal dynamics of the faculty and the conflict of authority and power between certain members and the principal (each teacher acting independently doing whatever each wanted to do). She knew this had to be resolved and began working to bring about a change so that there was harmony and a unity of purpose and goals. She began to work to establish the necessity for leadership authority and power to emanate from the principal.

3. She was constantly encouraging each teacher to take the initiative and responsibility for his leadership and success through the use of his own uniqueness, potential and talents. She worked patiently with each teacher gently nudging, recognizing and encouraging his individual efforts. Carrie wanted each teacher to be responsible for his success with the students through his own initiative and leadership action.

4. Good teaching to Carrie meant (1) preparation, (2) imparting knowledge and basic skills in ways relevant to the learner, (3) motivation, (4) involvement of the student, and (5) warm student-teacher relationships.

5. Carrie had uppermost in her mind her goals and what her purposes were in being a principal. These purposes and goals became the criteria by which she made decisions and provided leadership.

6. She worked continously to find ways to communicate with and stimulate teachers to purposeful, productive action.

7. Carrie recognized that the parents are the first and most important teachers in the lives of their children and she worked with her staff to find ways to involve them intricately in the education of their children at school and at home.

8. She operated on the principle that if results were not being produced you don't continue doing things that fail. But what you do is stop, step out courageously, reevaluate and look for new ways to accomplish your goal.

9. Carrie worked with teachers both on an individual and group basis and patiently waited for leadership to merge from each individual. Carrie nurtured this leadership development with each teacher by giving ideas, encouragement and opportunities for its use. She kept a perspective on this process giving time for the leadership to develop in its own unique way with each individual.

10. She found ways to praise and recognize the best work and achievement of individuals, (teachers, students, aides, secretaries, custodians. cafeteria workers, etc.).

11. She encouraged each teacher to share their successes with others.

12. Carrie encouraged each teacher to use her uniqueness and talents in appropriate and acceptable ways to achieve success with each student.

13. She found ways to demonstrate and model for teachers the best and highest quality of work being done in the classroom.

14. Carrie built an inner core of staff who identified with her and who worked with her cooperatively with dedication and commitment in support of her efforts. Then, she delegated to each of them meaningful and purposeful goals to achieve.

15. She was aware constantly of each person's uniqueness, motivation, talents and abilities and helped them to find ways to put them to productive use in the school.

16. Carrie had (and still has) a deep conviction that each student can learn and can succeed regardless of the past or present situation. She believed there was a way to help each child succeed beginning with today. This positive expectancy of success was transmitted eventually to each teacher and to each student.

17. Carrie believed that each classroom had to have order and purposeful, quiet activity. If achievement was to happen each student had to be goal-directed, personally motivated, positively oriented and responsible for wise use of time. The students were expected to demonstrate self-management and self-government in their learning activities. Each student was taught to be personally involved in his/her own learning.

18. In Carrie's mind the ideal teacher was a self-motivated, self-directed person who was involved in sharing, helping and contributing to the success of others on the staff and who had a dedication and commitment to doing his/her best in teaching and who showed in daily action a concern and care for each child.

19. Once a commitment was made either individually or as a group at Grape Street School each person became personally responsible for appropriately carrying out this commitment through his/her leadership. Commitments made by individuals and the staff through Carrie's leadership brought about the unity of purpose and action, the harmony, determination, persistence and work which eventually led to Grape Street Schools success.

20. Carrie focused everyone's attention on the productivity of the student-was he working and producing results? Did he Know what he was learning? Did he know why he was learning it? Did he know how it would benefit him now and in the future? Was he achieving goals on a daily basis? was he learning what was expected? If the student was not learning, she expected the teacher to find a way to change this by working with the student to bring about his personal responsibility and action for his learning and success.

21. Carrie set aside time each week for the teachers to dialogue and share with each other on how to achieve success with each student: dis-

cussing, studying and planning together ways to make the classroom work for the success of each student.

22. As a principal she learned to take constructive criticism in stride, assess it and use what was valuable feedback to her in being more effective in her leadership and management. She was not defensive or overly concerned with the negative aspects of criticism. When one is a self-governing person one can effectively handle criticism and make it productive.

23. She found ways as a principal to structure time each week into the schedule for teacher sharing sessions and structured staff training sessions. These two activities she kept purposeful, relevant and goal directed drawing upon the talents, abilities and motivation of her teachers to provide leadership. This weekly sharing and training increased the productivity of each individual and the staff as a whole. These activities helped to unify the staff and to bring about the desired success in the school in the shortest possible time. They helped to develop from within the internal, positive leadership necessary for the success Carrie wanted for each student at the school.

24. Out of the staff sharing and training sessions, plans of action were developed by individuals and groups. These plans were then implemented by the teachers to solve the problems and overcome the obstacles and roadblocks to student achievement and success at Grape Street School.

25. One of the most important strategies used by Carrie in working with others was to find out where each teacher was in his interests, talents, abilities, knowledge, motivation and skills and then to begin to work with him from where he was and then to take him where he needed to be in order to teach most effectively. When Carrie arrived at Grape Street Street School, you will see that the students had little or no motivation, interest or desire to learn. As you read what Carrie wrote, keep in mind this problem and see how she brings about change. Once she obtained the right kind of interest and motivation by the students, the staff had to devote more time to the content to be taught. Keep in mind this principle as Carrie works with the individual teachers and the staff as a whole.

26. Carrie looked for what was best of what was happening in the classroom. She recognized it and then found ways to share it with others.

27. Carrie is now 68 years old. She is still learning and setting new goals. She still is constantly seeking knowledge, ideas, and methods which can be put into practice in the classroom. A characteristic of a leader in education which is a must is that of goal setting. A teacher or a principal models best by setting and achieving challenging goals in every area of his life.

28. She recognized that each person had something to contribute and looked for ways each individual teacher and staff member could recognize that he was contributing to the overall success of the school. Each staff member felt that if he did not make his particular contribution a void would be left in the accomplishment of success.

29. Carrie worked to help each teacher find ways to make content-knowledge relevant to the child's present level of knowledge and experience. She wanted each child to know the meaning and the value of what he is learning and to be able to relate it to his life.

30. She wanted the teachers to involve the child in short and long range projects in order to teach him how to set goals and work to achieve them on a daily basis.

31. She helped teachers learn to structure the classroom into an environment that was rich in content, orderly and calm, and one that had purpose and goals to guide its activities. The teacher was given the responsibility for their learning and success and were held personally accountable for their achievement. The teacher was responsible for instructing, disciplining and directing the student so that the student had direction and purpose to his learning.

32. The teacher was responsible for integrating the subjects so that they were not taught in isolation from each other.

33. Carrie's aim was to develop self-governing learners who had mastery of the basic skills. She had her teachers teach intensive phonics integrated with language development experiences and found ways to make math meaningful and logical to the students through practical applications and experiences. She wanted for her students not to be dependent upon others for their learning but to have the necessary skills to learn and gain knowledge on their own.

34. The staff found ways to use the parent conference to intricately involve the parents in the teaching-learning process. Students achieve when parents keep the primary responsibility for educating their own children.

35. Carrie recognized that each community is unique and that it must develop its school along its own course. She believes that the parents and teachers must draw upon their own potential and talents to develop the school to met the particular needs of the parents and students of the community. Carrie recognized that if the school were to succeed, the leadership must come from within the school with the participation and cooperation of the parents. She believed that no one has a greater concern for the success of its students than the parents and teachers of the school. She operated on the belief that the school that develops its leadership from within the school and its community is the one that will ultimately succeed.

36. Carrie realized as the principal of Grape Street School that she was responsible for weeding out and selecting teachers and for developing the staff into a cohesive, harmonious and goal-directed group. She selected her teachers and staff carefully looking for individuals who were self-governing, who had purpose and direction in their lives, who had confidence and determination built into their character and who were willing to share and participate cooperatively with her and the staff. It

took Carrie three years to develop and stabilize the Grape Street School staff into a cohesive, harmonious and productive unit. A principal cannot succeed in meeting the purposes of the school unless the staff is cohesive and together in its leadership and management.

37. Carrie involved, involved, involved her teachers in problem-solving, goal setting and planning through the weekly sharing and training sessions. As plans developed, she delegated authority and responsibility to individuals and groups for carrying out these solutions.

38. Carrie found that multi-age classrooms encouraged personalization of learning with the individual student and provided stability and continuity to the students progress from one year to the next and contributed greatly to the students continuous progress and success.

39. Open education meant to Carrie: direction, structure, organization, involvement, order and purposeful activity.

40. Carrie brought the school staff in for 1 or 2 weeks or longer if necessary before school started for staff training, sharing, planning and organizing for the new school year. During the school year she continued this process through weekly sharing and weekly training sessions.

41. She had teachers evaluate individually, each year, every aspect of the school operation and then she responded to each teacher personally and applied those suggestions and ideas which were most needed to make the school work for the parents and students of Grape.

42. Carrie made the office the place where achievement was recognized and where students received positive support and encouragement for their leadership and success.

Undoubtedly, as you read through this book you will find more ideas you can use. Enjoy reading this book but keep in mind that what Carrie did in the 1970's is still what needs to be done today in our schools through the leadership of the principal.

The Unusual Life That Led to the Writing of
"GOOD NEWS ON GRAPE STREET"

SCHOOLING EARLY

During my lifetime of educational experiences I have found that too many elementary students, especially Black children, are being denied a sound foundation of basic academic skills. I count myself among those who were fortunate.

When I was three years old my mother was asked to come to substitute at Le Moyne Grammar School which was located one hundred yards from the home in which I was born in Memphis, Tennessee. She qualified for this assignment because she had completed the eleventh grade at the Tougaloo High School in Mississippi some years before. Her education terminated at this point because a tornado destroyed their home on my grandfather's farm.

The above, along with others throughout the South, were sister schools which were established by the American Missionary Association sponsored by the Congregational Church. Most of the teachers were unmarried women, six White and one Black. Because I was large for my age, it was agreed that I could attend the kindergarten class during the time that my mother substituted in a second-grade class from the third week of September until the end of December. Thus my formal educational life began. I adjusted and by the time my mother's interim assignment was completed I was an accepted class member.

EARLY SCHOOL ENVIRONMENT

Very vividly I can recall the activities and involvement in my kindergarten, first, second and third grade classes. There were never more than twenty-five students in a room. The environment was alive, cheerful, and meaningful. The teachers brought materials. Parents brought materials. Students brought materials. We were taught to read. We were taught to write. We were taught to solve problems. We went out in groups to find four-leaf clovers and classify the grasses on our campus.

We dressed in rain clothes, walked in the rain, and returned to study the water cycle. We held pieces of black cloth to catch the falling snowflakes, enjoy, and study the intricate artistic patterns. We made ice cream from snow, hot chocolate and from the canned condensed milk we brought from home. Reading recipes, cooking, and serving were fun. We watched and interviewed the telephone-pole climber as we did other workers who came to or near our school grounds.

We planted, cared for, cooked, canned and ate vegetables and fruits. We got a very vivid concept of a waterfall when our second-grade teacher took us out after a torrid downpour to observe a flow of water rushing over a mound. We were taught phonetic and structural analysis, as well as being taught to read for comprehension.

Penmanship was taught in cursive. Everyone of my primary teachers exhibited exemplary handwriting. But Corinne Wilder, my Black third-grade teacher, displayed a handwriting that could only be labelled calligraphy. I enjoyed going to school. I enjoyed learning. So did my classmates. There is no recall in my mind of truancies from these classes.

EARLY TRAGEDIES

My father had been robbed and shot in his grocery store several years before he married my mother. His health was on a slow decline. Because he felt I had received a good primary education and because his finances were becoming a little more questionable, he decided that I should enroll in public school in the fourth grade. I did and was totally lost in a class of forty-two. There was a fire drill on the fourth day of school. I moved out with the other mass of humanity to form a straight line with my class on the sidewalk in front of the large brick elementary school building. I was awed. Children and teachers seemed to be everywhere separated by a three or four-yard distance between each class.

Suddenly, my classroom teacher, I shall never forget her name, tapped me on the shoulder and reprimanded, "Stop your talking. You'll get a swat in your hand when we get back to the room." I was astonished. I hadn't opened my mouth. I didn't know one other student in the class. I had just followed whatever was being done. I was bewildered. When we were all returned and packed in our seats, she remembered. "You, the tall girl in the back seat, come up to the front of class." I walked up shivering. "Hold out your hand." I did. "This is to remind you not to talk when we have a fire drill." She gave me a lick. It wasn't that hard, but I was humiliated and that lick colored all my future attitudes about the administration of corporal punishment.

I didn't want to return to that school and I made that very clear to my mother. On Friday she came for a conference with the principal. On Monday he sent for me to come to his office. Personally, he diagnosed my capabilities. I read through the fourth-grade texts, I read through the fifth-grade texts, I read through the sixth-grade texts. I solved all the arithmetic problems he gave me on those levels. And, I spelled the words he called out correctly. His conclusion was that I was on the seventh-grade instructional level and I was seven years old. I have distinct recall of having him take me into a seventh-grade class announcing, "Here is a young lady who may not look like a peach, but she has the brains to take her wherever she wants to go." I am not sure how the decision was made, but the next week I was back in my fourth-grade class where I belonged at the Le Moyne Grammar School.

I was eleven years old on September the 9th, when I arrived for my first day in the ninth grade and was summoned to return home at 9:00 a.m. because my father had died a few minutes after I left home. My mother became bedridden after his interment. So it became necessary for me to take over the management of our grocery store and rentals. Remaining out of school for a month, with some adult and relative assistance, I arranged to send my mother to recuperate at her father's farm in Mississippi, employed help for our business and assisted in getting our family members situated. I returned to catch up and complete my high-school education between Le Moyne and Tougaloo High Schools in Memphis, Tennessee and Tougaloo, Mississippi.

EARLY ROLE MODELS

During our high school and college years, we listened daily to the classics and symphonies of Bach, Beethoven, Mozart, Mendolson, and Tchaikovsky and others as a daily routine. I shall remember always sitting in a small group listening and asking questions of George Washington Carver about all of the products he made from the peanut and had on display for us.

Marion Anderson's once-in-a-lifetime beautiful contralto voice still reverberates in my ears as I recall her singing Ava Maria in the Memphis Civic Center Auditorium. Our school had attended as a group and my mother accompanied me backstage to meet her.

My preference for wearing red and my decision to become a writer some day stems from the day I sat among a small group in our school auditorium, literally at the feet of Langston Hughes, and listened to him recite to us, among others of his poetry, The Little Brown Girl in the Red Dress.

Meeting Mary McLeod Bethune in person made me feel that I was in the presence of a saint clothed in ordinary apparel. What an inspiration, role model and legend she remains for so many of us Black women.

The night I thrilled from the reverberating voice and saw Paul Robeson playing *OTHELLO* instilled me with an invigorating pride in my heritage. Meeting and getting to speak with him personally on two different occasions made me feel I knew this multi-talented Black man who was born so many years before his time.

There were other, local and national Black men and women to whom we were exposed as a part of our educational program. To my parents who gave me a solid foundation for living, my teachers, and to each of these great people, those mentioned and many others not mentioned, I shall be grateful eternally for helping to guide and shape my personality, my characteristics and the focus of my life.

Both of these institutions grew and expanded so that I was able to enroll and complete my bachelor of arts in English, Magna Cum Laude, at Le Moyne College. My English professor and advisor, Dr. Hugh Gloster, is presently president of Morehouse College in Atlanta, Georgia. I had good teachers and instructors throughout my educational life. Teachers make a difference in the lives of their students. The difference may be good, bad, or negligible.

MY FAMILY

My own four children received a good basic academic education. They had good teachers in the primary grades. Then I suffered through the agony of observing classroom conditions deteriorate in the neighborhood schools of each of my four grandchildren. Fortunately, each had a good kindergarten teacher. After kindergarten their parents began to send them to private schools.

The oldest grandchild, April Chapple, bornDecember 21st, on my birthday, received a four year volley ball scholarship at the University of Tennessee in Knoxville and at this writing is playing professional volley-ball in Milan, Italy and is learning to speak Italian fluently. Michael Minor has completed his college work at De Vry Institute in Arizona with a major in Engineering and is now employed in his field. Daniel Chapple is a sophmore at El Camino Junior College and works part time on a school play ground. Rachel Chapple is a junior and an honor student at St. Bernard's High School. My youngest Melody Moon Minor, a two year old has begun her education at a special school, Dominguez Hills Development Center for the Handicapped. This beautiful little jewel brings a special radiance into the lives of our family as she responds to the endearing love, care, and nurturing being showered upon her by my son and daughter-in-law.

BEGINNING TO TEACH

My teaching career began in Buffalo, New York where I taught a first grade class for four years. I came to Los Angeles in 1950 and began teaching first grade at Compton Avenue Elementary School for Los Angeles City Unified Schools in 1952. I became a member of a staff that was dedicated and committed to teaching boys and girls. It was an accepted fact that teachers cared, planned, and implemented a sound educational program on that staff.

Teachers arrived on time, performed yard duty, lunch-bench duty, walked students to their areas, to the gates, and taught the basic concepts, skills, and processes as prescribed by the Course of Study. I was never aware of a clock-watcher during my five years of service there. The Head Custodian frequently reminded us to leave before six because he locked the gates at that time. One afternoon one of our little roly-poly White EMR class teachers worked past this hour. She told the joke on herself that it was necessary to climb the six-foot wire fence to get out to her car.

MY ETHNIC GROUP EXPERIENCES

In 1957 I went to teach largely Mexican-American children at Eastman Street for two years. This was a large well-organized school. Transiency was a major concern. As soon as a teacher became acquainted with many of the students they would transfer away.

I returned to teach Black children at the 118th Street School in 1959 as the only permanent primary teacher on the staff. All of the others were either substitute or probationary teachers. Those few among the group who had passed the teachers examination were looked upon as prodigious. There was as much concern about status as there was about teaching. There were gross misconceptions about the teaching role. One day a teacher explained in a grade-level meeting, "When our principal comes to visit if he hears the beginning of a sentence in my room, he will expect to hear the end of it in your room next door." She was serious. She was desirious of planning and implementing so that all would be "together" for the principal's visitation. I knew better. I had worked with this principal before. But this teacher looked upon me as an intruder and I found it difficult to allay her concerns.

To round out my ethnic background of experiences I was assigned as a training teacher to teach lower to middle socio-economic White children at Catskill Avenue Elementary School in 1959. Because I wanted to broaden my experiences, each year I was given the opportunity to teach a different grade level. Each time I made a change, Black men were summoned to move my instructional materials. The fourth time this happened one confided in me, "Teacher, I don't think they want you here the way they keep moving you around. Pretty soon, they'll be moving you out of this school."

BECOMING A SUPERVISOR

Two weeks before the Watts Riots in 1965 I placed number thirteen on the vice-principal's eligibility list. In the spring of 1966 I moved out to become the vice-principal of 111th Street Elementary School. The teaching staff there welcomed my efforts to upgrade the educational program. Many dedicated and committed teachers were on the scene planning and providing interesting and challenging studies for the boys and girls. This was also the year that many "talent search" teachers were being employed. These were teachers who had received a bachelor of arts degree in anything other than education. Naturally, some of them would be persons with potential. Also naturally, many of them were persons who had failed in their intended fields and were looking for work.

Because the principals of the area had committed themselves to developing some racial or ethnic balance on their staffs, most of the "talent search" teachers were White. Teacher advisors were employed and assigned to provide direction and guidance to these new employees. One Hundred and Eleventh Street received its fair share of this group. School pride and peer pressure aided me and the teacher advisors to help most of this new personnel to "shape up" or "ship out" of this environment. Staff concern for the children was paramount and parental support was solid.

BROADENING MY EXPERIENCE

To gain a different experience on the administrative level I was assigned to 95th Street Elementary School as a second vice-principal for the fall 1968-69 semester. This was a large institution. Upgrading the curriculum of the primary grades was my responsibility. The capacity and concern of this almost unwieldly staff ran the gamut. Some came to teach, some came to kill time, and some came to draw a pay check. Some were eager and willing to accept constructive suggestions. Some were doing many things well. Others were closed minded and didn't want to be bothered.

I remember one young White third-grade teacher who insisted that she teach her students a Black Studies Program which her secondary teacher-husband had developed. She contended that this was far more important to them than reading, writing and arithmetic.

Some teachers planned and were ready for their students when they arrived. I recall that on two different mornings our area superintendent arrived unannounced at the beginning of the school day. On each occasion, she observed teachers in the first three rooms visited, climbing and scrambling through cupboards to get books to provide assignments for pupils before she got there; each one was too late. There were teachers who planned well and taught so that their students achieved. A few of these teachers participated willingly in doing demonstrations for others. More and more teachers became conspicuously concerned about upgrading their classroom management skills. Some remained late in the afternoon questioning, searching, and planning.

AT LAST, GRAPE STREET

In the spring of 1969, I placed number one on the principal's eligibility list and was assigned to Grape Street School. It is one of Los Angeles City's 436 elementary schools located in the heart of Watts. Nestled in a cove surrounded by railroad tracks on four sides, it is vulnerable to social, economic, and academic ostracism. The school's premises comprise a rectangular block bordered on the east by Grape Street, on the west by Wilmington Avenue, on the south by 112th Street and on the north by 111th Street. The majority of students come from the Imperial Courts Housing Projects. The pupil population is 98 percent Black and 2 percent Mexican-American. Over 85 percent of the pupils are from families on welfare and almost the same percentage are one-parent families.

Before my arrival as a new administrator, the faculty had established its own dynamics and in its own manner and style made it known that they did not wish to accept an intruder. A teacher whom I had known previously, promptly designated herself as an informant. Her first message delivered surreptitiously in my office behind the door which she closed was, "He's telling the teachers, 'Don't do anything to make her look good'." Teachers locked their doors. Nevertheless, I entered and visited.

The inadequacy of most of the teaching that I observed was dismaying.

Only a few dedicated teachers were effectively implementing even a semblance of a positive program for pupils. The majority were lacking in motivation and were doing a variety of extra-curricular or personal activities. Some of the tenured teachers frightened the newer ones with threats that they would receive unsatisfactory ratings if they dared speak up about anything, including any need for assistance. Unrest was prevalent. Vandalism occurred with regularity. Most of the news media exaggerated these incidents. Some teachers transferred, some took leaves, and others remained to suffer with the desolating environment.

In the fall of 1969 the pressures were such that I found myself afflicted with Bells Palsy, a nerve condition that lowered the left side of my face three quarters of an inch. The neurologist I visited prognosticated that "the condition might last for two weeks, for two months, for two years or it might never leave." I missed one day from school. I returned, closed my door and worked inside my office for nine school days. On the fourth day of my affliction, the teacher informant knocked, came inside and recited, "They say that they are really working on you to get you down." Fortunately, R. C. Ola Brown, a fellow-organization member who had had some physical therapy experiences, came to my home, gave me encouragement and taught me some facial exercises that proved helpful. With determination of mind, an unswerving faith in God and this effort, I opened my office door and walked around void of any facial distortion after two weeks.

The effort made to upgrade the curriculum and provide a sound educational program by a dynamic and dedicated staff with the support of parents and interested community persons is chronicled in the book I felt compelled to write, entitled: GOOD NEWS ON GRAPE STREET, The Transformation Of A Ghetto School.

Carrie Ayers Haynes

Table of Contents

1

POSSIBILITIES UNLIMITED

As the sun set slowly on July 14, 1950, our damaged car coasted to the front of the address we sought in Los Angeles, California. Two weeks before, at about the same hour, our family of six had loaded the car in Buffalo, New York, for a trip across the continent. On the third night out, we were involved in a freak accident. A car, making an effort to avoid an overturned trailer, had swerved and crashed into our car broadside. Manuevering to avoid a collision almost sent us over an embankment. In the process, and without our knowledge, the oil pan in our motor was punctured. This led to a series of repairs and mishaps that ended with my ailing husband, our four small children, and myself arriving at our destination with twenty-five cents in our pockets.

I immediately began looking for an elementary school teaching position. In spite of my successful past experience back East, I soon learned that it would not be a matter of walking out of a classroom in Buffalo into a classroom in Los Angeles. After several disappointing face-to-face encounters, I resorted to using the telephone. One day I called a prominent teacher placement bureau. A most cordial voice answered and listened to a recital of my qualifications and experiences. Before I could finish I was informed, "With your qualifications, there should be no problem getting you placed. We have a number of openings. What would be a convenient time for you to come in for an appointment?"

I hesitated for a moment, wondering should I or should I not. I caught my breath and decided I would. "Oh, by the way, I think I should ask you something before I come in. Will it make any difference if I tell you that I am a Negro?"

There was a very distinctive moment of silence, then an audible gasp. The voice tightened, become resolute, and came through distinct and clear. "Why, yes indeed, it does make a difference. My dear, you should know yourself how limited your possibilities are." The words were bitter and they stung. But they were true, and I knew it. I also knew that there were prefixes, and I intended to place the prefix *un* before *limited*--that inflected word that sounded so devastating to me at the moment.

With persistent, insistent, and a never-say-die commitment, I became a teacher in Los Angeles in the spring of 1952. During the following fourteen years, I taught every elementary grade level, regular and special,

1

served on every school committee and most district ones, led institutes, taught in-service training, worked in local, state, and national organizations, served as an administrative trainee, and passed the vice-principal's examination in 1965--a week before the famous Watts riots. I was placed at 111th Street Elementary School in the spring of 1966.

After serving two and one-half years as vice-principal, I was transferred to 95th Street Elementary School on the west side of the city for a different experience.

In the fall of 1968 I experienced the trauma of a competitive examination that placed me number one on the principal's eligibility list. In the spring of 1969 I was assigned to be principal of Grape Street Elementary School.

2

A SCHOOL IN TROUBLE

Grape Street Elementary School, one of Los Angeles City's 436 elementary schools, is located in the heart of Watts, the notoriously publicized ghetto. Nestled in a cove surrounded by railroad tracks on four sides, it is vulnerable to social, economic, and academic ostracism. There are no recreational facilities in the community. The one Safeway Market, as well as most other small businesses, were burned during the 1965 riots. A barbecue restaurant, an independent meat market, store front hot dog stands, and a few small groceries are interspersed throughout the neighborhood. Transportation services are almost nonexistent. Bus service is erratic. Taxicabs refuse to enter the area.

The school's premises comprise a rectangular block bordered on the east by Grape Street, on the west by Wilmington Avenue, on the south by 112th Street and on the north by 111th Street. The majority of the students come from the Imperial Courts Housing Projects. The pupil population is 98 percent Black and 2 percent Mexican-American. When I arrived, there were two White pupils among the nearly one thousand enrolled. Over 85 percent of the pupils are from families on welfare, and almost the same percentage are one-parent families.

Scattered   throughout the neighborhood are an amazing number of well-kept homes occupied by the owners, who are mostly parents of children who are now grown. Also spotted throughout the area are houses with broken windows, trash in the yards, rags hanging from windows or roofs, and surrounded by broken bottles, empty cans and scattered debris. The occupants of these houses are often transients. Watts is sometimes an entry port for large displaced families. Antics and misbehavior such as rock throwing, bottle breaking, foul language, property defacement, and similar activities frequently caused the older residents to live in apprehension and fear.

Since the after-school playground, which is open only two hours after school for children of elementary school age, is the only accessible area for playing within the school community, many of the young people resort to the streets. Partly because the school was an institution some regarded with hostility, partly because it was an obvious public building upon which to vent frustrations, and sometimes because of an urge to acquire salable items, Grape Street School was under continuous attack. Vandalism and theft occurred regularly. Every weekend there was a break-in. Every Monday morning the question arose, "Where and what is the extent of the damage this time?" Often it was of the malicious mischief type. Rooms were entered, papers, boxes and files were scattered. Mixed paints were frequently strewn and splattered around. Glue was added to the mixture on occasions. Cleaning up the mess generally delayed class-room occupancy for some time into the day. Other entries involved theft. Typewriters, records players, tape recorders, and other items with buyer or pawn shop salability were stolen. Such activities were not confined to the weekends. Often during week nights our own students, sometimes accompanied by older brothers, sisters, or friends entered and left the offices or classrooms in disarray.

When I arrived, the administrative offices were located in an old two-story brick edifice that housed six classrooms. There was a fenced-in kindergarten unit with four classrooms, a primary unit with six classrooms, and six bungalows with double classrooms. The three Black and three White clerks, including the office manager, were not speaking to each other.

I will never forget the astonishment on the face of Mr. Weber, the plant manager, when I was introduced as the new principal. For a time I though he would topple over. I wondered if it was because I was a woman or if it were because I was Black. I only know that I could never desire a more supportive custodial staff than these four Black men and one Black woman turned out to be. They worked against tremendous odds. Students and passers-by threw papers and broken glass about the grounds. Windows were continually being smashed. Vandalism and theft were routine. Each one of Mr. Weber's staff was busy, but the school remained dirty almost all the time.

Complicating the custodial work was the Central Kitchen. To the west of a new two-story building being constructed, a gray stucco building housed an auditorium, a cafeteria, and a teachers' lunch room. The cafeteria contains the large equipment necessary for preparing lunches for twenty-two other city schools. Trucks arrive to deliver foodstuffs and to pick up prepared lunches to take to the other schools. The boxes, papers, cans and other refuse form this operation is extensive. Trash often overflowed from the bins. Cafeteria personnel sometimes parked cars so that they interfered with gargabe pickups, which were scheduled irregularly

There were times when this cafeteria area became so cluttered and malodorous that neighbors complained. Several times fires were set in the bins or cans. Fortunately none of these spread.

Around the entire perimeter of the school block was a six-foot high wire fence. Gates were locked when school was not in session. Many children relished the challenge of scaling the fence when coming to or from school or the playground rather than walking through a gate.

At the time of my arrival the faculty had established its own dynamics, and it was obvious that they did not want anyone to interfere with the status quo. At that time there were thirty-nine Blacks and five Whites; thirty-eight were women and six were men. The faculty chairman was an enterprising young Black man who had married into my family. During the first week he came in for a formal interview. The following week the community newspaper carried an extensive article entitled "Grape Street School Gets New Principal" under his by-line. The piece was quite complimentary and extended a warm welcome, but the atmosphere in the school was inconsistent with this printed word. Two weeks after my arrival, a teacher I had previously known surreptitiously entered my office, closed the door, and whispered, "He's telling the teachers, 'Don't do anything to make her look good'."

Most elementary school faculties organize. Generally a president or a chairman, along with the other necessary officers, is elected. The basic intent is for the elected leader to collaborate with the administrator on matters relating to faculty welfare, school concerns, and the educational program. The young man this faculty had elected chairman seemed popular with the students, the teachers, the parents, and the community. He was a candidate for a political office in an adjoining smaller city. Many of the school staff and school community supported him, but his classroom left much to be desired when I arrived. He had teaching expertise, but he had become lackadaisical as he openly focused on other matters. He served as a junior minister in a comunity church and used the title of reverend in a column he wrote for a local newspaper. In brief, he had many skills.

"Whenever you want to, you can teach," I remarked to him frequently. His eyes would twinkle, and he would chuckle knowingly.

It was difficult to ascertain what his objectives were. It was obvious that he was searching for power. I remember that in discussion with the former principal reference had been made to the mystics of his behavior. I made many visits to his upstairs classroom in the old building. On the first two occasions I discovered him at his desk typing material that appeared to be other than classroom assignments. The third time I unlocked the door and entered, I discovered students viewing a film and attempting to take notes in the darkened room, while their teacher typed with a desk lamp lit.

"This is injurious to students' eyes, and what kind of guide have they been given for note taking?" I asked.

"Oh, it isn't going to bother their eyes, and they know how to take notes. Come, let me show you some of their work. Laura, pull out your folder. Let Ms. Haynes see your handwriting." Laura and several others tugged at the many materials stuffed in their desks. It took effort to remove the requested folders. The teacher reached for one. "You see, we do research, and we are learning to record in good handwriting. Who else has a good folder to show? You see, here's another one."

I visited four other times during that first semester and never found him teaching. Yet at Open House time his was a model of good room environment with students' work on display. When a principals' meeting was held at our school, he organized the staff so that we looked as if we were an exemplary school for that day. He took his leadership role seriously. He counseled staff members openly and surreptitiously. Whenever an opportunity presented itself, he would assume a key role. He would then fit his performance to his mood. There were times when he worked effectively and with precision. At other times it seemed his intention was to disrupt. It was difficult to predict the direction he would choose to take. Whatever his decision and for whatever the reason, he could count many followers among the staff.

Visiting classrooms had been a major involvement for me during my years as vice-principal at the 111th Street and 95th Street Schools. Teachers in these schools had welcomed observations and teaching supervision. This was not so at Grape. As I traveled from room to room, I found many doors locked. After taking a survey of activities going on inside the classrooms, I tallied too many that were bleak, bland, uninviting and meaningless for children.

During recess the children literally ran wild. On my first day, I walked out to the yard during the upper-grade recess. A handsome, husky boy came running full speed over a plankway the construction men had left. I extended my right arm to check him as I cautioned, "Young man," He sidestepped my block, whirled, glared, and helled, "God damn you black son of bitch, what you trying to do? Trip me?" I was stunned. He never stopped. I noted his clothes and an hour and a half later located his fifth-grade classroom. I attempted to elicit some information from his teacher. "Oh yes, that's one bad boy. He's just plain no good. Every teacher who's had him has had trouble with him. He's driving me up the wall. I want him transferred out of my room."

"Have you talked with his parents?" I asked.

"What's the use? The whole family is no good. I can't do anything with him. I want him out of here."

"I'd like to have some time to visit in your room and observe his activities," I responded.

"Oh' that's all right. I think I can manage with him. I've been doing it all year."

6

Daily I walked onto the yard at the recess periods. At first few, if any teachers reported for yard duty. I kept appearing. By the second week, as I moved out into the yard, teachers seemed to emerge from the woodwork.

Sending children to the office with or without referrals to be reprimanded, or preferably swatted, was common policy. When these students were interrogated, it was frequently discovered that no one knew why they were there, whether some other child had reported them, or whether their misbehavior had been provoked. I began accompanying each student or group back to their classroom, observing for a period, and later offering constructive criticism that might help prevent recurrences. The word spread. Office referrals decreased appreciably.

One incident involving a Black male teacher was typical of many. He came panting into the office, holding two angry boys by their collars.

"These boys were fighting in the yard. George started the whole thing. That young man is just asking for it. He needs some solid swats."

"He hit me first," yelled George.
"I didn't. You hit me first," shouted Philip.
"Did you see the fight?" I asked the teacher.
"No, but John did," explained the teacher.
"How do you know who started the fight if you didn't see it?" I inquired.

"John came and got me and told me all about it. John is in my room, and he is a reliable boy. Come here, John, you tell the principal what happened."

"I didn't see what happened, but I told you the way Anthony told me. It was like this. He said..."

Teachers' meetings were held each Tuesday. During these sessions the permanent tenured teachers and I talked. There was continual rationalizing on why these 'culturally deprived' students couldn't learn, the multiplicity of equipment, materials, and supplies needed in each classroom, and the support needed from administration in the form of swats.

Because I continued my classroom visitations, I was dubbed "the walking principal." There were times I felt totally frustrated after a round of classroom observations. In some rooms desks were so cluttered that one might expect a family of rodents to emerge at any time. It was common custom for some teachers to give classes a mass assignment and then retreat to their own desks to write or type a term paper, a political speech, a newspaper article, a letter, a sermon, a grocery list, or some other personal matter. Frequent assignments were "Find all the compound words you can," or "Arrange words in alphabetical order." The majority of students were not even able to do these simple tasks accurately.

On too many occasions it was obvious that classes were viewing innumerable films and filmstrips without prior briefing or follow-up. Often when I entered, the teacher would walk over to explain what the children were supposed to be doing. Clearly they felt this was necessary because otherwise it was generally difficult to ascertain what the assignment was. Only a few dedicated teachers were effectively implementing even a semblance of a positive program. The majority were preoccupied, lacking motivation, and involved in personal activities, not teaching.

Within my mind, I searched for ways to try to work out some ways of communicating with and stimulating the teachers. When Richard Smith, the affable, outgoing principal, had attempted to orient me, he intimated that there was a quiet storm brewing. I am still appreciative of his endeavor not to frighten me. Here I was in a position for which I had worked and struggled for years with one major aim in mind. My goal was to provide an opportunity for boys and girls to learn how to learn, so that their possibilities in life would be less limited. Here I was--here were the boys and girls--but so little was happening to affect their lives academically in a positive way. Only a short time before there had been a hue and cry for Black administrators in Black schools. I certainly fitted the color scheme, but my blackness was working no magic for me.

Betty Coleman, the Child Welfare and Attendance Supervisor, was working fairly successfully organizing parents in a Block Club. They met in the Club House of the Imperial Courts. It seemed wiser to go to meet students' parents on their home ground. Yugo Fukushima, who was then vice-principal, and I met with a group of thirty parents duing my second month in office. The meeting went well.

I left the Imperial Courts Housing Project that evening feeling that maybe we were about to make some inroads. Already I had developed the habit of setting my clock-radio so that it would awaken me with the morning news. Already I was conditioned to listening for reports of vandalism at Grape Street. The school was not lacking in publicity in this area. The Los Angeles Times made much of most incidents. The assessed monetary amounts of the damage were usually ballooned out of proportion by at least one additional digit.

The radio announcer's voice came on with gusto. "Last night the 112th Street Elementary School was hit by vandals, and extensive damage was done. Twenty rooms were vandalized, several were burned, and a piano was taken from the auditorium and beaten into splinters. It seems that the vandals had a key. Doors to classrooms were entered, rooms were senselessly disarrayed and left locked, and undetermined amount of equipment was taken. Present property damage is estimated at $50,000."

"Oh, my," I sighed. "Poor Duane Danielson." He was principal of the victimized school. We had shared many such experiences for our schools had taken turns making vandalism and burning news. Today, it

8

was his turn, and I knew how to empathize. I began wondering what I could say to him when I met him a few hours later at the superintendent-principals meeting scheduled to be held at his school. I wondered if the auditorium had been left in a usable condition. I wondered if it would be necessary to change the location of the meetng. Just as I was pondering whether or not I should offer Grape's auditorium since we were in the immediate vicinity, my telephone rang. The voice on the other end of the line was that of the faculty chairman, "They've torn Grape Street up. They really got us this time."

"What do you mean? They couldn't have gotten two school on the same night. I just heard the radio announcement about 112th Street School."

"I don't know what happened over there, but I do know they've gotten Grape Street and they got it good."

As I replaced the receiver in the cradle, I heard the radio announcer describing the vandalism at Grape Street. Hurriedly, I dressed and drove to school. When I reached the front of the school, all doubt about where the vandalism had occurred vanished.

It was early--about 7:15 a.m. There was no place to park. Never in my life have I encountered so many of the news media. Almost every television channel and most radio stations were represented. Confusion reigned. Among the crowd was the faculty chairman. Many parents were arriving. They came to help--and they did. Mr. Weber had called for maintenance assistance. The workmen came. It was heartwarming to see all these concerned individuals working to clean up the mess.

The six upstairs classrooms in the administration building had been entered, vandalized extensively, and left locked. The one classroom downstairs had been totally burned. Records, books, tables, chairs--everything was charcoal. It was necessary to move Bennie Wyatt and her fourth-grade class to a bungalow. Workmen, parents, and teachers, though dismayed, joined together to re-establish some order out of the chaos. During all this activity, I noticed the faculty chairman busily attending to the news media. Each time someone attempted to speak with me, he broke in, "Oh no, she doesn't want to talk." I was busy trying to re-establish enough order to begin school on time. But the obvious attempt by the faculty chairman to take over the supervision led one teacher to remark, "I wonder who is the principal of this school."

At nine o'clock when the school bell rang, all teachers led their classes into their rooms except the faculty chairman. He was still busy conversing with newsmen and parents. Reverend W.J. Broussard, a concerned parent, had taken off from work to volunteer assistance together with his wife and many others. Parents were disturbed. They made it quite clear that they

9

were ready to organize to try to avert any future disasters of this nature. We discussed planning a night meeting.

Most of the news media had gone or were leaving. I couldn't help wondering why there had been so much news coverage. Vandalism was no rarity in many Los Angeles schools. The vandalism and arson had been bad, but I could cite others at different locales that had been far more extensive and costly. And, as usual, the publicity given had been exaggerated-- the number of classrooms involved had been inflated, and the piano, which had been pushed from the auditorium, was intact and had been pushed back into place. It had not been splintered.

I was summoned to the telephone. The public information office of the school district was calling. "Newsmen are reporting that you are not responding," I was politely informed.

"I've been busy trying to get things in order and get school going. I've tried to answer their questions in passing."

"Channel 7 called in requesting an interview with the principal. We would strongly suggest that you cooperate."

The newsman was sitting in his well-marked cab in front of the school. As I approached the door, he got out and came forward. We conversed. He brought his equipment and set it up in the office. I prepared myself. Anne Renshaw, the office manager, sat in the background to lend moral support. With mixed emotions, I made my debut on television. The commentator was benign. I had informed him that if I appeared, I would prefer to be asked questions that would help correct some of the erroneous reporting that had been broadcast earlier. He did just that. I braced myself and got through that first interview.

After the news media left, there were security and police reports to be made. I looked through the broken pane in the front door and saw a parent I knew placing some battered typewriters on the sidewalk. "These were taken last night. I know where there are more. I told them that they'd better get them back here."

Before completing my conversation with the parent, I looked up to see the faculty chairman. "Where is your class?" I asked.

"Oh, they're covered. My neighbor is supervising them. I just wanted to tell you the press conference has been called."

"What press conference? What do you mean the press conference has been called?"

"You remember you gave me permission to call a press conference."

"I gave you permission to call a press conference after all the news media we had here this morning! When did I give this permission? When will this conference take place?"

10

"Twelve o'clock today in the library." We were interrupted.

"Ms. Haynes, the public information office wants you on the phone," a clerk informed me. I picked up the receiver. A seemingly understanding voice inquired. "Ms. Haynes, we're calling to find out who is calling a press conference at Grape Street School." There is no way to describe the he humiliation I experienced at this moment.

"The faculty chairman has just informed me that I gave him permission to call a press conference." There was no further discussion. I was thankful. What a nonsensical explanation. But, it was the only one I had. It was accepted.

My mind cleared. I asked the faculty chairman what he planned to say. He pulled out four typewritten pages. Scanning the text, I noticed the word "conspiracy" throughout. I asked for the pages, read them, edited them, and returned them with the admonition that, "Nothing should be said that wasn't written on that edited paper." He agreed. "My word," I thought, "what about the faculty! They had already endured enough." But I had to face the fact that this conference had been called and I had no time to cancel it. Hurriedly I wrote a note announcing that the faculty chairman had called a news conference to be held in the library at noon. All who wished to be present were welcome.

The newsmen returned. The faculty came. I sat on the sideline. The faculty chairman was in the spotlight on television.

That day finally ended. I couldn't help wondering if I had missed some sessions in my administration courses for I could not remember ever having been taught or read anything that would have guided me through such a day. Well, there would be tomorrow. And tomorrow the parents would meet in the library to organize and plan strategy to help counteract the vandalism. A crisis had occurred, and parents did not want it to happen again.

The parents were true to their word. Around 8:30 a.m. they began assembling. "Black is beautiful" was being heralded as a slogan. It is true. The beauty of black is embodied in the elegant Dr. Josie G. Bain, who was then my South Area Superintendent. She knew I was having trouble. Somehow, I knew she would come to give me moral support. If I had had time, I am sure I would have wondered if she were disappointed with me. In less than two months what shameful events my appointment seemed to have precipitated.

"Ms. Haynes, did you know the parents are picking up a throw-away newspaper as they go into the library? asked Doris Wooten, one of the Black clerks.

"That's OK,", I answered.

"But Ms. Haynes, have you read the headlines?"

"No, I haven't but your voice tells me I should."

"Yes Ms. Haynes, I really think you should."

I walked into the hall and picked up a paper from the bundle stacked at the library door. There in heavy bold type was the headline: BLACK CHILD CHOKED BY WHITE TEACHER.

Immediately I walked among the parents and asked if I might retrieve the papers they had picked up. They complied willingly. The bundle was removed. I retreated to my office to read the two and one-half pages of what had to have been internal reporting. The by-line gave the name of an unknown reporter. Explicit, lengthy, and gory details eulogized one of our Black boys and damned a White male teacher.

I called the area office. Dr. Bain was out, but her assistant endeavored to give me some guidance. He suggested that I direct the White teacher to come to the area office at the end of the school day. I felt this was a dangerous course to take. Dynamite was in the air, and I felt it could blow up at any time.

Just as I decided I'd better return to meet with the parents, Dr. Bain walked in. She had come to see the damage incurred.

"Well," I greeted her, "I was taught at least one thing that may be of benefit to me now. That is the need to be ready to rearrange priorities, and I think we have that need now."

I presented her a copy of the newspaper. She read the lengthy article and sighed, "Let's get that young man over to my office right away." I agreed wholeheartedly.

The White male teacher came down to the main office. He knew about the article. Everyone did.

"Well, he threatened he would ruin me with that paper, and this is what he meant. I don't want to leave here. I want to stay and fight it out."

We explained that we felt it best for him to accept a transfer to another school for his own safety. He cried but he reluctantly understood. What an unfair situation this was. It was true that I had not had time to determine the quality of his teaching and the account in the newspaper alleged activities that had taken place before my arrival. I had made several visits to his classroom. It was colorful; each bulletin board had been painted a different pastel color. His own commercial printing of the alphabet, numerals, and mathematical processes were abundantly displayed. Some students' arithmetic work was in evidence. On the three occasions that I had visited his room on different days and at different times, his students were well disciplined and involved in math work. Each time I had entered I found him moving around assisting students. It seemed that mathematics was his major focus. Nevertheless, I had never actually seen him teach. I knew very little of his temperament. I never knew whether the alleged accusation was true or not. He reported, "This is all a big lie. He's been after me for a long time. He said he would get me moved out, and now he's going to win." He left.

Later, we met with parents. They volunteered to patrol the school's premises and made plans to schedule a night meeting to formalize an organization.

Who will be next was the question in the air. Were White men the only target? There were only two left. Speculation about who contributed the information for the newspaper article was covertly discussed. Apprehension and concern abounded.

While driving to school the next morning, I began wondering what could be done to relieve some of the tensions. The uptight atmosphere was more than apparent. I arrived without receiving a brainstorm. There was much to do, and I began. At exactly 8:20 one of the clerks answered the phone to hear, "A bomb is in the building. It is set to go off at five miutes after nine."

"Was the caller a man or a woman?"

"It was a man."

"Do you remember anything else about the call?"

"Just that he hung up with a bang as soon as he finished."

My God! I needed strength. Strength came. I summoned Yugo. We planned strategy. The clerks got busy calling the school disaster office and the area superintendent and alerting the fire department. Nolan Porter was signing in, and he agreed to brief the five other male teachers on the staff. They would organize baseball teams and get a game going with students and teachers as spectators. Everyone was to be kept out of and away from the building. It was agreed not to announce the bomb threat. The teams played, and the school population cheered until the bomb squad declared the school all clear at 10:20 a.m. The remainder of that Friday passed without a major incident. That afternoon I sent a note around giving information about the circumstances and went to each room to personally thank teachers and children for their cooperation.

Later I had a long talk with Dr. Bain. What an inspiring human being! I could have felt so ashamed, but she never allowed me to. She was never didactic. At the end of each conference that seemed to have no solution, she would calmly predict, "Now, Carrie, I know you'll find a way." What confidence! Each time she said that I was groping in the dark, but each time she made that statement, I knew that her prophecy would be fulfilled.

On Monday morning I sat in my office reading a communication when I heard, "Ms Renshaw, how many more days do I have?"

"Let me check. I do know that whatever the number is, they are half-days."

When the teacher left, I inquired, "What was she asking?"

She wanted to know how many more days she could be absent with pay. Most of them keep close check. Most of them use up all their days every year."

I went to the library where the teachers were assembled for an 8:30 meeting. I had written a statement chiefly to clarify my relationship to the faculty chairman. His activities had been ambivalent. I was told that he had confided to some people that we were cousins and that if they wanted a good rating, they should accept his guidance. He reportedly told others he knew all the politicians and that they would take care of me for him when the time came. Rumors were rampant during those three traumatic days. Intentionally I read my statement. All the teachers were present except the faculty chairman. When he arrived at 9:00, as he regularly did, the meeting had ended. Since the message involved him, I asked him to read a copy. He scanned the pages and offered them back to me as if unimpressed with the content.

"There are other copies. Keep that one for your record. You may wish to refer to it again some time," I offered.

"Oh, well, if you wish," was his nonchalant response.

Later in the day, I visited classroom. Terrezene Brown, a young woman who had been an Olympic champion, was also a champion in her classroom. I walked around to see what her students were doing in each of her three groups. Preparation, motivation, and involvement were evident. Warm student-teacher relationships permeated the room. Oh, for a school of teachers with her concern and commitment.

Down the hall I entered another classroom. The teacher was absent. The students were busy supposedly writing compound words.

"Where is your teacher?" I asked softly.

"She had to take care of some important business," a child cautiously replied.

"She got a call," one clarified.

"Did she go to the office?" I inquired.

"Oh, no. She just went to the phone in the bookroom."

That is how I found out that there was a private line almost hidden away at the end of the bookroom. Some of the upstairs teachers frequently left their rooms to engage in private conversations. These children had not meant to tell on their teacher. They had tried to choose their comments wisely. Most of the students felt a fierce loyalty to their teachers.

I walked around the room looking at papers. Few had identified compound words. I asked one girl to read her words to me. She read: "ta-ble, flo-or, pic-ture, mo-ney."

The teacher returned. She became very busy helping a student. I left and went to the room from which the white male teacher had been abruptly transferred. A white male substitute had served there for two days. After entering the room, I could not locate him. The class was noisy and out-of-order. "Where is your teacher?" I asked.

"We don't know. He just walked out."

And that is just what he did. He just walked out, and we never saw him again. Another white male took over this class the next day. He lasted until 10:30 a.m., when he walked into the office and announced, "I'm checking out."

Security agents were still working on the vandalism case. A suspect had been named. We summoned an EMR (Educable Mentally Retarded) boy to the office. I sat with the officer as he sternly asked the boy for the

14

school's master key. The boy reached into his back pocket and placed it on the desk. I was shocked that he had it and gave it up so easily. He admitted that he had had it for a year and that he had used it for previous entries.

That afternoon the boy's mother called me and made vicious threats against the security agent. Several evenings later during a community meeting, I started to go to my office to fetch some papers. Nolan Porter blocked me saying, "No, stay inside Ms. Haynes."

I complied but wondered why. I later learned that three teenage brothers of the EMR boy were waiting outside to get "that damn Black woman principal who got our little brother in trouble." I never saw them. I was told that teachers reasoned with them and they went away.

On Tuesday night a mass meeting was held in the auditorium. About fifty parents and community friends came. The Grape Street School-Community Advisory council was organized, and Reverend W.J. Broussard was elected president. One of the custodians had invited his minister, Reverend P. J. Jones, and he was elected vice-president. The discussion focused on ways of providing continued protection of school property. Parents had been voluntarily driving around at designated intervals.

William Vickers announced that he would accept a major responsibility in this area. He knew two young men in the community whom he could involve.

Reverend Jones rose to suggest, "If this man is going to accept this responsibility, we should pay him. I'm putting down the first five dollars. Who else wants to contribute? Nobody needs to feel embarrassed. If you don't have money, you can render other services. If you do have money and don't have time, come and give."

Several people moved to the table. More came. I knew that the administrative guide prohibited the collection of money without a civic center permit, but again here was a situation for which I was not prepared. I felt I could not afford to stifle their enthusiasm and effort. The mood of the meeting was for positive action. The people present were giving support in the only ways they knew, and our school needed support. The money was already on the table, and help was needed to curb the vandalism.

"Let's turn the collected money over to the treasurer," I brazenly suggested. "And, hereafter, we can plan to carry on money-raising activites off the school grounds and have Mr. Vickers and the young men he engages patrol the streets and sidewalks around our school. If any of them sees any suspect on the grounds, they are to call security section." That settled it. The group agreed. Thereafter, rummage sales were held regularly in a parking lot of the Imperial Courts, and the young men were paid to circle the school at staggered hourly intervals. Vandalism subsided appreciably.

Three months later the police captain came by to tell me about the mysterious events that occurred on that night of the major vandalism. He reported that there had been two simultaneous entries in which neither group had been aware that the other was present. One group of EMR boys used a master key. They unlocked the doors of the auditorium and pushed out the piano. Then they came over to the main builidng, entered, and went into each of the six upstairs classrooms, vandalized them and left, locking the doors behind them. They came downstairs, vandalized the classroom, and set it afire. At the same time a group of young community adults took the butt end of a shotgun and shoved out a pane in the front door. Reaching through, they released the lock and entered. Their objective was to steal equipment, and they did. They hauled away all the office typewriters, record players, radios, the two film projectors and screens. As the sirens of the fire engines wailed and the truck turned a corner two blocks away, one of the fellows dashed back into the burning building to get the second film projector to go with the second screen he already had in his possession.

The new building was being erected. The contractor was delayed from time to time by vandals. He reported that it was not unusual for this to happen in other areas while construction was in process, but it delayed his progress and it continued to worsen. One day he came to relunctantly inform me that he was going to bring in two patrol dogs to guard his fenced-in area. The dogs were trained not to bite, but he hoped that their presence and their barks would deter intruders.

"My," I thought, "what danger will the dogs pose for our children, and how will parents react to dogs being on the school grounds?" After thinking it over, I asked him if he would wait until I sent a bulletin home to inform the parents. He consented.

As I walked out to my car the first afternoon the patrol dogs came, I observed a group of young EMR pupils shouting, hurling rocks, and antagonizing the dogs.

"Children, why don't you just look at the dogs? They are here to protect our school. Soon we'll have a nice new building to move into. Won't you leave them alone?"

"Dem dogs don't know how to bite. That man put 'em in dare just to scare us. Humph, dey don't scare me."

"Me neither."

"Me neither."

Their molestation subsided as I walked away, but I understand it began again and continued until late into the evening. On the fourth day the dogs were not returned. I learned that someone outside the immediate neighborhood had brought over a battle-scarred bulldog, placed him in the confines with the two patrol dogs, and sicked him on them. He fought them mercilessly. A concerned neighbor called the posted telephone number of the patrol dogs' owner, and he arrived in time to save them. This incident left us all with a feeling of hopelessness.

Then Nolan Porter had an idea. He suggested to the contractor that he consider paying a community person the amount he was paying for the service of the dogs. He pondered the idea, decided to give it a try, and contacted Mr. Vickers. The men came to an agreement. Thereafter the building was completed with only minor vandal incidents.

After the Block Parent Club was organized, signs bearing a large purple "G," representing Grape, appeared in windows throughout the school community. A few senior citizens, parents and concerned community neighbors scheduled themselves to drive around the school or patrol corners in the mornings and evenings when students walked to and from school. Fights, debris throwing, and disturbances diminished. The patroling of the premises throughout the night decreased the vandalism. Minor sporadic incidents did occur, but they were rare. Parents were concerned.

The School-Community Advisory Council met the second Thursday of each month in the evening; an average of twenty-five membes attended each session. The Block club met once each week at the Imperial Courts in the afternoon. Parents were involved.

Basically, parents maintained a blind faith in the school. On the whole they felt that whatever the school did with their children was right for them. If teachers made telephone contact with a home, generally the parents recommended, "Just give him some swats. You have my permission. And you just let me know, and I'll give it to him when he gets home."

Swats and discipline were synonomous for too many teachers and parents. There were some parents who became incensed about teachers slapping, pinching or hitting children on places other than their bottoms. Over and over I listened to irate parents detailing reports of physical punishment to students. In meetings, in bulletins, and in the Teachers Handbook, teachers were continuously reminded that they should only administer corporal punishment in the presence of an administrator, and an administrator should only administer corporal punishment in the presence of an adult witness.

"Whenever you feel it is absolutely necessary to give a swat, bring the child to my office so that I can witness the act," I announced. A few teachers accepted my offer. Others continued their efforts to make children behave by administering corporal punishment in the classroom or on the school grounds without a proper witness.

California Assemblyman Leon Ralph (D) had learned Grape Street School was having trouble. A representative from his office had come to participate in the School-Community Advisory Council organization. One day he and Dr. William Lucas, an administrative coordinator, visited. They toured some classrooms, noted some of our needs, and recognized some of our efforts. The intent of the visit was to insure us of his office's support.

After they left, the phone rang. Ruth Persley answered, and the voice at the other end informed her, "This is Assemblyman Ralph's office calling. He asked me to inform you that your flag is flying upside down."

How embarrassing. Ms Persley left her desk momentarily to check something. Briskly, she returned, and announced, "You know what? When a flag is hoisted upside down, it is a distress signal. Shall I return his call with this information?"

"Please do," I approved. "Tell his office that maybe this is a subconscious gesture. Our flag is signaling that we are a school in trouble."

3

THE SANCTITY OF PERMANENCY

After those three consecutive days of trauma, I had hoped we could concentrate on teaching children, and I continued my classroom visitations. In almost all rooms total class assignments were still being given. There was seldom any evidence of groupings, and very little students' work was displayed. While in the classrooms, I saw many words misspelled by teachers. Subject content and basic skills were vague or absent.

In desperation I decided to ask all teachers to formulate reading lesson plans for three groups. When I mentioned the idea to Yugo Fukushima, he recoiled and cautioned, "Oh, Carrie, I don't think I would do that."

I was aware that theory advises against making abrupt changes, but after brief contemplation, I replied, "You know, Yugo, we are about as far to the bottom as we can go. And since we can't go any further down, if there are any repercussions, we can only move from side to side."

He just stood listening.

I concluded, "I understand what you are saying to me. I have no assurance this move is going to help matters, but I've got to take the plunge. And if need be, I'll go it alone." He did not reply--he didn't need to. Without his sustained coadministration, it would have been almost impossible to have gotten through the difficult and trying days and years ahead.

At the next teachers meeting I announced, "I am asking you all to prepare reading lesson plans and submit them as follows: On Monday, plans for your second group, your average readers; On the second Monday, plans for your third group, your slower readers; On the third Monday, plans for your first group, your faster readers, and each Monday thereafter plans for three groups will be expected."

Sighs of resignation, disgust, and exasperation ensued.

"Why, what nerve, asking permanent teachers for plans."

"I've had my credentials for years, and no one ever asked me for plans before."

"You know, I think it's time for me to get a transfer."

"I've had sixteen years of experience and have been doing all right without lesson plans."

"Well, we were here when they came, and we'll be here when they are gone. I'm not running anywhere. I'm permanent anyway."

The reaction pause had given me time to take a deep breath. The wheels had been set in motion, and they were turning and turning fast. There was much mumbling, but no questions were asked. I explained a basic procedure for teaching reading. The meeting ended, and teachers huddled and chattered all the way down the hall. For a long time I did not see Yugo. When he later walked into the office I asked, "What happened?"

"They cornered me down the hall with questions about how to write lesson plans. When you started talking about phonetic analysis in there today, they thought you were speaking Greek or Latin or some other foreign language."

Evidently many teachers did not even understand the sequence of the teaching procedure, even before I reached the explanation of teaching a phonetic skill.

On Monday many of the teachers submitted lesson plans. Most of them were meager, unclear, and inadequate. One of the permanent teachers proclaimed, "These plans are a waste of time. We will be teaching your way when you are in the room and our way when you are out."

"Are you suggesting that I should be in your rooms most of the time?"

"Oh no, no, no. All this just seems so unnecessary."

After attempting to read the plans, I began to see what she meant. Much of the writing was illegible, an incredible number of words were misspelled, grammar was mutilated, and the sequence of the reading procedure was confused. Some were unnecessarily copious for teaching one group. Most of the permanent teachers were frustrated but would not admit it. Most would have preferred to ignore my request as the faculty chairman did.

The general admonition from the permanent teachers to the nonpermanent ones was to keep quiet, ask no questions, admit no weaknesses, and seek no assistance from administration. Should they ever do so, they were told that they were certain to receive an unsatisfactory rating from the administrators. The nonpermanent teachers worked in continual apprehension and fear. It was impossible to relate or communicate with them. The permanent teachers had agreed to speak for them to protect them from a catastrophic evaluation. And speak for them they did in teachers' meetings. Consistently any conversation that took place was between the permanent teachers and me, for the permanent teachers contended that they were safe from retaliation.

Never did I hear a concern about the quality of teacher performance. On researching why this attitude was so prevalent, I learned that the majority of Black teachers had taken the Los Angeles City Schools Teacher Examination on the average of four or five times, so passing this examination was considered a major accomplishment. After they served their three years of probation and became permanent (or tenured), they considered themselves above reproach by the school administration. Research also showed that White teachers who served in the ghetto school generally either came as missionaries to save the souls of poor little Black kids or needed an entry port where they would endure their three years of probation. It was almost a foregone conclusion that near the end of the third year a transfer would be submitted by most.

The climate among a segment of the Black teachers wasn't aiding this situation. The four Whites left on the staff were probationary teachers. The total school was permeated with a sense of negativism. Most Black teachers supported the premise that Grape's ghetto children would not respond to positive treatment. They believed that any administration that refused to inflict wholesale corporal punishment as a disciplinary measure was weak. Many contended they couldn't teach without this type of administrative support.

The permanent teachers were involved in the lesson plan endeavor as well as the nonpermanent teachers. Fortunately, there was no open fighting. Efforts to comply were becoming more and more frustrating, and guidance was needed, but I knew that I'd better muster every ounce of tact and diplomacy possible in giving it. At the next teachers' meeting I announced, "Some teachers are spending far too much time developing plans for one group. Because you have two other groups to teach and other subject areas to cover, I am sure you do not want to give an excessive amount of time to planning for one group with whom you'll be spending only about twenty minutes of the school day. So, I have developed a simplified form that will help you present concise plans, which you may extend as you follow them."

The forms were distributed. "Let's go over them. If there are questions, we can discuss them" The legal sized sheets presented the following guidelines for groups 1,2, and 3.

Reading Lesson Plan

TEACHER　　　　　　　　　　*GRADE TIME ROOM NUMBER*

Group II-Instructional Text	*New Words*
Story Title	*Directed Lesson*
Objectives	*Words Study Skill*
Type of Lesson	*Generalization*
Follow-Up	*Independent Activity*

This presentation was received fairly well, and no antagonism was expressed during this session. On the Monday of the third week, five complete well-developed plans for the three groups were submitted. I displayed them on the teachers' bulletin board. There was no way to miss them. Naturally there were mixed reactions.

"Oh, that's the way she wants them. Oh, I see."

"Well, my word, who ever heard of teachers' work hanging up on a bulletin board."

"At least this gives us some idea of what she's talking about. I haven't done lesson plans in so long, I've forgotten how."

"I still think this is all unnecessary."

"Well, well, well. Whose plans are those? Who made the bulletin board?"

Initially there was considerable sarcasm about teachers' work being exhibited. But fortunately the five teachers whose work was displayed were surprised and pleased at the recognition of their work. Their attitudes did much to shape a desire to succeed in others.

After the first shock, teachers seemed to avoid studying the displayed lessons plans as if they were a plague. On rare and erratic periods during the beginning of the week I noticed a single person standing at a distance surreptitiously eyeing the content. As the week neared its end, teachers came more frequently and went closer. By Friday only a few seemed hesitant. Groups moved in to find out how each of the five did their plans. The display paid off. On the next Monday, there were sixteen diversified but good plans. All sixteen were posted. There was no effort to suppress the feelings of satisfaction of those whose papers were displayed. This procedure continued until almost all of the plans submitted were posted. Thereafter, the teachers agreed to display on a rotating basis plans with new and interesting concepts and skills. A small amount of concern for teaching was surfacing.

Paper plans were a beginning, but implementing them so that children learn is the true proof of the pudding. So, another endeavor was devised. It wasn't a new idea. It was one I had used when working with teachers at 111th and 95th Street Schools when I was vice-principal and one I am sure many others have used many times. But it was new to Grape Street School. The procedure calls for one teacher on a grade level to plan and teach a lesson to a group of students while teachers of the same grade level observe. This is followed by a brief evaluation which only one or two points are highlighted.

I approached several teachers and asked if they would initiate these demonstrations. They were very reluctant for peer pressure and insecurity, even among those few with skills, discouraged them. Eventually three permanent teachers from grades one, three and five consented. Schedules were developed because all the teachers of the grade level of the teacher doing the demonstration would be invited. Generally our arrangement was to have one teach⸝ ⸝m another grade level take the released four to five classes either ⸝ ⸝itorium for a film or to the playground for outdoor activities. ⸝ ⸝ demonstration twenty-five minutes before the mornin⸝ ⸝e the most propitious time. Each of the first thre⸝ ⸝detailed plans than requested on the pre-p⸝ ⸝ initially we reviewed together the pro-⸝ a production, but our staff develop-

⸝ssion in which the teacher had gone through the ⸝ ⸝⸝ically but well. When she was ready to teach the phone⸝ ⸝ote the word PLEASE on the chalkboard and explained, '⸝ ⸝s and girls, this word is please. Please begins with two consonant⸝ ⸝e consonant is a p, the next consonant is an l. Whenever two consonants go together, they lose their identity and you call them a consonant blend. Now close your books. We'll finish our story tomorrow.''

This was a teacher who was really trying. She had involved the group in the reading of the story through questioning. But when she began to teach the skill, she just told--and the information she told was incorrect. This was quite typical of much of the teaching. Our staff development efforts were calling attention to many such areas of deficiencies.

Each week there were one or two demonstrations. During the first month I asked teachers who seemed most ready. Later teachers began to volunteer.

One very positively oriented Black male permanent teacher asked if I would come to observe him teach a reading lesson. He indicated that he wanted to prepare himself to do a demonstration. I was delighted. He set the date and time. On the designated morning, he reminded me again so that I would be sure not to forget. One minute before the set time I left my office and walked into his room. The teacher's back was turned, his body leaned forward, and his fist was in the air, "Boy, if you don't get yourself over there in that seat, I'll knock your block off. And that goes for everyone of you. I told you that the principal was coming to hear us read. Now get ready.''

Sensing the unreadiness, I quickly backed out and stood outside for a few minutes waiting for the pandemonium to subside. I don't believe he ever knew I was in the room during the commotion. I didn't even hear the children inform him as they often do. When the air seemed clear, I reentered and was ushered to a seat. It was impossible to remain seated. With laborious effort he read the questions he had written on his cards. Then he read the answers he had anticipated from the students. He became obviously confused and began reading the story. The children began to fidget. The ones in the other two groups started getting out of hand, so I walked over to assist.

"Would you please come back tomorrow?" he blurted out.

"Yes, I will," I promised.

Help in various forms was given this teacher. Arrangements were made for him to observe others. Yugo and I both worked with him individually. He was most receptive for he really wanted to be able to teach, but during that semester, he did not acquire the skills necessary to demonstrate teaching one group to read.

There were some, especially among the permanent teachers, who looked upon these efforts with ridicule and sarcasm. Slowly and laboriously we tried other ways to upgrade and adapt the curriculum to the needs of the children. Progress was painfully slow. During our weekly meetings, only the permanent teachers continued to converse with me. Some light broke through one day when a permanent teacher remarked, "Ms. Haynes, you don't care a thing about teachers. All you care about are children."

"At last, I do believe, we are about to begin to communicate."

A party was given in the home of one of the dedicated Black male teachers. It was announced as a get-acquainted party, but few came. The faculty chairman presented me a beautifully wrapped package. Upon opening it, I found a paper plate with the words LESSON PLANS inside--these were the only ones he ever submitted to me.

Later in the evening, seemingly impromptu and spontaneously, he and a Black female permanent teacher met in the middle of the floor about four yards from where I was seated and began hitting the palms of their hands together in pitty-pat fashion. They began chanting, "I'm permanent, I'm permanent." Then they locked arms and skipped clockwise around continuing, "We're permanent, we're permanent. And you can't touch us."

4

LET THE SUN SHINE IN

*I*n the spring of 1969 there were six educable mentally retarded (EMR), often termed special training classes in Los Angeles--one precompulsory, one primary, two intermediate, and two upper grade rooms. No less than twelve and no more than fifteen students should be enrolled in the precompulsory class; no less than fifteen and no more than eighteen should be enrolled in the other classes. Placement is supposed to ensue after each child has been individually tested by a psychologist, has been determined to have an intelligence quotient of seventy-five plus or minus four, and parent approval has been given. The funding allocation for these students exceeded the average daily attendance amount for students in the regular classrooms. These classes had been kept filled over a period of years without strict adherence to the specified guidelines. They were all housed in bungalows and were physically and psychologically detached. The students were labeled "dumb" by many peers in regular classes.

The intent was to provide these identified slow learners individualized programs in small group settings, but this was not happening. In almost all these classes bedlam reigned, and when these children were released to the playground, they literally ran wild. Although playground areas were assigned each room, seldom could the children be located even near their alloted areas. During the recess periods these boys and girls habitually ran in between the bungalows, pounded on classroom doors, yelled into windows, rampaged throught the kindergarten yard, threw rocks, broke bottles, and behaved in a manner inimical to their own welfare and that of others. One day as I was visiting classes, I observed a number of the young EMRs playing in and around the bungalows during class time.

"Where is your teacher?" I asked.

"She's in the room. She's looking at her television show," one child answered.

I unlocked the door. She jumped and quickly reached up and pushed the button to turn off the soap box opera *Love of Life*.

"We are on our way out for physical education," she explained.

"Are you scheduled for physical education every morning directly after recess?" I rhetorically asked. She scurried outside.

On the following morning, I unlocked the same door and stepped inside. The students were there. Mild disorder was evident among the ten boys. The four girls sat beside the teacher in a back corner enthralled with the day's episode of *Love of Life*.

About two minutes passed before anyone noticed me. Suddenly there was a click. The teacher moved rapidly announcing, "Now, boys and girls, get your books. Get your books and let's come over to the circle for reading." The boys and girls scrambled, and each picked up a *I know A Story*. They tumbled over each other, and each sat in one of the fourteen chairs.

"Sit tall now. Let's read 'The Three Bears.' Let's read 'The Three Bears' for our principal."

I left and that afternoon informed this teacher that the television set would be removed from her room.

The following week I walked over to this room at about the same time of day. No one was inside. I went looking. After exploring for some time, I unlocked the door of the auditorium. There, occupying thirteen of the one hundred and forty-four seats in the auditorim, were the teacher and the twelve pupils present that day looking at the day's episode of *Love of Live*. I turned on the lights. The teacher was chagrined, to say the least.

"Come on, children. We have to go back to our room now," she announced resignedly. They followed.

That afternoon I told this permanent teacher that I would come to her room to observe her teach reading the next day at our now established time. When I returned, they were there and they were ready. They had delayed their reading until my arrival. All children were present that day, all sitting in the reading circle holding a copy of the same book.

"Now, boys and girls, Ms. Haynes came to hear us read. We are going to read her the story of "The Three Bears.' Now, boys and girls, sit up tall. Ready begin."

"Once-a-ponce-a-time there was" they chorused. Together they chanted and read on and on. Some were mouthing. Some were repeating. Some were echoing. One held his book upside down.

About two weeks later, I stopped by this room early in the afternoon. No one was there. Again I went searching. On entering the auditorium, I found several classes looking at a movie. The corner of my left eye glimpsed a ray of light behind the cracked door of the small equipment room. I looked in. There huddled the teacher intently viewing *Edge of Night*.

A male teacher of an upper-grade EMR class came relunctantly to the office one morning to admit, "Something rather serious has happened in my class. It is something that needs some special attention right now." His class of sixteen children were with him. He moved into the office with four students and explained, "This girl said these three boys raped her."

"Um-humph, um-humph, um-humph, We did," they gleefully acknowledged.

"Where did this happen?" I asked.

"On the schoolyard," the girl replied. "Right beside those bungalows out there. And they got me all wet, too."

"When did this happen, before school?" I inquired.

"No, just a few minutes ago they told me," explained the teacher.

"Well, it's 9:20 now. Is this supposed to have happened since school began at 9:00?"

"Yes, it just happened. They just reported it to me."

"Then where were you?" I inquired of the teacher. "If this happened after the bell rang, you should have been supervising them."

"Yes, I know. But I had to come to the office to get some supplies. I told them to come with me, and they got away."

After four hours of interrogating, listening, and investigating by the vice-principal and myself, it was determined that the four had run away from the teacher. They had had a tussle outside a bungalow. The boys had fallen on the girl, but she had gotten herself up. She was not wet and had never been. The ten-year old girl shrugged it off with, "They always meddle me in the room and outdoors, too. I wanted to get them into some kind of trouble."

In making a check, Lydia Daniels, the counselor, discovered that many of the pupils in the six EMR rooms were improperly placed. Records showed that scores made on the Kuhlman-Anderson Intelligence Test given in group situations were used as the criteria for placement in many instances. There were children enrolled in these rooms without signed parental consent. Ms. Daniels proceeded to administer the Binet or the WISC to individual pupils using the proper procedure. As a result, some children were returned to regular classrooms.

That same spring of 1969, Jerome Parks, a third grader in Grape Street School was identified as a gifted child with an I.Q. of over 130. He was a rarity. The feeling existed that the school was indeed blessed to have one child with his talent. The concept of superior achievement had received little if any consideration. Ms. Daniels developed and disseminated among the staff a list of possible characteristics of gifted children. Teachers were encouraged to be observant and refer any child evidencing potential intellectual ability.

Beverly Washington submitted the name of one of her kindergarten girls. Ms. Daniels administered the test, and Latanya Austin was identified as a gifted child. What a day of rejoicing! What a magnificent discovery! Now Grape Street School had two identified gifted children.

Anne Renshaw, the office manager, was a reservoir of information for me as a new principal. She was able, ready, and anxious to keep me informed about the way things had been done in the office. Her efforts to provide guidance didn't seem out of line at first, but gradually an insistence to do things according to the established pattern began to emerge. Subdued resentment seemed to smolder as I endeavored to bring about minor changes.

As the spring semester neared its close, I was informed that Ms. Renshaw had filed for a transfer. I knew the child welfare and attendance supervisor and the nurse would be leaving. Now, the office manager wanted out. My philosophy has always been that people should only work where they choose and where they can be happy. So when people want to leave, I create no stumbling blocks. I was aware that in the fall the walls of the old administration building would come tumbling down and that an office manager with expertise would be direly needed in the new administration building. Our program would become more complex the following year. I began wondering if there were any one who could or would be willing to take on this challenging responsibility, especially with the kind of negative publicity that seemed to be Grape Street School's lot.

It did seem that walls were tumbling down in more ways than one. Clerical interviews were scheduled. The personnel office made it clear that I must accept one of the three interviewees willing to take the position. Ms. Renshaw, Mr. Fukushima, and I interviewed each candidate. The first to arrive was an attractive, seemingly mature and competent young Black woman. She was acceptable to each one of us, but, the next day she called and left word that she would not accept Grape Street. There was no explanation, which seemed odd. But so many deflating things were happening that this was just one more added to the list.

Two days later, three interviews were scheduled. The first person was a small, almost elderly Caucasian woman. When she entered my office and faced the three of us, she looked as if she felt she were a mouse caught in a trap. She explained that she hadn't known that the drive would be so far and she had had no experience with special programs. She was obviously anxious to complete the interview. If the first candidate seemed nervous, the second one appeared nerve-wracked. She was a tall, lanky, middle-age Caucasian woman, who wore a long orange doubled necklace. I kept wondering how long that string of beads would survive. She clutched them with her right hand and rubbed them up and down with sporadic jerks. This was her third interview, and she would go to the bottom of the list if she turned it down, but she wasn't sure about a school in this area. She knew nothing of special programs and had only worked in a small office with one other clerk. It was late in the afternoon. She left by a side door, didn't look back, and made a fast getaway.

I breathed a troubled sigh. Yugo muttered, "The third time has got to be the charm." It was. He ushered in a ray of sunshine. She was Naomi Gilbert. She was professionally mild mannered but obviously interested in becoming involved. Questions, answers, and discussion flowed freely with this third White candidate.

Then she asked, "Ms. Haynes, just what do you expect of your ofice manager?"

Yugo insightfully responded, "Everything." We all chuckled. Here it was in a nutshell, and she accepted it.

In the fall she came ready to work as did Marion Oliver, the nurse, and Novel Stokes, the child welfare and attendance supervisor. With Lydia Daniels, the staff counselor, what a team we made. Without the support of this office and special services group, I could not have survived the turbulence of the 1969-1970 school year.

5

SPECIAL PROGRAMS

*T*he Elementary and Secondary Education Act introduced by Congressman Adam Clayton Powell of New York and Carl Perkins of Kentucky, which was passed by Congress in 1965, has been the most far-reaching educational legislation ever enacted in the United States. The major provisions dealing with elementary and secondary education are detailed in the first five of its eight titles.

Title I provides funding for solving urban and rural problems of impoverished school districts, Title II for library and textbook materials, Title III for supplementary centers, Title IV for research centers, and Title V for grants to strengthen state education departments with state matching funds. Although Grape Street School benefited in some manner from each of these, it directly received funds from Title I and Title III. Although Title I was the main source of funds for compensatory education throughout the nation, in Los Angeles the school system combined additional state and district funds with Title I to create a larger coordinated compensatory education program to avoid duplication and provide support for larger numbers. In 1969-1970 Title I funds at Grape Street School were combined with the Miller-Unruh Reading Act, Assembly Bill 938, the Teacher Employment Program, and district inner-city funding.

A Title III program, a supplementary and innovative program, was functioning at Grape Street School on my arrival. A city-wide proposal had been submitted and was in effect in two units in Los Angeles-the Jordan Educational Complex in the south for Blacks and the Garfield Educational Complex on the east side for Mexican-Americans. Each complex derived its name from the high school central to its satellites. In the Jordan Complex the five elementary schools were Compton Avenue, Grape Street, 111th Street, 102nd Street, and Ritter Street.

1968-1969 was the second year of the program, which then encompassed kindergarten through grade two. During 1969-1970 it would include the third grade, and there it would stop. The program focused on individualization of reading. The Early Childhood Coordinator for Grape Street School was a young astute Black woman. Education aides assisted teacher, and substitute teachers came so that regular teachers could be released to visit classroom elsewhere that were purported to be individualized.

Each complex had a director. Laverne Parks was ours, but Grape was not her favorite school, since we had difficulty conforming to the strict guidelines of this innovative program. Toward the close of spring of 1969, a team from the Compensatory Unit of the California State Department of Education came to Los Angeles to review the Title I programs. Fred Tillman, a Black interviewer, visited our school.

The principals of the schools visited later learned that this team concluded that the compensatory funds were being spread too thin and diluted throughout too many schools, thereby resulting in too little achievement anywhere. They recommended that the most needy schools be saturated with funds. With the two major criteria being poverty and low achievement scores, thirty-nine schools were identified. Grape Street was number four. Its budget was allotted $300 per student with $50 deducted overhead expenses. We were given a shopping list of prices for purchasable items. With nearly nine hundred students enrolled, exclusive of the EMR children who receive no Title I funds, we felt rich--but what a responsibility. Now that we had some money, we wanted to spend it wisely. We were told we should begin involving the staff and the School-Community Advisory Council to which any parent or interested community person could belong.

We held discussions with the faculty and the School-Community Advisory Council and began to plan a budget to finance the program that would be implemented during the 1969-1970 school year. The six components covered in the budget were: reading and language arts, mathematics, auxiliary services including counseling, health, and attendance assistance, parent involvement, intergroup relations, and staff development.

Late into many nights, Yugo and I worked balancing the budget and writing the program description. To upgrade teaching procedures, we decided to budget for two consultants. The Early Childhood Coordinator for the Jordan Complex, Helen Clemmons, was taking a maternity leave, and Rosaleigh Wilson, a young woman who had outstanding competencies that I had seen her demonstrate in the classroom, accepted this position. Her responsibility was to work only with language arts in kindergarten through second grade. Anything that might relate to arithmetic, social studies, or science was a no-no, and she adhered to the guidelines. Gwen Wykoff was asked to leave the EMR classrooms she was so effectively teaching to become a consultant for kindergarten through third grade in all subject areas except language arts. To me, this seemed an awkward arrangement, but it was necessary to work out the program the best way possible, to satisfy the guidelines of both the Title III and Title I programs. Fortunately, these two young ladies were compatible, worked well together, and, at least for the first part of the year, offered teachers who were receptive some assistance.

When I worked as vice-principal at 111th Street School, Bernadine Lyles had been asked to leave her classroom to assist me in coordinating and upgrading the curriculum. Her teacher demonstrations and observations had proven high successful. I asked her to become Grape's third consultant and to work with upper-grade teachers as we had worked together previously. The year before she had taken a sabbatical. During this time she had designed a program based on strength teaching in social studies and language arts. Strength teaching involves assigning teachers subject areas in which they have special skills and interests.

Morning hours were to be spent teaching reading to students in their own classrooms. Ms. Lyles personally administered diagnostic tests in math and divided students into five learning levels. After the reading period, students were to move to the teacher responsible for their level of math. In the afternoon the students were organized so that they went to a teacher with strengths in social studies or language arts. The organization was intricate and complex. Ms. Lyles had worked it out in detail. She presented the procedure to teachers and asked for suggestions. They had none, but gave superficial consent to participate.

At the beginning of the school year we had moved into the new egg-crate shaped two-story building containing twenty classrooms, a library, two faculty rooms, and an administrative unit with offices to house the secretarial staff, the Child Welfare and Attendance Supervisor, a conference room, the nurse, a students' cot room, the counselor, the vice-principal, the principal, and an outer office. Most floor areas were carpeted. Although the architecture is extremely austere, the interior of the building seemed luxurious to us. So that every child could spend part of his or her school life in the new building, we began by allotting space to grade six and moved backward.

One third-grade class was assigned to the new building. That became Mayme Sweeney's room 5 where she began implementing an open classroom. There were so many problems around that very little attention was paid to her effective teaching methods. When she moved in, many people asked, "When will she ever stop bringing things in? Where in the world did she get all of that junk? And what is she going to do with all that stuff when she finishes getting it in there?" The program she was implementing was one she had envisioned while out on leave. It materialized into an open classroom model.

Bernadine Lyles worked tirelessly planning and trying to get a program off the ground, but very little clicked. The two out-of-classroom teachers assigned to assist her circumvented their responsibilities. They wanted to pull out small groups of students to teach reading. They refused to go into classrooms as the program designed required.

So the implementation of the strength teaching began to falter. Nevertheless, Ms. Lyles continued her efforts. Among the new teachers upstairs were Andrea Roberts, a young Black teacher just out of college, and Patricia Douglas, a White teacher just out of a convent. They didn't know each other prior to their assignments in rooms next to each other. Although, naturally, there were vast differences in their personalities, there were some outstanding similarities. They both had potential, both came with a positive commitment, both related well to the students, and both were ultra-traditional. In their rooms every table and every chair faced the chalkboard, every lesson I saw each teach was to the total class, and every child used the same textbook. Both maintained control, and both were good teachers, but evidently neither of them had had experience with grouping. They both seemed unaware of student differences in abilities and achievement.

They both wanted to be left alone, but they were new and were a part of the upper-grade program. Whether this particular program or some other program were being implemented, there was a need to train the staff to provide for individual differences, so I requested that Ms. Lyles work with them, as well as with others, in the area of diagnosing and prescribing for individual needs. A pattern developed. Ms Lyles went in and rearranged furniture to facilitate grouping. The next morning, each teacher arranged her room back into the original traditional setting. This happened about four times. Feelings began getting edgy. These were two of the twelve classes involved in the strength teaching. Efforts to implement the program were being sabotaged, unwittingly or otherwise. Few of the classroom teachers complied with the plan with any semblance of regularity. Some would detain their students. Some would send them late; some would send them early. Some made excuses. Others just didn't bother. A few tried. Some gave attention to students as they transferred to other rooms; others allowed them to run helter-skelter through the halls in a stampede. Some children kicked holes in the plaster of the new walls. There were periods when pandemonium reigned.

Ms Lyles continued her efforts. She went into classrooms to assist teachers in developing learning center environments. Time after time, Ms. Roberts, Ms. Douglas, and other teachers rearranged their classrooms back to the original barren, traditional settings. Over and over this happened. There were times Ms. Lyles understandably became discouraged. She made herself available for group or individual conferences, and she led workshops regularly. Some teachers came and participated, some came and sat, and some didn't come. One day after a workshop session she exploded to me, "Why don't you *make* these teachers cooperate!"

I had to explain that it wouldn't work that way. One can't "make" human beings implement any program. The basic need at Grape Street School at that time was to develop a positive attitude toward students and a desire in more teachers to want to facilitate learning. Before the end of the first semester, we had overreached the saturation point. Neither departmentalization nor strength teaching was going to work for us, so I called it off.

The Jordan Educational Complex was an imposed program that created many problems, many meetings, excessive paper work, and the rigid guidelines of an innovative program. Many teachers expressed concern about whether allegiance was due to the director of the complex or the principal of the school. Their philosophies differed considerably. The complex director directed teachers to write behavioral objectives and post them at each learning center. Some teachers tried, and some never did.

Because I still felt some obligation to try to comply with the different mandates, I asked the first and second grades to go on a divided-day session. In this organization one-half of each class arrived at 9:00 and were taught reading for an hour. The remaining half arrived at 10:00. After the entire class had a twenty-minute recess, each first and second grade returned to its classrooms to study social studies, math, and other subjects. At 2:00 the children who arrived early were dismissed, and those who had arrived at 10:00 were taught reading or an hour. The intent of this schedule was to allow teachers to individualize with few students present. Because the second-grade teachers seemed to be making some effort, I planned to assign first and second-grade teachers to double classrooms with doors opening between them so that they might work cooperatively. The first-grade teachers rebelled at this idea; they didn't like the divided-day proposal either. Reluctantly, they agreed to try this program with first-grade teachers housed in the double classrooms, but frustrations were scarcely abated.

The Jordan Complex Early Childhood Coordinator worked continually helping those who were receptive to learn how to write behavioral objectives, set up learning centers, make reports, keep records, and give tests. Tons of paper were dittoed and distributed. Ms. Wilson kept a full-time clerk busy day in and day out. When visiting classrooms, I began to notice the teachers' written behavioral objectives splattered with paint, scribbled upon, torn loose, stepped upon, or desecrated in some other manner. I also noticed that teachers were busy but that little was happening to advance the learning of students. Too many unrelated activities were going on. Teachers were increasingly making more effort, but the desired results were negligible.

Ms. Wykoff and Ms. Wilson planned and conducted outstanding workshops. They went into rooms to assist in developing learning centers and room environments. Some teachers were outspokenly resistant. Rooms kept changing. On some days they vibrated with the consultants' touches; on other days, they returned to disarray and bleakness. Resentments and hostilities filled the air, although some teachers were trying. I was told that some consultants entered rooms announcing, "We're arranging the classroom environment the way Ms. Haynes wants it done." It had been my intent to have the consultants work closely with teachers to plan and develop meaningful room environments, and this was what I had planned with the consultants, but they had encountered so much resistance, perhaps they felt the need to use this tactic. They were making real efforts to work with teachers, and some teachers were working with programs, but overall it was disjointed and detached. This went on throughout 1969-1970.

In December school closed for a two-week vacation period.

"Merry Christmas, ladies," I called out "You are really going to make the holiday merry for some families, aren't you?"

"We hope so, Mrs. Haynes. You know we have such a long list of really needy families. Mr. Stokes, our CWA Supervisor, checked the list out for us so that there won't be duplications," explained Ms. Broussard.

It was about dusk on a Saturday afternoon. On the chilly auditorium stage a group of PTA women were busily packing baskets from foodstuffs contributed by children, staff, and community agencies. Thelmarie Gray, Luella Burton, Inez Henderson, Alecia Jackson, Doris Washington, Willia Moore, and Margarette Broussard were the nucleus of our volunteer parents. Each served as a member of the Block Club Parents, School-Community Advisory Council, and Room Mothers, but still found time to work with teachers in the classroom as well as recruit others to do so. For three years Ms. Moore had fought a one-woman battle to secure no parking signs indicating specified hours for regular sweeping of the area's streets, and she finally succeeded. These parents knocked on doors and gave residents telephone numbers to call if they suspected vandals were on the school's campus. They asked local grocers not to sell candy during school hours, and they called parents of children who brought candy and threw papers on the school grounds. They recruited resource persons to share their experiences and skills with teachers and children in classroom and assembly programs. They attended scheduled meetings and brought others along. In short, they supplied much needed support.

The education aides already employed in the Title III Jordan Educational Complex program lived outside the school neighborhood. When the Title I program was planned, we budgeted for twelve additional education aides. The School-Community Advisory Council had approved and the chairperson had, as required, signed the budget. Together we had also developed guidelines indicating that Title I education aides must live within the school community boundaries. An evaluation board with representatives from the school and the Council interviewed applicants, most of whom were parents who had volunteered their services to the school throughout the years. A ranked list was developed, and each person on the list went for a health examination. Several weeks after school began they were cleared and came on duty. Most were welcomed; the others were accepted. Six weeks after they arrived and were settling into their tasks, received, with no forewarning, a notice instructing me to terminate the twelve at the close of the next week. They were to be dismissed before they could become permanent and were to be replaced by persons from the district list who lived in various areas throughout the city. I didn't believe what I was reading. There was no way--just no way that I could call in these twelve neighborhood women and tell them that they no longer had jobs at Grape Street School, but there was no way I could avoid telling them if their pay stopped. What a dilemma. This was one of my very lowest points. I telephoned, and wrote letters. At first I was told they could not possibly remain--they had to be replaced by persons from the district list. Community involvement was the heralded slogan of the day, and these inconsistencies were too much to endure. How ironic! I kept at it. My problem reached the Associate Superintendent, Dr. Robert J. Purdy. I understand that almost everyone on "The Hill" heard about Grape and its problem, and I heard that some rules were bent, twisted, and changed. I do know that if those education aides had not received an assignment order, which showed a printed correction of their termination dates, that they would never have know that their jobs hung in a precarious balance for what seemed to me an interminable period.

From the beginning and throughout this school year, vendors and salesmen called and came. Entrepreneurs made contacts. Book publishers inundated us with mail. School supply companies mailed, called, and came. Invitations for luncheons, for dinner, and for cocktails arrived. Displays and sales talks accompanied each. There were individualized reading programs--kits of materials--teaching machines--audio-visual equipment--encyclopedia sets--programmed materials--instructional teaching games. There were foolproof materials and teacher-proof programs. And on and on it went. Word had gotten around that the schools had money, and the salespeople came in droves.

What seemed difficult for some of the public to understand was that the school did not have money. The Title I schools had budgets that had been planned and approved during the preceeding school year. Once the school year began, we operated with the approved budget, with the actual money being paid from the central office. Most of our funds were being spent for more personnel, and we just couldn't go shopping any time we wanted to do so.

I remember that once a number of Jordan Complex elementary school principals were invited to the Los Angeles County Multipurpose Health Center, a neighborhood facility near the Jordan High School. The meeting had been arranged by the Mothers of Watts. Following the riots, a group of young men from the neighborhood, who had police records or some encounters with the law, had organized as the Sons of Watts to involve themselves in positive activities in the community. Their mothers or female relatives had organized to support these and other community efforts.

California State Assemblyman William Green (D) was present with a White gentleman who had a math program to sell. Reprints of news articles about the program's successes with groups in other counties and states were distributed. The speaker presented his program eloquently and explained the cost per pupil. The mothers present were convinced that this was the program every school in Watts needed. Two of the mothers became incensed when the principals tried to explain how a budget worked, that their budgets were already decided, and, even if this were a program of interest, they would need to involve their own staff and councils in the decision to buy it.

"You principals have money. Our children are behind. You aren't teaching them anything. Here is a good program. We called this meeting so that you could buy this program now."

I felt sure the ladies, who were well meaning, had some misgivings about most of us when we left.

During the fall of 1969, some of our students brought their lunches, some bought nutritious lunches in the cafeteria, some went home for lunch, and a few brought no food, bought no food, and had no food. Those who brought lunch ate it at the beginning of the recess period. Bringing money for lunch often posed problems. Sometimes the children lost their money, and some times other students extorted it. Too frequently children stopped at a neighborhood store to purchase potato chips, Fritos, peanuts, candy, or some other snack, and they often left the grounds without permission during school hours to go to a store. Often teachers sent students to the office when they observed that they had come to school without breakfast and had no food for the day.

Every noon about two hundred pupils sat at tables under the pavilion eating either the lunch they had bought or the one they brought. Noon duty directors were parents or persons from the community employed to supervise the lunch and noon recess periods. Teachers are not assigned duty during the lunch hour unless it was a rainy day or there was some special need.

In November 1969, the National School Lunch Program began at Grape Street School. We sent home an information sheet and an application for everyone of the almost one thousand pupils. This was one form parents lost no time returning. It took hours and hours of work to process the returned applications. Lunch tickets were prepared for every child. We were admonished not to differentiate between those who received a free lunch and those who paid. Only a few did not qualify for free lunches. The teachers distributed tickets to every child each day before going to lunch. It was imperative that a ticket be collected for each lunch served, so Florence Bottorff, the cafeterial manager, diligently collected and counted the nearly one thousand tickets herself.

Ms. Bottorff was White. The thirty-two other workers were Black, and they respected her. The cafeteria operation was run well, and the organization of the free lunch program looked good on paper. More tables were ordered, and more noon duty directors were employed. Most of the education aides chose to work one-half hour during the lunch period so that they might leave school half an hour early at 3:00 P.M.

38

On the first day the primary lunch period was hectic, but we survived it. When the primary children went out to play, the upper-grade students arrived. There was a delay in the service because the cafeteria wasn't equipped with enough ovens for preparing food in that quantity. The waiting period was disastrous. The simplest way to describe that lunch period would be to say, "All hell broke loose," Students yelled, pushed, chanted. When the meals were served, they decided they didn't want ground meat over rice. They threw food--they threw milk. All the tables were filled--there weren't enough seats. Some children poured food on others or poured food on the ground. Somehow the staff got through that lunch period. The cafeteria was left looking as if a rock group had camped in it over a weekend. The garbage cans and trash bins overflowed. There weren't enough to hold the waste.

The next day hot dogs were served. The students liked them. As they ate, they discovered the accompanying small plastic bags filled with mustard and started having a heyday. They pinched holes in the bags, aimed, and squirted them onto other children, the walls, the floors, the tables, and the grounds. They stomped the packets with their feet. By the end of the day, most of the walls of the buildings were spotted with mustard, and the cafeteria manager was frustrated. More lunches had been served than tickets collected. Some youngsters found ways to use the same ticket twice, some extorted tickets from others, some bought tickets from others, and some lost tickets, got a duplicate, found the original, and then used them both.

One day an outspoken parent stalked into the office demanding, "I want to see the lady with that mole on her nose, and she's got that big bushy natural."

Pauline Bryant, our very calm and poised little clerk, called, "Ms. Cole."

Glorious Cole, one of our most amiable school clerks, who was spending hours at school and at home at night sorting and counting tickets and attending to many other accounting matters, came to the counter.

"May I help you, Ms. Walters?"

"Yes, my daughter came all the way home to tell me you won't give her no food to eat, and she's hungry."

"But Ms. Walters, Diane has lost her ticket two times already. And the rule is not to give the children more than three tickets."

"I don't care what the rule is. You give my child something so that she can get her lunch. And I don't want to have to come up here to see about this kind of matter anymore."

Confusion reigned. Counting and packaging tickets daily was a chore. Sometimes there was more than one ticket for each child; sometimes there weren't enough tickets. Members of the office staff took boxes of tickets home to sort and package, so that they could place them in teachers boxes for distribution on the next day. At faculty meetings we tried to discuss ways to alleviate the situation. Some teachers complained about the menu.

"It doesn't matter if the food is free, they don't have to feed them slop."

"I wouldn't give that food they are serving to my dogs. That cafeteria manager doesn't care what they serve these kids."

"There aren't enough garbage cans. They fill up before the primary children finish."

"Where do you expect the children to sit? Maybe they should bring out their chairs."

"My children didn't even get served until ten minutes before time to return to class. I had to stay out and let them play for a period."

"I told the noon duty directors to let mine play first. They've been standing and waiting so long every day."

I had checked the food. There were two menus that didn't look too good, although they were nutritious according to health standards. We had ordered more tables, and some had arrived. We had also ordered more trash cans, but there were not enough.

I called Harry Redoglia, director of food services, and he came out personally, surveyed the situation, and gave immediate assistance. He arranged to replace the ovens with larger ones. We received more lunch tables, more garbage cans and another large trash bin. We chose two other menus to replace those that seemed less palatable.

Then it was the staff's responsibility to work with the students to help them with table manners, eating habits, and a sense of appreciation. We did so after a fashion. Gradually, the lunch periods became tolerable.

One morning in May 1970, Ms. Bottorff informed me tht she had found the electric plug disconnected from the refrigerator when she arrived at 6:30 a.m. No one knew what had happened, or how long the food had been without refrigeration. We did not deliberate about what should be done. Every morsel of food in that refrigerator was packed, wrapped, put into the trash bins, and covered until it could be hauled away. Fresh food was ordered and delivered quickly, but, understandably, the meals for Grape Street and the other schools serviced by the central kitchen were delayed. The staff was informed about the circumstances. It was another inconvenience, but they seemed to accept the "it's better to be safe than sorry" attitude.

6

INSIDE SOME CLASSROOMS

*E*ach morning and throughout each day, without fail, Yugo Fukushima, Lydia Daniels, Marion Oliver, and Novel Stokes went to a certain class in a bungalow. They went individually, in pairs, or in groups, and periodically I dropped in too. There was always one condition on which we could count--chaos! This was the clasroom of a Black female permanent teacher.

Many destructive things happened in that room. The clock was pulled from the wall repeatedly, rungs of chairs were broken, holes were punched in the ceiling, and furniture was defaced. Obscenities were written on the floor, door, walls, or elsewhere. Windows were broken, and children climbed in and out of them at will. All of this went on while the teacher was in charge and in the room.

The vice-principal, the counselor, the nurse, the Child Welfare and Attendance Supervisor, and I constantly tried to assist and offer suggestions. The composite skills we had to offer were of little, if any, avail. Trying to have the guidance committee work with the situation was a waste of time. A typical explanation offered during any conferences was, "Well, what can you expect from these children? They don't have any home training."

On another occasion, during the 1969 summer school session at 111th Street School, two students supposedly supervised by this same teacher had had a fight. One left the school grounds and returned with an irate young uncle and four juvenile relatives bearing lead pipes. I sent for the teacher to come down to the office. She came, nonchalantly faced the outraged group, and calmly commented, "Oh, any doctor can pull that cut together with two or three stitches. After all, she started the fight, and I guess she had it coming to her." After an extended period at Grape Street School, making no apparent progress, this teacher chose to transfer.

One day I took a visiting administrative coordinator into some classrooms. We opened one bungalow door and walked in. The permanent teacher was sitting on a piece of carpet on the floor, nodding and wiggling his toes through his stocking feet. Three groups of students from this room had been purposely scheduled to study simultaneously with the Miller-Unruh reading specialists in their labs. About ten boys were jumping, running, throwing, and having a heydey in the disarranged areas. As we stood there, the teacher awakened startled, glared up, and haltingly explained that the remaining students "were having a period of exploration which would help develop their independence."

A little later we learned that a probationary teacher was suspending pupils, sending them home at any time of the day at will, and daring them to inform the office. This teacher maintained a rigid, traditional classroom, and anyone who deviated from his stated rules were in trouble. Almost every day at least one child was sternly instructed to leave by a side door and to go home without benefit of a note or knowledge of an administrator.

The students in this classroom were regimented at all times. Everyone was instructed to, "Sit up straight, keep your mouths closed, and do your lessons."

All tables and chairs faced the chalkboard. I can't remember seeing this teacher ever smile. In the initial interview, I remember him shaking his shiny brown bald head, looking me straight in the eyes, and warning me, "If anyone tries to prevent my becoming a permanent teacher, I will take him to court and I will sue. I will sue." This teacher evidenced a desire to become a strict, staunch, traditional teacher.

He came to teach, and he did just that. He gave no consideration to children's learnings. No talking was allowed. His hand-writing looked like chicken scratchings. He wrote briskly and filled the board with questions. Many times his letters and words were illegible, and students dared not ask for clarification. When I attempted to suggest relaxing the rigidity, he explained that he couldn't let those children get out of hand. Then he ended on a totally irrelevant note, "The police have traced me from my last job here. Someone here must have informed them where I'm working now." I think the regularity of the unannounced suspensions ceased, but little else changed in that room that year.

Fifteen school journeys or field trips were purchased as a Title I budget item for the 1969-1970 school year. They were planned to be outdoor classrooms where learnings were to be extended. These trips supplemented the seven trips allocated by the district for each semester. Only one class could go on most district trips, which usually meant around thirty-five pupils. The Title I trips transported seventy-nine passengers, so with our three norm reduction teachers--teachers who were added to the staff and paid from Title I funds so that all classes would have less students--each bus would accommodate two regular classes and an EMR group. With this arrangement, every class participated in at least one field trip a year and many were involved in two.

One day the stern Black male teacher just described, the faculty chairman, and an EMR teacher, their three classes, and two education aides boarded a bus for a day at the beach. The parents of the children had signed permission slips for them to be away from school under the supervision of their teachers. The slips indicated the 9:00 a.m. time that the bus would leave and the return time of 2:00 p.m.

At the beginning of the day, there was very little communication between the two male teachers. By the end of the day, obvious hostility had developed. My understanding is that the faculty chairman and the driver announced the time the group was to leave and return to the bus. After arriving at the beach, the faculty chairman supposedly informed the other male teacher of a twenty-minute later change in the return time. He took his class and they went on their exploring activities. After lunch, according to the new schedule, there was a half hour for play. At the appointed time they formed a straight line and marched like soldiers to the door of the bus. There sitting, waiting were all of the other passengers. The bus driver gave the teacher a public tongue lashing, reprimanding him for the delay and reminding him that the return time had been announced clearly to the total group before they left the bus. The faculty chairman sat smugly smiling and never revealed that he had informed the other teacher of a time change.

About two-thirty that afternoon, those of us in the office began to be concerned. The minutes ticked away. We called the Transportation Section, who told us there had been no accident and that the bus assigned to our school was on schedule. This really didn't tell us anything. Our children had not returned, and it was past time for them to go home. Parents began calling. Agonizingly the minutes passed. The information we could obtain told us nothing of the whereabout of our classes. The phone kept ringing. Parents came to school, but we asked them to wait at home. We remained calm because, generally, we reasoned, when an accident happens, one is informed immediately.

At 5:25 p.m. a relieved parent called me exclaiming, "Ms Haynes, the bus just stopped in front of my house. The driver is delivering the children home." And that is just what he did. It seems that when the bus driver was ready to load the bus for the return trip to school at 1:30 p.m., the faculty chairman called to arrange with the Transportation Section, in the name of the administrator to have this bus driver leave his passengers at an adjoining beach and return to pick them up at 5:00 p.m. Blithely, after delivering the children, the five adults descended from the bus. The stern Black teacher was silent, but he was generally that way. Three of them signed out and bade us goodbye.

The parents were satisfied; their children were home. The faculty chairman had explained at each stop the advantages of this extended experience. The children had enjoyed themselves at the amusement park.

The parents accepted his reason for the late return, I needed some further explanation. The faculty chairman evasively bounced up.

"May I speak with you a minute? What happened?" I inquired.

"Oh, we just got permission to stay longer. They said you approved it."

"How could I approve something that I knew nothing about? You should have called me to make this request."

"They said they would call you. Anyway, it worked out all right."

"You know, you seem to have a propensity toward administration. Are you interested in studying and involving yourself so that you might go into administration properly?"

"Naw, child, I ain't got no interest in letting these niggers kill me."

One afternoon I opened the door of a double bungalow and walked into a third-grade classroom. The children in the first room were sitting at tables busily coloring turkeys. There was order, and every child seemed involved. The teacher stood in the open doorway supervising her own class and the one in the adjoining room. I walked through into the second room, where the students were watching a filmstrip of Goldilocks. One of the children was operating the filmstrip projector. On the table beside the machine was a box holding three other filmstrips of fairy tales ready to be shown in turn.

"Where is their teacher?" I asked.

"She had an emergency," the attending teacher answered.

"Is she ill?"

"No, I don't believe she is."

"Did she get a call from the office?"

"I don't believe she did."

"Do you expect her back today?" I kept trying.

"I'll keep her class until she gets back," the teacher calmly replied.

She didn't return that day. I checked in the office and she had not reported that she was leaving school. In the OUT time slot opposite this teacher's name someone had signed 3:30.

Although she arrived on time the next day, she avoided coming into the office. When I stopped by her room, her elegant coiffure seemed to substantiate the fact that I had heard that she had had a 2:00 p.m. appointment with her hairdresser the previous day.

Two weeks later, I walked through several third-grade classrooms in the afternoon and counted one, two, three, and four vacant. I looked out on the yard, but they were not out for physical education. I went to the auditorium, and found the four classes there looking at a movie. Only one teacher was present. I looked in the teachers' dining room, but no one was there. I asked the teacher in charge, "Where are the other teachers?"

"I'm supervising the classes," I was informed.

"Yes, I can see that, but are the other teachers returning to pick up their classes?"

"I don't know. I promised I would take care of them."

I sat through the movie until 3:00 p.m., when the teacher dismissed the children and told them to go home. The other three teachers did not return that day. Some weeks later, through a queer quirk of circumstances, someone mentioned, by name, seeing one of the absent teachers with two other persons at the race track.

In the fall of 1969 Mayme Sweeney returned from a leave. I was really amazed that such an affable, positively oriented teacher would choose to return to a school so openly infected with acrimony. Nevertheless, she did. When she moved in, she brought a lot of things with her besides her effervescent personality. There was a cash register, an adding machine, a typewriter, a variety of weighing scales, turnstile bookracks, stationary book holders, a menagerie of animals, cardboard boxes, pieces of wood, bottles, tops, clothespins, magazines, catalogs, advertisements, books, styrofoam, regular school supplies, state texts, paperback books, comic books, and innumerable other items she used as instructional aids. The comment, "How junky," was frequently made to describe room 5, but personable Mayme Sweeney taught, mothered, and opened the minds of her classroom brood.

Her students came early, stayed late, and made all kinds of excuses to remain in during the recesses. Wood constructions began taking shape. A "WATTS GROCERY" sign was hung, and the cash register was filled with play money. The children and their teacher filled the shelves with cans, boxes, and wrappers that once contained food. These either retained or were marked with realistic prices. Advertisements were used for verification. Then a "GRAPE STREET BANK" sign went up. Boys measured and cut out a window for a teller's cage. Play money was placed in denominations in tin pans used as money holders, and play coins were counted into muffin tins. Some children helped design simple deposit slips and checks. These were duplicated and placed in stacks. The bank was ready to open.

"SCHOOL LIBRARY" was posted over the corner where books were stacked and piled. Two turnstile bookracks stood here along with two tall-boy stationary racks. The students categorized the books for display by arranging them in alphabetical order of their own design: *Animals, Bugs, Cars, Dogs, Eyes and Ears, Family, Games, Houses, Ideas, Jokes, Kites, Laughs, Men, Noses, Owls, People, Quiet, Rain, Sky, Tall Tales, Umbrellas, Voices, Women Xylophones, Years* and *Zoo*.

What involvement those children had deciding these groupings, and then what decisions they made while determining where each book would be placed! It took six weeks for six children to organize the library, and what an abundance of learnings took place during that time. Deciding where each of the one hundred and eighty-two paperback books were to be placed was a tremendous task. Not only titles needed to be considered, but the content of the book was of high significance, they found. One day while visiting, I listened:

"I can't find any book named xylophone, can you? What is it anyway?"

"It's a musical instrument. Maybe that's what we can do, put books about musical instruments under X."

"Oh, no, that won't fit right. Wow, you know X is a hard one. Maybe we should change that title."

"Change it to what? At least, we have a name for X. Do you think we might find a story with an xylophone in it?"

"Oh, you know what, I saw xylophone for X in one of those ABC Books."

"Well, that's it. Let's see it. Yes, let's put it under X."

"But how would anyone know xylophone is under X in this book. The title says ABC Book."

"That's right. We'll have to figure something out."

"I've got it. Let's type out a strip to paste on the front. I'll type 'WITH X FOR XYLOPHONE.' We'll cut the paper and paste it right under the title ABC Book. Then it will say 'ABC Book With X for Xylophone.'"

"Yeah, I think that's about the best we can do for X."

And that is what they did.

A carpenter shop, a zoo, and a local hospital where children and animals were nursed in turn were also developed in this room. Many of these children had more than their share of academic and emotional problems. Case study files had been compiled on nearly half of them. While in their classroom milieu, however, the problems they had or brought with them seemed to lessen and dissipate. The children continually discussed their need to take care of business in their room.

One morning I heard Maldonado Hankins, a well-known hyperactive third grader pleading in his usual plaintive tone, "Ms. Sweeney, we don't have to go back to structure today, do we? Do we, Ms. Sweeney? Do we have to go back to structure?"

"That depends upon you and the group, Maldonado. If I recall correctly, I believe, according to our contract and what happened yesterday, your group will begin with structure this morning." Structure for this group meant program planning by the teacher. Other students who had become self-motivated and self-directed were allowed to choose the times, or to contract for their projects and basic subject study skills. When contracts were not honored or children found it difficult to follow through on their schedules, then Ms. Sweeney planned their day and worked very closely with them throughout each session. Although she was always available to anyone in need, certain periods were designated for direct instruction to small groups or individuals.

In a conference one day Novel Stokes, the Child Welfare and Attendance Supervisor asked, "Did you know that there is one room in this school that maintains perfect attendance?"

"Yes," I answered, "I can guess. It's room 5."

Later at a PTA Meeting I related, "There is one teacher on our staff whose room maintains 100 percent attendance. Frequently she has to send for me to help persuade her students to go out for recess, come for lunch and to get them to go home in the afternoons. One day a boy in this room became ill. The nurse found his temperature to be 101 degrees. His mother was called, and she came, but the boy ran away. He circled the new building and darted in between and around the bungalows; he allowed none of us to go near him. We sent for Ms. Sweeney, and she went outside. She called Frank. He came to her, and she reasoned with him. They walked back together. 'Frank has agreed to go with his mother to see the doctor. He says he will take care of himself so that he can come back to school as soon as he is well,' she explained. Meekly, the usual little bully took his mother's hand and followd her away. The next morning he returned to class with a normal temperature....The children in this room just can't seem to stay away.''

As I finished the audience began to chant, "Room 5...it's room 5."

"Yes, it is room 5. Something is happening in that room that makes children want to come and stay in school," I concluded. Most teachers were unaware of this and accepted my explanation. Two became indignant and felt their efforts were being over-looked. One nurtured her grievance to the point of using it as her reason for requesting a transfer.

Joan Dunning, a young Black teacher, called from her room to ask for permission to take her second graders for a walk around the school block. It was granted. In an orderly, nonregimented line the children walked, talked, and filled their bags. It was obvious that there had been preparation for this field study trip. Two days later when I entered room 28, I saw the trash and debri the girls and boys had collected, displayed above carefully lettered stories. Some of them read:

Jeannette Greenwood   *November, 1969]*

We went for a walk around school.
We found lots of trash and dirty things.
Can you see all the paper wrappers I found?
Paper trash makes our school look dirty.

Ronald Brim   *November, 1969]*

Miss Dunning took our class for a walk.
We walked around our school.
Miss Dunning gave us some brown paper bags.
We picked up trash and put it in our bags.

Carlos Castanon   *November, 1969]*

Our class took a walk around our school.
Children and grown-ups throw down too much trash.
I picked up candy wrapper and frito bags.
I picked up cigarette packets and cigarette butts.

[Yvette Clark   *November, 1969]*

Today our class went walking around our school.
We saw lots and lots and lots of trash.
I picked up leaves and papers and bags and beer cans.
My teacher told us not to pick up glass it might cut.

Every word in these stories was correctly spelled. The teacher had pro
vided the proper guidance. Other stories showed learnings by other stu
dents in different subject areas. Frequently throughout the year this class
went on excursions, each time for a different purpose. On different
occasions they collected rocks, wood, debri from the construction area
litter from the yard around the old building, bottles, cans, plastics, and
discarded items of all types. In this room, also, pupils were quietly bu
purposefully involved.

Carol Reiss, a White teacher, was new to the school that year. She
was dedicated, committed, and seemed unafraid of hard work, but he
fourth-grade class was difficult. Regardless of how she planned, regard
less of how she tried, discipline problems interferred with the implemer
tation of her program. She sought assistance from the supportive staff and
made regular contacts with parents. One mother whose son was late
identified as EH (educably handicapped) agreed to come to school almost
every day. Only when his mother was in the room did her son maintain
any semblance of control. The departmentalization and team teaching
efforts were additional disruptions, but Carol Reiss worked on, experienc
ing few successes or satisfactions that year.

Through the school year, in too many classrooms too little teaching
had gone on, but in the spring, about two weeks before Open House
housecleaning and "work-to-show" began appearing. It was like magic
Classrooms were transformed. The permanent teacher who liked to tell m
secrets came again. This time what she had to say was no secret. Severa
teachers had commissioned her, she said, to tell me, "There is a teache
with pictures high up on the walls--way up above the children's eye level
We thought you needed to know this. We thought you'd want to know be
fore people come in to see it that way." She didn't say who the teache
was or where the room was, but her eyes focused on the southwest corner.

I recalled having spoken about placing displays at students' eye leve
when I was endeavoring to help teachers develop some meaningful roor
environment. Obviously the teacher's intent was for me to find and crit
cize someone. Joan Dunning's room was in the southwest corner, so I wer
there to see what the hullabaloo was all about. When I opened the doo
I was propelled into an enchanted classroom. Children's language
math, science, and art experiences were displayed from the ceiling to th
floor. My eyes feasted. Everthing I saw was relevant. All around me wer
those many discarded items transformed into meaningful and creativ
works of art. There was no doubt that the children had been involved i

48

research. Tissue paper sunsets, roving thread birds, plastic bottle pigs, painted volcanic rocks, and other scenes were portrayed in authenic colors. Among the many hangings and three-dimensional displays, was a large heavy old wooden gate that was now termite riddled. The teacher had guided the students to make a study of the neighborhood. Each day different groups were assigned to identify the function of a business or institution in the school area. Each day different students took turns using a black felt marker to sketch on this old gate the library, the fire station, a church, a grocery store, a barbecue stand, a meat market, a stationery store, a liquor store, a doctor's office and others until the gate represented a map of the neighborhood. This black on black work of art was captioned, "WATTS."

I was so impressed with the total display in this oasis of a classroom that I insisted that the Art Supervisor come to take a look. I am sure she felt something was wrong with me. It was difficult to convince outsiders that there was any quality teaching at Grape Street School, yet here I was announcing that there was a teacher successfully using art as a medium. Nevertheless, the Art Supervisor did come. One look and she was as impressed as I had been. She asked that the work of this class be displayed in the South Area Art Room. We were delighted, and this classroom's art show remained on display there for two months.

Slowly and dejectedly I closed the door behind me as I walked away from Elois Taylor and her twenty-seven first-graders. This was my fourth visit to her classroom in the last four months, and the same situation prevailed each time. In October when I entered, she sat with her back to the chalkboard and the class sat altogether on and off the pieces of carpet on the floor. On the chalkboard Ms. Taylor had lettered:

This is the family.
Father is big.
Mother is big.
The baby is little.

She moved her right arm under each line as the students chorused the words. At least, some of the students chorused. Two played patting hands, two pushed each other with their legs, two played catch with a shoe, and three on the periphery rolled in and out. The room was bleak, although several commercial posters had been hung.

That afternoon I spoke with Ms. Taylor and asked when she planned to divide her students into groups. She replied that she was getting ready to do so; she was trying to work out a way to individualize.
Elois Taylor is an affable, delightfully emotional and highly involved person. She radiates warmth or depression as the occasion warrants. At this time it was obvious that she was frustrated. A month later when I visited again, the room environment was the same, and on two later occasions when I visited this room again, the same situation prevailed.

This morning after Open House early in the month of April, I received a note that summoned me to, "Come to room 29 right away." "Why," I thought to myself, "had I missed visiting that room when I made my school walk on the afternoon before? How could I have missed it?" Because of the disappointing previous experience. I guess I subconsciously had missed visiting this room on Open House Day.

I left everything and literally ran to room 29. When I walked in, my amazement was only surpassed by my disbelief. The environment was alive and rich. The well-delineated learning centers looked practical and functional. As my eyes circled the room, it was apparent that all basic subject areas has been encompassed in this planning. What challenging questions and tasks were provided! I looked long and hard. Then I looked at Ms. Taylor and her students. There she sat proudly, and there sat the children in the same spots and the same positions I had seen before, only this time, all eyes were sparkling and looking expectantly at me.

My voice came, "Ms Taylor, this room has truly been transformed. You have certainly developed a rich learning environment for your children. I am happy you invited me over to see it. But, what would please me more, would be to see these boys and girls working in these centers. When may I come back to see them at work with these well-prepared and well-planned centers?"

Ms. Taylor's response was filled with pathos but emphatically clear, "You know what, Ms. Haynes, if I ever let these children get their hands on those centers, they will never be the same."

Later I asked Ms. Taylor, "What do you think will happen to your boys and girls when they are permitted to become involved in that rich environment you have provided?"

Her infectious smile predicted what was to come. She did learn to involve her children in the centers, and now you can't find a happier, more animated teacher as she works among and with her students. She'll tell you, "They'll never be the same."

7

TIME OUT FOR STRIKING

*D*uring the years I taught in the Los Angeles school system, I was actively involved in the Elementary Teachers' Club. I was affiliated with the California Teachers' Association and the National Education Association. Before I became an administrator, the Los Angeles Teachers' Association, LATA, was organized and separated from the Affiliated Teachers of Los Angeles, ATOLA, the organization that had originated as an umbrella entity. In 1969 the majority of teachers chose to join the United Teachers of Los Angeles, UTLA, and became unionized. A few chose to remain members of the depleted professional organizations.

UTLA began negotiations for higher salaries and better teaching conditions. A trial one-day strike was called, and it was somewhat successful for the union. A large number of teachers throughout the sprawling city remained away from school for that one day. Later that year representatives from the New York City United Federation of Teachers came to tell our teachers of their strike successes. The newly unionized teachers voted to call a major strike. The decision to walk out or stay in was an agonizing one for many teachers. The reasons for the strike remained unclear to most participants from the beginning to the end. It was my duty to say to our faculty, "The strike is illegal. The decision to go out or remain in rests with you as an individual. But I will assure you that whatever course you take, there will be no recriminatory action taken by this administration."

On the eve of the announced day of the strike I received a telephone call from a comparatively new, apparently naive young Black male teacher, "Ms. Haynes, would you call an assembly tomorrow and encourage the teachers to stay home?" It was difficult to believe that he was serious, but he was.

"Didn't you hear me explain my position at the meeting this afternoon?" I asked.

"Oh yes, I heard you, but I thought if you would tell the teachers to stay home, it might carry some weight with them and more of them might come out on strike."

"I guess you just don't understand." I reiterated my position again to him.

"Well, I hope you'll wish us luck," he concluded.

The teachers strike began on April 13, 1970. It lasted twenty-three days through May 13, 1970. About one-half of the Grape Street staff went out. The two consultants and the Jordan Educational Complex Coordinator joined the "out" group; substitutes embellished the ranks of the "in" group. Although the students population fluctuated, we were able to hold school. On the first morning, some of the "out" teachers went into the community and encouraged children to come to school. They came in hordes and droves. The intent was to overwhelm the depleted staff with numbers. Some of the striking teachers joked with me through the fence as they elaborated about their strategy.

"Why don't you close school?" one teacher asked. Why don't you close up school so those other teachers will come out?"

"Ms. Haynes, you ought to come to one of these union rallies. You should hear this sharp young man from New York. Ms. Haynes, if you would just come to hear him speak, you'd come out on strike, too."

Somehow we managed to have enough certificated personnel to take care of the crowded classrooms. Education aides were on hand to assist. Some of the union teachers sent sympathetic non-school personnel inside to see if any classes were being supervised by education aides or other classified personnel. They found each class properly supervised by certificated persons. Two persons were sent from the area office to assist in filling our teaching positions.

The following morning, a different tactic was used. The same teachers knocked on doors and walked down the street to shoo children back home. That day only a few students attended school.

An erratic pattern of these strategies was employed. We only knew whether there would be many or few students after school began each day. A few teachers who went out initially, returned within a few days or two weeks. A few teachers who did not go out on the first day drifted out during the strike period. Teacher attendance and pupil attendance were uncertain and differed each day.

Among the fraction of the staff present each day was the former faculty chairman. I understand that he was outside with the striking group each morning, passed out doughnuts, teased and "jived" with them, and promptly at 8:59 jumped the fence so that he met his class at 9:00 every morning. I continued to be amazed at his presence. But he was there each morning. He willingly accepted students assigned to teachers who were now on strike. Whenever a teacher is absent and there is no substitute to take the class, the pupils may be assigned to other classroom teachers who will receive what is called replacement pay. For every six pupils replaced in another class, the receiving teacher is paid for one hour above his regular salary. The former faculty chairman accepted all the sixth graders of other teachers who came to school, and he also received commensurate pay over and above his regular pay.

The strike went on. The pickets came each morning. One morning a young lady whom I had known when I was at 95th Street School entered the building and came to talk with me. I had known Ms. Pat Riley as an interested parent who had no hesistancy verbalizing her concerns about the deficiencies of the schools. Fortunately, we had developed a good relationship.

She sat down and began, "Ms. Haynes, why don't you close down the school, so these teachers inside can come out on strike? You know, I'm out here supporting the striking teachers. I'm out for the cause."

"I see you are, Pat," l responded. "You know, as I explained to the teachers, the strike is illegal. The boys and girls here need their education. They can't get it if schools are closed. I can't even consider closing the school. I see another strange face in your group this morning. Is she a sympathizing parent, too?"

"Oh, no, Ms. Haynes. She's a teacher from the other side of town. She's the only one striking at her school, so she came over to picket with us."

"Have you looked at the situation critically, Pat? Doesn't it seem that the largest number of teachers on strike are from the Black schools? The one White teacher out there with your group came all the way over to the Black section to do her picketing. The White pupils in her school are in session. What children are being denied their learning, Pat?"

"Well, I see your point, Ms. Haynes. But I certainly hope the teachers get something out of this strike."

There were level-headed understanding persons on both sides with whom the staff was able to maintain a reasonable relationship. On cold days we served the "outs" coffee and doughnuts; they reciprocated by inviting us to lunch. We accepted, and took turns on two occasions. And, as usually happens when dealing with human beings, someone took advantage of the situation. Word came that we were taking sides with the "outs." It was easy to convey to some of the strike leaders that we would necessarily discontinue our relationship until they returned to the inside. It seems that this was understood and accepted.

When the teachers returned, Coy Roberson, the faculty chairman at this time, asked that I come to the faculty lounge to talk with them. It was a beginning of an opening up. Nonpermanent, as well as permanent, teachers participated in the rap session, and there was true verbal interaction. This was the first time non-permanent teachers openly communicated with me.

"What are you going to do about our salary monies?" a female teacher asked.

I knew what she meant, and I replied, "Until now I really haven't given much thought to the unpaid salaries accumulated during the strike. But now that you've returned, I'll make a decision. If, and when, that money is offered, I will not accept it. Should I do so, it would be necessary to make choices between the 'ins' and 'outs' as recipients. It seems that the best way to pull together is to go forward from here letting bygones be bygones."

My explanation was accepted. Some of the striking teachers returned announcing they had won a victory. Others admitted it would take a long period for them to recover financially. There was no evidence that negotiations had won anything for anyone, so conversations about the outcome became muted. It did seem that the teachers returned with the intention of being more positive. Some evidenced a greater commitment. Nevertheless, much of the year had slipped away. Efforts were affirmative, but there wasn't much time left to attain conspicuous achievement.

As the 1969-1970 school year came to a close, it went without saying that there had been very little achievement on the part of Grape Street's students. The standardized test scores substantiated this.

There were some teachers who cared about what had happened to their students. Carol Reiss came in for a conference. She was concerned because she recognized her inability to cope with some of the fourth graders with severe problems in her room. During our conversation we agreed to transfer her to a first grade in the fall. One day during the summer she telephoned me at home and said she would like to come over and talk with me.

"You know, Ms. Haynes, I enrolled in a workshop this summer to try to get some help for my new primary class. Yesterday the director of the International Center for Educational Development, Dr. Virgil Howes, announced that he was looking for an urban ghetto school that wanted to develop an open classroom program. He said that he had three schools and needs one more to complete the project. I believe the teachers at our school would want to develop a program like this. Would you look into this for us, please?"

"Yes, I will. You know we already have a model among us. Mayme Sweeney's room is an open classroom. Other teachers frequently comment about how involved her students are. If enough teachers are interested in following suit and developing open classrooms in their own way, then we'll give it serious consideration."

We did. The program was called the Open Classroom Environmental Education Project.

8

SEEDS OF CHANGE

A District Advisory Committee was established for the Title I schools of Los Angeles. Members of local school councils and people from community agencies servicing poverty areas were chosen to serve on the committee. They met once each month with the Title I staff to receive information, offer advice, and suggest directions. A Principals' Advisory Committee was also formed. Three representatives from each of the areas serviced were elected. This group met once a month with the staff. Representatives from each of these two groups formed the Advisory Cabinet. I served on the Principals' Advisory Committee and the District Advisory Cabinet. During the first year, the meetings were informative, and expenditures of the overhead monies were generally a major consideration.

Near the close of the 1969-1970 school year as the Advisory Cabinet was assembling for a meeting, I sensed an unusual tenseness in the air. It was obvious that the parents present were disturbed; they seemed to know something the principals didn't.

When the meeting began, a parent asked, "Bill, has that proposal already been sent to the State Department?"

"We are meeting to discuss a proposal," William Anton answered. He was the director of the Title I programs in Los Angeles.

"Could we be filled in?" inquired one of the principals. "Some of you seem to have some knowledge others of us don't have."

"A sizable amount of unused Title I funds have accumulated. Guidelines have indicated that these funds must be spent by June 30th," Mr. Anton explained.

"Hold it, hold it, hold it," interruped another parent. "That isn't true. We've already check with Leo, and he says that the time can be extended." Leo was Dr. Leo Lopez, State Division Chief of Compensatory Education.

"Come on, Bill, let's get down to the nitty-gritty. Haven't the powers-that-be already made a decision on how that money is to be spent and haven't you already sent the proposal to Sacramento?)" asked Mrs. Dorothy Rochelle, one of our community-activist leaders.

"You see, the time element is crowding in upon us fast," explained Anton.

"What decision was made?" Rochelle inquired.

"Yes, we want to know what decision was made," a community member confirmed.

"One of the urgent concerns that has been voiced all year is the opportunity to have staff development for teachers," announced one of the administrators.

"Oh, no, you won't," resisted one parent.

"Oh, no, you bet your bottom dollar you won't," agreed another.

"Why do you have us come all the way down here for a meeting, when you've got everything all signed, sealed, and delivered?"
"That's the game they always play," sighed a local community member.

"Please, let us in on what is happening," interjected another principal.

"At the beginning of this school year, all the Title I schools budgeted," Mr. Anton began. "Because the program was new, many schools were not able to fill many of the positions until late in the year. Every pay period that a position remained unfilled, funds accumulated. We now have a sizable sum of money that is designated to be spent by June 30th. Because in past meetings one of the main concerns of principals was staff development, we felt that this was the best and most logical way to spend the funds."

"How much is that sizable sum?" a parent inquired.

"Around one million, six hundred thousand dollars is involved," was the answer.

"Well, now, this is it! This is the time! This is the time to get parents involved. Too many parents don't know a thing about ESEA. Some parents don't know anything about Title I. Now that there's some money to pay parents, you want to spend more money on the teachers. We're going to get into the act this time."

"I don't believe the Board members will approve a massive parent-in-service," one of the administrators conjectured.

"Never mind the Board members, I'm going to call Leo," announced Ms. Margaret Wright. She rose quickly from her chair, left the room, and went to a telephone. She dialed Sacramento and reached Dr. Lopez. An effort was made to proceed, but everyone really sat stunned, waiting in anticipation. Ms Wright had made herself well known on many previous occasions concerning the schools and the community. Whatever her convictions, she made them known in her own eloquent style.

She either wore her hair natural or wrapped and tied with a colorful scarf. Her dress was always neat, generally loose fitting, and worn in a manner that indicated its wearer was championing the cause of grass-root people. It was an acknowledged fact that when she got on a case, some sparks could be expected to fly. She knew how to articulate her concerns and had no hesitancy or misgivings about doing so.

After a lengthy long distance conversation, Ms. Wright returned and announced, "Let's get on with the business at hand. Leo said the time for spending the money could be extended. Let's get on planning for a parent-in-service. Bill, call or get somebody in here to help us start the planning and get this show on the road."

Discussion began and continued. Delaying tactics weren't going to work. We met all that afternoon and into the night; we met again on Saturday and again on Sunday. The parents were persistent.

A Community and Staff Development Program was planned and implemented. Ms. Wright insisted that William Bailey, at that time with the Office of Urban Affairs, be the director. By this time the large District Advisory Committee was divided into smaller advisory committees for each area. Representatives from each of these advisory committees worked on planning the in-service program. The groups were so diverse that some basic principles had to be formulated, and then each area committee proceeded to decide its own way of implementation.

It was agreed that each school would be allowed a certain number of participants, who would attend twenty hours of sessions and receive a stipend of fifty dollars. Participants would include parents, education aides, teachers, principals, and other involved community and school personnel. Each area held its sessions on different days and at different times. During that summer over four thousand people were involved in the largest community and staff development program ever held in this country. All participants interrelated in large and small sessions, which were well organized. There were problems, points of disagreement and agreement, questions, and misconceptions, but there was information. It was a learning experience for all who attended. Only a portion of the accumulated funds were expended. The remainder was carried over to the next year.

The Open Classroom Environmental Education Project began in the fall of 1970, under the direction of the International Center for Educational Development and funded by the Ford Foundation. The schools involved were Grandview in Manhattan Beach, Palomar in Chula Vista, Kew-Bennett in Inglewood, and Grape Street in Watts. By design these four schools were in diversified settings, with varying socio-economic and ethnic backgrounds. Each school agreed to work to develop its own brand of open classroom education using the environment as a focal point.

This relationship was good for Grape Street for it provided motivation. To be assured of the cooperation of the teachers, I called a summer faculty meeting. Thirty-nine came in slacks, in shorts, with bathing suits covered, with sun visors, with sun hats, and other casual summer attire. I wasn't sure why the response was so large and so willing, but, needless to say, I was gratified. We had tried so many approaches--departmentalizing, some team teaching, and individualizing. There had been indifference and resistance to everything. After the strike, there was evidence of a desire for a change of some kind. It didn't seem to matter what or how. There seemed to be a groping or a reaching out for some sense of direction, so I felt the time was propitious. It was.

Dr. Howes, the director of the center, came to that faculty meeting too. We discussed the project, and many questions were asked. Grape already had two special programs; how would this new one affect the others? How much money would this program provide? It was made clear that the school would receive no money and would relate occasionally with the other three schools involved. Grape would begin developing open classrooms and synthesize the other programs so that they would complement each other. What pleased me most during this meeting was the fact that the teachers were demonstrating a concern about their teaching.

"Ms. Haynes, there's one very special thing we'd like to know."
"Yes?"
"If we decide to go into this program, will we have to write lesson plans?"
"No, in an open classroom setting you will not be required to write the traditional type lesson plans."
"That settles it," announced a faculty leader. "We want to join."

"All right," I announced, "will everyone who is in favor of joining this four school project and who is willing to commit himself or herself to developing and using an open classroom approach, please sign this sheet."

I quickly wrote a heading on the paper and passed it out for signatures. Thirty-eight teachers signed. The stern gentleman who had conducted the traditionally rigid classroom walked over to me and asked, "May I have papers to sign for a substitute leave?"

"Yes, you may," I replied. He was the eleventh person who sought to leave the school by requesting a substitute leave or a transfer. When Carol Reiss had contacted me two days earlier, knowing the difficulty she had encountered with discipline in her fourth grade her first year, I had thought, that even though we had agreed for her to change to first grade, she was calling to request a transfer. Happily I was wrong.

The teachers who were working during the summer session seemed pleased with their decision. Anticipation of the new program gave some added zest to their efforts for the remainder of the summer. The other teachers left the meeting feeling that they had made a decision to do something positive. There seemed to be much enthusiasm. I realized that the majority did not really understand what an open classroom entailed or what their commitment truly meant, but the commitment had been made, and we would work to implement it.

That summer many well-meaning teachers went shopping and spent their personal funds to purchase materials for their classrooms.

During what we call 1-B time, the two weeks the office staff comes to work before the teachers and students return, I found myself in a dilemma. The city school system had been reorganized. Instead of areas being designated geographically, as previously, they were now assigned alphabetically. Grape Street was no longer in Area South; it now belonged to Area A, Sector II. Richard Lawrence was my new superintendent. Grape's participation in the Environmental Education Program had been negotiated during the summer while it was in Area South and Dr. Josie G. Bain was my superintendent. Now Dr. Bain was on vacation, and I had to explain the school's commitment to my new superintendent. He and his assistant, Henry Dyck, listened as I explained as persuasively as I knew how. Naturally they asked many questions. After convincing them that the project would be developed as an innovative program, that there would be no conflict with the Los Angeles City School philosophy or curriculum, and that no funds were involved, they gave the go-ahead signal.

Attrition had taken its toll. The school year of 1970-1971 opened with many new teachers on the staff. Others had asked or had been advised to change grade levels. Although few had been openly receptive to the preparation of lesson plans and the demonstrations, some teacher learnings had occurred. The concept of grouping had been implanted, and the learning center idea had circulated. Teachers returned with a determination and a commitment to go "open". There was much hustle-bustle.

I endeavored to convey to the teachers that they should begin by using any acceptable methods with which they felt comfortable, as long as it resulted in student productivity, while gradually phasing into the open classroom approach. My message was misinterpreted by many.

Carloads of purchased and discarded materials were moved in and arranged in classrooms. There were many commercial games and activities, and some gleanings from our own past school staff development were apparent. Learning centers were developed. Mayme Sweeney's room 5 was an open classroom model. Joan Dunning developed a learning laboratory with ordered freedom in her room while Elois Taylor was at ease with her new room environment. Carol Reiss filled her room with materials she had constructed and accumulated. Andrea Roberts and Patricia Douglas, who had both structured their classes traditionally, now arranged their tables and chairs in groupings. Veronica Morris had planned, organized, and developed a meaningful enriched environment, and Wilnora Ewell's room was obviously developing into a newspaper office. There were other teachers too who were putting forth a real and sincere effort. There were also eleven new classroom teachers, all of whom had committed themselves to the open classroom approach.

When visiting classrooms, it was obvious that a majority of the learning centers used games. There were checkers, dominoes, decks of playing cards, Old Maid, Tiddley Winks, jacks and balls, racing cars, racing tracks marble games, puppets, comic books, Monopoly, and similar types of activities. In some rooms centers were almost totally devoid of academic content and skills activities. There were still a few rooms in which every student faced the chalkboard and used the same text. There were a few teachers who were frustrated and provided close to no environment. Two of the new teachers had read or heard of Dr. William Glasser's *Reality Therapy* and *Schools Without Failure,* and they implemented discussion circles as their program. There was one thing for sure--Grape had diversity. This was so apparent that one day an out-of-classroom teacher walked down the hall and proclaimed, "This open classroom business is really something. You just do anything you want to do."

This was the explanation given to some classes. The children, in turn, reported this to their parents, several of whom called to ask what was going on. Because the groundwork had been laid with the Advisory Council and the PTA and because we had endeavored to keep parents informed through *Happenings Along the Grapevine,* a periodic newsletter, it wasn't difficult to clarify the misconception. It was common knowledge that the school staff was discussing, studying, and planning together ways to use the open classroom approach.

The Los Angeles Unified School District allows each school staff an option of using ten shortened days each year for staff development. During the shortened days grades one and two are dismissed at their regular hour and grades three to six are dismissed forty minutes early. With our superintendent's approval, we chose to devote the first ten Wednesdays to inservice training. We made every effort to communicate how this time was being used, so most of the inquiring parents accepted the situation. One openly rationalized, "Well, whatever is happening, my son likes it, but I do hope it will not throw him behind in his studies."

There was reason for concern. Most of the children were more involved than they ever had been, especially in game activities, and they were having a good time. Tic-tac-toe was being played on paper, small chalkboards, regular chalkboards, and sometimes on the walls. Cars raced over plastic tracks, down boarded inclines, and around and across classroom floors. Balls were thrown into the air, jacks were picked up. Students played games with regular decks of cards, others played Old Maid. Checkers and checkerboards were in demand. Rules for games were improvised, designed, and created.

The first staff development sessions were largely dialogues, and for a time many were diatribes, but at least the nonpermanent as well as the permanent teachers were talking. This was progress.

At the eighth meeting I announced that grade sheets and report cards would be placed in the teachers' boxes. Teachers were bewildered about how to grade and evaluate what they had taught and what their students had learned. Naturally, a few had formulated objectives and had included content and skills. Evaluation posed no major problem to these few, but to the majority, it did.

Out of this frustration developed an effort to focus on a curriculum to be used in our open classroom approach. Rather than say, "Throw out what you have and begin again," we concentrated on ways that content and skills could be incorporated into what was already in the classrooms. Simultaneously an effort was made to slowly introduce other acceptable instructional aids. Most of the teachers had utilized the learning center concept, so we thought of ways to make them more meaningful academically.

Even before this meeting it had become evident that we were going to require more time for staff development--we had so many needs. Our request for an early dismissal day to develop an innovative program was granted. Once approved, the entire school was dismissed each Wednesday at 2:00 p.m. By that time we had begun to ascertain our needs. We knew we needed to become involved with teaching basic skills. We took a survey of what was on hand and began there.

Task cards were developed for race car centers. For example, a designated number of students would take turns rolling a car from a given point. Each would measure the distance traveled, and these might be charted, graphed, or recorded in a variety of ways. Obstacle courses were developed. Car books of various types were written as a result of research. Math and language arts moved in.

The checkerboards became versatile tools by which word recognition and structural and phonetic analysis skills were developed and reinforced while playing the game. Tic-tac-toe became a word building or math computational process. Imagination flourished with the use of dice. Travel and other games were created to teach or reinforce innumerable skills in almost any content area.

Comic strips were read, and skills were taught from them. For instance, the ballooned quotes were cut out, and children wrote their own narratives. Several teachers had puppet stages in their classrooms, and some had bought puppets. Others had the children design and make stick, paper bag, stocking, cloth, or other kinds of puppets. Fairy tales, folk tales, tall tales, fables, and familiar or creative dramas were performed before student or any available audiences.

These were a few of the many ideas teachers could begin utilizing with what they had. I presented some other practical, personalized starters that would be easy, such as using a *TV Guide*, the telephone book, advertisements, magazines, catalogs, calorie counters, automobile club maps, directories, and an infinite number of other discarded materials. I also suggested ways I thought the children could be meaningfuly involved. Periodically these suggestions were typed up and placed in the teachers' boxes. It would be almost impossible to relate the variety of ways teachers used these seed ideas.

Initially I tried hard to visit every room at least once a week. When I observed unique ideas, I asked the teacher to present them in the teachers' meeting. At first there was some reluctance. In several cases, it was necessary for me to make the presentation and give the credit to the teacher. Gradually, teachers began to work to have their efforts recognized. This was a healthy trend. Teachers began taking pride in sharing their creative ways of teaching or the instructional outcomes produced. Word got around that the first-grade teachers had developed challenging and interesting environments. Their classrooms were visited, and the teachers explained their programs. Their ideas were extendable, and upper-grade teachers left with many concepts they were able to modify and implement with their own classes.

One week I asked three primary teachers to share with the others. Annie Hill displayed a bulletin-board size sheet of orange butcher paper. Magazine pictures depicted a variety of mathematical concepts. Her children had cut out pictures to clarify sets of more than, less than, equal to, equations, sums, and products. It was colorful, meaningful, and evidenced that students had been involved and that learning had taken place.

Ruby Helire shared surveys her students had taken among themselves. Each child had chosen a number of his friends to interrogate. Some of the questions were: "Do you live in an apartment or a house?" "Do you like hamburgers or hot dogs?" "Were you born in Los Angeles or not?" "Did you go to any other school beside Grape?" "Do you eat in the cafeteria or go home?" All students handled their findings in their own ways. Most prepared graphs, but there was much variation in each child's project.

Then it was Elois Taylor's turn. She came in bringing her student-made television set. Behind her came one of her first-grade student, dressed in his best outfit, followed by his mother. Ms. Taylor pulled out some sentence strips and some flash cards. Then she and Anthony Dunn put on a real performance for us. He read the call letters, matched them with the TV channels, related on which channels programs of interest to children were aired, read the o'clocks from the flash cards she held, commented on his favorite programs, read the titles of other programs from the sentence strips, told which friends like those better and why, and turned the television to show and tell what program was on each channel at 7:00 p.m. on Tuesday. After eighteen minutes of listening spellbound, spontaneous applause resounded as Anthony announced, "The End." This really crystallized the staff into a sharing faculty.

Two classrooms that were developing differently but spectacularly were those of Andrea Roberts and Patricia Douglas. In Ms. Roberts' room, tables and chairs were arranged in orderly groupings, with carrels sectioning off different areas. Practical task cards were posted. Colorful curtains fluttered at the window, and a table lamp lit up a reading corner where children relaxed on pillows as they read. Students planned trips across country on maps, researched occupations in which they were interested, and described the soul foods they ate at home in a cookbook. These were a few of the many activities taking place simultaneously in this formerly formal classroom. Now, it was open. The sixth graders enjoyed being involved in their own planning, their own contracting, and their own learning.

Every day tables and chairs were placed in the hall outside Ms. Douglass' door. Every morning she arrived early, unloaded her car, and added something to her room environment. She frequented odds-and-ends shops and found discarded items to serve as display cases or filing or posting spaces. The children in her fifth-grade class became interested in measuring themselves and their classmates. They made facsimiles of a driver's license, using their own photos. They went to the nurse's office to be weighed and measured. They used catalogs and ordered clothing for themselves or gifts for family members. They planned menus, made shopping lists, and wrote checks for their pretend purchases.

Ms. Douglas amassed a group of dolls from different countries, and boys did research on the countries to earn a doll. Her room was becoming a beehive of purposeful activity. One day one of the largest, most boisterous boys in her room pulled over a chair, stood on it, reached up to the shelf, took the doll from France in his arms, cuddled her, kissed her, and affectionately whispered, "Oh, you lovely, beautiful doll. Won't my little sister love to have you for her very own!"

At this time, we were meeting on two consecutive days. Tuesday was designated as faculty meeting day, but we avoided administrative matters as much as possible. Tuesday became the day teachers shared, while Wednesday's staff development sessions were planned by consultants in collaboration with me. Staff development activities were as varied as our needs. Sometimes classrooms were visited and discussed, sometimes the consultants led workshops, or sometimes mini-sessions based on interests were held. Sometimes grade-level groups met together, and sometimes resource persons led total or mini-sessions. Gradually teachers became more receptive to on-going learning. We had three on-staff consultants who planned workshops that proved highly profitable.

Suggestions given in this manner could be accepted, personalized, and individualized to fit the needs of any class. On some days groups worked to develop subject area ideas dealing with food, clothing, family, people, houses, cars, sports, television, radio, school, home, health, travel, air, pollution, animals, or almost any familiar subject. Ways of working so the content would be relevant to the children were explored. Some instructions were lettered, some were written in cursive, some were typed, and some were printed.

It was amazing the way rooms began to fill with simple to more complex, short and long term tasks and projects. Many rooms became quite full of materials. Gradually requests began coming from parents, "Ms. Haynes, would you put my child in one of those rooms where all that junk is, please?"

Ms. Minix was a parent who maintained regular telephone and in-person communication with the school. On each occasion she engaged in verbal battle with at least one of us. One day I was startled when I lifted the receiver and listened to her clear sophisticated voice volunteering, "Ms. Haynes, I just called to tell you how happy I am with whatever is going on in Ms. Roberts's classroom This is the first time I can remember that David has wanted to come to school and has been so happy and satisfied about it."

All along it had been interesting to watch the halls. Sometimes a table and chair were pushed out into a corridor. On another day almost all of the furniture would come out of some room. I can only say, "Thank God for our custodian." Edmund Weber has been one of the most understanding and cooperative persons on the staff. "Whatever is good for our children," is his motto. As furniture was abandoned or requested, he and his staff responded and accommodated. Rugs, sofas, pillows, turnstile bookholders, various types of bookcases, cardboard cubicles, cardboard boxes, dividers, pegboards, clean used clothing, and various other discarded items began appearing.

Some people who knew or heard about Grape's endeavors began coming for a visit. Changes were becoming evident. Many teachers still practiced secure traditional methods, but most of them were giving students some options for at least one period a day. Most teachers were holding steadfastly to reading, math, and spelling periods. Some were setting up isolated learning centers and allowing children to use them as a special privilege. Some set up five or six learning centers and followed a strict rotation system throughout the day.

The Wednesday staff development meetings were beginning to pay dividends, but scheduling became a concern for many. Coordinating a variety of learning activities for all the children often posed a problem. At a dialogue session, teachers shared their unsuccessful attempts as well as ways that worked. Teachers came away from these discussions with a nottion of at least one way to try to schedule classroom activities.

As word continued to get around that we were using the open classroom approach, visitors began to drop in at unannounced and frequent intervals. Many times they waded through a filthy entrance, broken glass, and seas of debris in the school yard. Nevertheless, once inside there were classrooms that held promise. Most teachers were trying. Learning and interest centers were appearing daily. Carpets and couches were being hauled into classrooms. Our nurse made frequent inspections. There were teachers who felt that a couch and rugs "opened up" a classroom. Much discussion resulted in more discriminating and practical use of these items.

One day Veronica Morris phoned the office to inquire, "May my class go down the street to pick up a couch? My children say a rest home is disposing of some furniture." The nurse went to inspect it and approve its use. The class carried, sanitized, and measured it. They cut plastic material to specifications and covered it. This piece of furniture was appreciated and used well.

Some teachers constructed cardboard carpentry items in classes. Ingenious ideas of how to make dividers for individual and small group carrels began to develop. Most used chipboard, some used pegboard, and some used both. Teachers were growing in their ability to develop personalized task and activity cards, although some commercially dittoed assignments were still in evidence. In some instances. children brought in items and designed relevant tasks.

A relaxed and calm atmosphere began developing in many classrooms. The noise was one of busy involvement. It was amazing that in most rooms the noise level was lower than in the former traditional classrooms. One day Ms. Douglas approached me with glowing eyes to report, "You know, Ms. Haynes, Charles came over today, tapped me on the shoulder, and whispered, 'Ms. Douglas, you're talking too loud. Your voice is disturbing us. Would you mind lowering it, please?'"

Staff development sessions supplied the key to opening up our minds. They have been as varied as our needs. Classrooms were visited for a variety of reasons. Sometimes a grade level of classes were visited, and the host teachers served as instructors. Some retained their students, with parent permission, to demonstrate how they taught a lesson. Consultants from our staff, Title I, our Area, and the Jordan Educational Complex were engaged when appropriate. It was always my business to orient those unfamiliar with Grape's program. I wanted contributors to understand that we were receptive to ideas, but I was also concerned that no one state that any single program, approach, or text was an only way to proceed. Another concern is that Grape's program be student-oriented with a focus on a humanistic, integrated curriculum. Learning tasks must involve subjects and skills that have the human touch and have some relevancy to the life of each individual child.

As time passed, some of the best leadership began to emerge from our own teaching ranks. Some outstanding sessions on ways of integrating art, music, science, social sciences, math, and dancing have been successfully led by Grape's own teachers. Ideas are freely shared.

Teachers and education aides seem to look forward anxiously to each session. They participate freely. During an earlier total group session, some one rather facetiously called out, "Whatever happened to our parties? We used to have one every week."

Another voice responded curtly, "We are teaching now. That's what happened."

The self-fulfilling prophecy has come to pass with the adults in these sessions as they bring it to fruition in their classrooms with their students. Only seeing is believing.

As more visitors trickled in, more classrooms began to change. Students noticed whose rooms were being visited and were totally uninhibited about discussing them. They equated rooms being visited with rooms where students were learning. Often I went to photograph unique activities. I remember one day I went upstairs with my camera and was able to capture several innovative scenes in four classrooms. When the last bulb was flashed, I returned to my office. As I walked down the stairway, I overheard childish voices: "There must not have been anything good happening in that room next door. Ms. Haynes didn't go in there. They must not be learning much. Sure am glad I'm in my room. Man, we've really got things going. We're really learning some things in our room."

"Now that we are teaching differently, the A,B,C,D, grades just don't convey the progress students are making in my room the way I would like them to."

Thoses are my sentiments, too. Maybe we should consider parent conferences instead."

"That would be ideal, but so many of our parents work, it would be impossible to get them all here, no matter how late you stay."

It was report card time. A group of teachers expressed their concern about a need for a change in reporting student progress to parents. A teacher from each grade level was asked to convene her or his group and present the following: (1) A narrative-type checklist reporting form developed by the Board be used at this reporting period, and (2) That each grade level convene and develop a report-to-parent form that would be comprehensive and acceptable to all concerned. There were no dissenters, and this plan was implemented.

At the next meeting of the School-Community Advisory Council this proposal was presented. Some parents objected. Many had saved report cards throughout the years and wanted to continue doing so. Some insisted that they knew very well what an A,B,C, or D, meant.

The teachers present took turns making explicit points such as: (1) We are working more with each student as an individual or in small groups; (2) We know our students' area of strength and weaknesses better; (3) We are guiding our students to become more self-directed; (4) Our students are learning to work together and learn from each other; (5) Our students are learning how to follow through on assigned tasks; and (6) Students are learning to evaluate themselves.
The parents listened. Then one queried, "Does this mean you aren't teaching any more reading, writing, spelling, and arithmetic?"

"It means that we are teaching reading, writing, spelling and arithmetic in ways that are meaningful to each child. It means that we are teaching each child to learn how to learn the skills he needs to know and to cntinue building upon each learning."

"What if we wanted a report card with grades along with that special report you are putting together?" a mother questioned.

"There would be no problem. You may get them both just by asking," I informed them.

"If that's the case, I don't see why we can't give it a try," concluded Reverend W.J. Broussard, the Advisory Board President.

At the next month's meeting, the finished forms were presented to this Council. It endorsed the three forms designed for kindergarten, first and second grades, and grades three through six with dispatch. We described our intent to use these new Report to Parents in the *Happenings Along the Grapevine.* We also knew that as our program developed, these report forms would need to be redesigned.

During the summer of 1971 I was one of three principals and a teacher from the project schools to be included in a ten-day study tour of London, courtesy of the International Center of Educational Development. Dr. Howes and Dr. Keuscher were the leaders of this group of about one hundred persons. It proved to be a good experience. We visited primary and infant schools, saw films, listened to lecturers, held discussions, and were superficially involved in some workshops. I visited six schools, all of which were quite different, but interesting for various reasons.

Near the close of the study tour someone inquired of me, "What have you learned form this experience?"

I replied, "I have learned that the British primary school cannot be transplanted to schools such as mine in America. The culture, the environment, the people, the children, and the schools are different. This experience has confirmed for me the fact that we at Grape Street School have gained our direction and have begun to develop a program unique to our own needs. I have also concluded that the only way any school can operate with an open classroom approach is to determine its own potential and needs and to develop from within."

9

TENSIONS AND CONFLICTS

*I*n the fall of 1970 I noticed a continuous stream of students from grades one through six climbing to the upper floor after lunch periods. The primary children were housed outside in bungalows, and there was no reason for them to go up to the second floor of the main building. I watched for about five minutes as youngsters continued to go up and down, and then walked over to a sixth-grade monitor and asked, "Where are these children going? It's one-thirty now, and everyone should be in his classroom."

"The teacher up in room 18 says these bad boys and girls are to come to his room to be disciplined."

Without commenting, I walked to room 18 and went inside. There they were. Ms. Helton, the music teacher, was busily teaching a song to the children belonging in this classroom, while lined up across the rear of the room was a group of varying ages and heights with their hands on their hips, bobbing up and down doing "the stoops." My pointing finger counted 18 children. The room 18 teacher, the former faculty chairman, was seated at his desk with his legs crossed counseling a nineteenth student. A memo was placed in this teacher's box inviting him to come in for a conference. He came. He promised to discontinue this activity, and to the best of my knowledge he did.

One day in the fall the area superintendent, Mr. Lawrence, came out to visit. It was obvious that Grape Street was on the move. As we traveled from room to room, even I was surprised to see that so many teachers were trying. The room 18 teacher, who had been maintaining a traditional classroom, was involving his students in organizing a project oriented to an open classroom. His students ably explained that they were building a radio station, a grocery store, a theater, a hospital, a mortuary, and a travel agency. They had been well prepared, and their classroom was becoming meaningfully exciting.

On another day we were honored by a visit by Congressman Augustus Hawkins and some of his colleagues. He could see the efforts being made, and he seemed pleased to have the other visiting Congressmen view Grape's program. He had visited the year before, and afterward he had sent the school a flag that had flown over the Capitol building. Naturally, we prized the gift.

We moved together from room to room talking with students and commenting on the activities in which they were purposefully involved. When we entered room 18, the teacher quickly opened a cupboard, pulled out a stack of duplicated lesson sheets, and began explaining classroom procedures explicitly for the Congressmen's ears. Very determinedly Congressman Hawkins backed away, moved over to me, and whispered, "Please, get me out of this rascal's room, quickly."

"We must keep moving," I announced. We walked briskly to the next room and took our time for the remainder of the tour. I couldn't help surmising that the two must have met before.

When we closed school for the Christmas holidays, the School-Community Advisory Council was concerned and planned to provide surveillance of the school and grounds. Reverend and Ms. Broussard took the lead. They scheduled a few other persons, but mostly these two took turns driving around the school at some time during every hour of each day and night. Ms. Broussard wasn't well during this period, but no one could stop her. She kept going.

Their watchfulness provided protection until 5 a.m. Christmas morning. At that time a group of community youths broke into the premises and tore most of the classrooms apart.

Grape Street has a good custodial staff, and with assistance they cleaned up the mess. The extent of the malicious destruction was scarcely noticeable by the time school resumed in the new year of 1971.

Happenings Along the Grapevine carried the following "An Open Letter to Our Parents:"

Sometime during the morning hours of Christmas Day our primary building, many of the bungalows, and the main building were entered. Mass destruction took place. I spent a portion of my Christmas Day looking into rooms through broken windows with tables, chairs, materials, and everything in sight torn and scattered all over. I could not help but wonder what satisfaction this activity had afforded the ones who had entered. Could they have younger brothers and sisters attending our school? Could they care for any of the students in school? What causes the bitterness that results in trying to prevent young children from learning?

Parents, no matter how we view this situation, its largely a community problem. If each one of you care enough and join with those who are already trying, a stop can be put to this wanton destruction.

We are making a real effort to have a Great School here at Grape Street--one of which the community, students and staff can be proud. We continue to plead that we need your help. Time lost in the classroom is learning lost for boys and girls. It can never be regained. Come and join with us to find ways to work and solve some of our problems. It is for the benefit of Grape Street boys and girls. Join the group that is showing we care.

70

On the first school day of the new year, Mr. Weber commented, "You know, Ms. Haynes, that's a real mystery. Rooms 31 and 33 weren't touched. The vandals got into twenty-one rooms. Those two rooms were in the middle of all of it, and they left them alone. It seems odd."

At the first recess period Ruby Helire entered the office to report, "I asked my children if anyone knew why our rooms weren't torn up as the others were, and one of my boys raised his hands and said, 'I know, Ms. Helire, 'cause I was there. I begged my big brother and his friends please not to tear up my room. Bobby in the next room was out there too, and he said the same thing.'"

During a holiday weekend, when I was out of town, one of my cousins held his yearly birthday dinner. I was told that the room 18 teacher had attended and boldly announced to my relatives, "I'm going to move Carrie Haynes out as principal of Grape Street."

One of my uncles responded, "I'll bet you won't. I'll just bet you won't."

At first this was shocking news, and I chose not to believe it, but as the play for power grew more apparent, I knew I had to face reality.

By February the school was definitely moving toward opening its classrooms and facilitating the learning of most students, but at the same time the flames of unrest were being fanned. This was the situation when a correspondent from *Newsweek* magazine was assigned to write a story about Grape's program. It was very apparent that Paul Brinkley Rogers was impressed with what he saw happening. Almost immediately he said to me, "I get the flavor of the British schools as we move through these halls."

I quickly corrected, "There may be similarities, but if so, it is purely accidental. Whatever you see here at Grape Street has been developed by us and therefore must have the Watts flavor." We laughed and proceeded. He informed me that after conferring with the administrators, he wished to go on his own to talk with staff, students, parents, and community people as he saw fit. He did just that, and I never knew the extent of his research until his article was published. Early in April a *Newsweek* photographer appeared, who took a large number of pictures and seemed to enjoy himself while doing so. Shortly after he left, storm clouds gathered.

The next time I encountered the room 18 teacher, I warned him that if his negative activities continued, I would begin documenting his actions with the intent of issuing an unsatisfactory rating. This was the first time I had taken this stand. Because he was a permanent teacher, most of the staff became concerned about the outcome of our confrontation. This man had himself proclaimed that once a teacher became permanent, he was secure from administrative evaluation. For years tenured teachers just didn't believe a permanent teacher could be given an unsatisfactory rating, so my action was a revelation.

A permanent teacher could receive an outstanding or an unsatisfactory evaluation any time either was merited, but substantiative documentation was required. In the process of issuing an unsatisfactory rating, the administrator must also show evidence of providing assistance and guidance in an endeavor to resolve or alleviate the problems. For exactly two years, I had tried in every way I knew, could think of, or could contrive to work with this volatile young man.

In an effort to persuade him to leave the school in peace, I asked my superintendent to offer him the opportunity to transfer for a new experience. He did, but the young man refused the offer.

It was already customary for me to write Memo-grams on self-duplicating memo forms to teachers as reminder, compliments, conferences records, or suggestions. Teachers were aware that when they received a note, I had a sensitized copy. So, I began writing memos to the room 18 teacher. He was informed that he was missed at a faculty meeting and a staff development meeting, which were held during regular school time. He was asked in writing for copies of his students' trip slips, for which he had been asked on innumerable occasions and which should have been submitted in October. He was informed that he should arrive and sign in at 8:30 instead of just appearing out of nowhere at his room at 9:00 each morning, and he was reminded that students should not be left unsupervised in his classroom. While walking with the fire captain one day, I had unlocked his classroom door and discovered three boys working and playing in the room during a recess period. He was asked to desist from transferring children from one class to another without administrative approval. After or sometimes before each of these written reminders, a face-to-face conference was held. He did begin coming to the office to sign in, but his signing out in the afternoon continued sporadic.

One evening about dusk, I was ready to let my mind hide in its foxhole as I had learned to do, when the telephone rang. I answered and heard the voice of a school parent, "Ms. Haynes, one of your teachers just knocked on my door. He asked me to sign a petition to have you moved out of Grape Street School. Some of my neighbors told me that he's been going around knocking on doors several evenings lately. So, you know what, Ms. Haynes? I told him that I had just signed a paper that the community got together to have *him* moved out."

"Well," I answered, "I guess there isn't much for me to say. I'm home and I'm relaxing and I won't be leaving home to knock on any doors. Thank you very much for your interest and your information."

I wasn't at all astonished about the first endeavor, but I was really surprised to hear about the community effort.

Before the evening waned I received six more calls. The content of each was somewhat similar and confirmed that a community petition was circulating. I didn't know whether the teacher was being successful in

72

securing signatures to have me moved or if his efforts really were boomeranging because of the community petition asking for his removal. I was aware that there was a sense of apprehension among the staff. It seemed to be an accepted fact that anyone who displeased this teacher would receive negative publicity in the community newspaper with which he was associated. I was in the process of documenting an unsatisfactory evaluation on him, and this provoked his anger.

Throughout the years a carrier brought the weekly community newspaper on an erratic schedule to be sent home to parents without charge. Generally when he came, he placed the bundle of papers inside the large entrance door. One day soon after the petition calls, they were brought and placed inside the office door. One of the clerks walked over and looked at them.

"Ms Haynes, the bundle of papers is here."

"So?"

"Ms. Haynes, I think you should look at the paper."

"Oh, so it's come."

I walked over and looked. There it was in the community throw-away: BLACK TEACHERS IN WATTS ARE LOSING JOBS, ASK PROBE BOARD OF EDUCATION--Children Lack Discipline--Grape St. School Target.

I had prepared myself for this. After turning a page, I paused and spontaneously asked that a copy be placed in each teacher's mailbox. It was the kind of sensational reporting that I knew no one would want to miss. The article was a full two and half pages, and I noted that every name was incorrectly spelled in some manner except mine.

Later I learned that Naomi Gilbert, the office manager, cried. I didn't see her, and I'm glad I didn't. The office staff was wonderfully understanding and supportive as were many others. Some whispered and elaborated on the adverse publicity. Somehow, an inner strength seemed to emerge within me, and the whole episode became a challenge. I guess this article brought me to the attention of many persons and groups. Many diverse reactions reached my ears. Some questioned, but most were empathetic.

Fortunately for me, the School-Community Advisory Council members gave me their unequivocal support. It just happened that the paper came off the press the day of the regular meeting of the Council. There was standing room only in the library, and the regular membership was astounded at the overflow attendance. The chairperson, Reverend W.J. Broussard, had had an opportunity to peruse the article and had become incensed. He lambasted the publicity and the publishers in no uncertain terms. Since there weren't enough papers to go around, Ms. Broussard and I volunteered to read it. At the conclusion, each person named in the article, except one, either verbally or in writing refuted the "facts" that had been presented. Sitting among the group was my Sector II superintendent, and he rose to express regret that anyone should have the need to feed this type of internal reporting to a newspaper. His support was total.

Ms. Broussard came to my office. "Ms Haynes, I've been fired."

"What do you mean, you've been fired?" I asked.

"My teacher just fired me out of his room," she explained.

"No teacher can fire you. I couldn't fire you. It doesn't work that way. What happened?"

"Ms. Haynes, just last week in the PTA meeting I announced that my teacher was one of the greatest teachers in the city. But when that newspaper came out, I confronted him. I told him that I remembered that other story about the white teacher when you first came here. And, now, all this ugly publicity seems to have a tie-in with the other. When I asked him if he had anything to do with all this writing, he said to me, 'Ms. Broussard, you are fired from my room. Don't come back to work in here any more. There is going to be a fight between me and the principal, so stay out, so you won't be in the middle.' So, here I am with no place to go."

"Oh, yes, you do have some place to go. There are teachers who have been pleading for an education aide to assist them. You may work here in the office until we make an adjustment and give you an assignment."

There it was in *Newsweek,* May 3, 1971. It began on page 60 under the caption DOES SCHOOL + JOY = LEARNING?" I read on. There was a phrase in the first paragraph describing room 18, but the teacher's name was not included. Then it hit me--in the second paragraph glaring undeniably at me were my own words lifted from a communication I had written my superiors. "What's more," says Principal Carrie Haynes, "it also had the heaviest concentration of incompetent teachers we have ever encountered on one staff." I had given the reporter a copy of this letter, and he had used it. I didn't blame him and I didn't blame myself, but I knew that this would fan the wrath of teachers who were taking sides with my adversary.

Inevitably at the next teachers meeting, the question was asked, "Did you make this statement quoted in *Newsweek* about incompetent teachers?"

I answered honestly, "Yes, I made that statement early in the school year of 1969." Most of the teachers were fairly willing to accept this explanation, but a few preferred not to do so. As the meeting proceeded, there were piercing glares as the room 18 teacher deliberately mouthed a subdued chant of "Incompetent, incompetent, you're incompetent," as he looked from one teacher to another. When a group walked out to the parking lot afterward, Coy Roberson, the present faculty chairman, commented, "If the shoe fits, let him wear it, whoever the him may be."

When the community newspaper next appeared, the headlines read, "GRAPE ST. SCHOOL TEACHERS INCOMPETENT: Mrs. Haynes Attacks Teachers in National Publication."

Later I received a second local newspaper dated April 22, 1971 with headlines, "POISON FOOD CHARGES--Asks Probe Grape Street School." The article began--"Los Angeles--In May of 1970, frozen hamburger meat left to sit out overnight and subsequently served to youngsters, caused many of them to vomit and to be sent home ill." I read that article several times before I noticed the date and only then recalled the incident of the unplugged refrigerator that had occurred the year before. No one at Grape Street School or at any of the twenty other schools served by our central kitchen had been served any food that had not been continuously refrigerated.

On the following week the paper that goes to Grape's school community proclaimed, "GRAPE STREET PRINCIPAL DENIES SERVING CHILDREN POISONED FOOD." Another paper's headline read, "PRINCIPAL BLAMES ELECTRICAL FAILURE."

The room 18 teacher was growing openly impatient with faculty chairman Coy Roberson. One day during the spoiled food accusation period I heard him say, "He's too soft. He's not calling any meetings or doing anything to protect teachers and their rights."

Almost daily the room 18 teacher was inviting parents and community people to come in to discuss the situation. For two days in succession this teacher had accompanied his sixth-grade class down the stairs, and from one end of the hall to the other they chanted, "The food is poison...The food is poison...The food is poison." The upper-grade lunch section had become so chaotic the day before that I had requested all teachers to remain on duty and supervise their classes as they ate lunch. I did not want to do this, but something had to be done to try to control the madhouse being created under the lunch pavillion.

Vonceil Edmondson went to the attendance office to get a pass to go home for lunch. Ms. Cole gave it to her and reported it to me. Ms. Broussard was working in the office, and she called Vonceil's mother. Ms. Edmondson told Ms. Broussard that Vonceil was afraid to eat the cafeteria food and they shouldn't eat it.

When she returned to school I spoke with her. Vonceil reported, "My teacher told us--the whole classroom--that the cafeteria had food from last year and flies were getting on it and they didn't wrap it up so it had gotten poison and made some children vomit."

"I think that was last week that he told us this. Monday I ate a hot dog and my stomach started hurting. I went to the room and it stopped hurting. My mother fed me some dry spaghetti and my stomach stopped hurting. I didn't eat Tuesday. My other friends didn't eat either. But they won't tell because now the teacher says we can eat it if we want to."

A noon duty director rushed into my office, "Ms Haynes, it's getting hectic out here. They say they're finding rocks in their food. They're yelling 'Don't eat the food. Don't eat the food.'"

"Thank you, I'll go out," I responded. As I walked out, the chanting became subdued.

The room 18 teacher walked toward me, announcing, "See, they just found this rock in their food."

"Well, at least that's a come-down from poison, isn't it?" I asked.

That afternoon parents and teachers gathered in the library. As I walked in, the room 18 teacher stood pointing to headlines in the community paper. He stopped talking, glared at me, and inquired, "Why are you coming in here?"

"I am a member of the faculty," I answered as I took my seat.

He resumed his speech, "I tell you that what is in this paper is true. I can document all the facts stated here. I can produce written proof of boys and girls who vomited and got sick after eating the poisoned food from that cafeteria."

Much irrational discussion ensued in which I participated. After about a half hour one perceptive young Black father arose and announced, "This whole thing just seems to be a fight between one teacher and the principal. They need to settle this between themselves." He and several others left.

Naturally, the morale of the cafeteria workers and the cafeteria manager was affected. A committee of workers came to me to indicate that they wanted to submit a petition indicating their confidence in and support of Ms. Bottorff, the manager. They did, and this served to sustain a congenial relationship among themselves.

Inspectors from the Los Angeles County Health Department were summoned. They checked on the school sanitation survey and inspected the entire central kitchen operation from stem to stern. They took samples of food being served back to their laboratory. The director of food services came out for interviews. On May 3, 1971, my office received an official inspection report that read: "No Sanitation Violations Noted At This Time. All refrigeration good."

There was no doubt that the *Newsweek* article had had an impact. Television stations and movie makers descended upon the school. The timing was propitious and helped prevent the program from disintegrating during this tense period. Parents continued calling to report that a teacher was knocking on doors, and petitions were being discussed by some teachers. Many were confused. In spite of the continuous agitation, the learning program thrived. The regular teachers and staff development meetings continued. During this period at least three major television stations filmed and aired segments about Grape Street School in special TV news spots. Several radio stations broadcast from the school grounds.

There was so much activity that it was necessary for everyone to stay alert, and the student programs grew increasingly open. Pride and shame walked side by side. One day as I walked briskly across the grounds, I look-

One day when I returned to school from a Title I meeting, I was met by Ms. Willis and Ms. Brown.

"Ms. Haynes, we've been waiting for you. We want you to see what that teacher did to our boys. Get him out of here. He isn't fit to be a teacher," exclaimed Ms. Willis.

"Get him out of here, and we mean right now, Ms. Haynes," added Ms. Brown.

The sons of these mothers had received obvious, though slight, injuries as a result of being struck by a Black male permanent teacher. Teachers had been repeatedly advised that they should only administer corporal punishment in the presence of an administrator. These two mothers knew the rules and were not going to be appeased. The teacher who had committed the offense admitted that the accusations were true. He also knew how these mothers could be. He had had similar encounters with them before, and they recalled the other incidents.

He came to me and voluntarily requested an immediate administrative transfer. He realized that there was no other way. Recognizing the crisis situation that already existed among staff, he also voluntarily agreed to tell the faculty. At the staff meeting that afternoon he explained, "I made a bad mistake. I struck two boys. Their mothers are angry, and they will make trouble. They will only be satisfied if I leave. So, voluntarily, I am requesting our principal to give me an administrative transfer."

"You see, she won't even back a teacher," exclaimed the room 18 teacher. "What did I tell you? She won't back you. You can't sit here and let parents pressure you out. Look at what's happening here. Who will be next?"

A faculty meeting was called. I was tired of meetings and didn't bother to attend. Five days later I received the results of the meeting, a petition signed by most of the teachers asking that the room 18 teacher not be removed as requested by the community petition.

At the time I made the decision to document an unsatisfactory evaluation of the room 18 teacher, I contacted Dr. Reginald Murphy, the area's legal advisor, who worked with and guided me. When completed the unsatisfactory notice was a polished document that had to be issued affect an administrative transfer from Grape Street School. The reasons documented were: unprofessional conduct, poor judgment in handling student problems, failure to comply with rules and regulations of Los Angeles City Schools and the administrative policies of Grape Street School, and failure to accept suggestions and to cooperate with the principal. There were twenty-two documented charges and twenty-one documented instances of assistance and guidance.

I presented the unsatisfactory notice to the teacher the morning of the last day of school with Yugo Fukushima as witness. He refused to sign or accept it.

ed up toward room 18 and saw a small hand give a surreptitious wave and then disappear from sight. During recess a sixth-grade girl sidled up to me with clenched teeth and furtively mumbled, "Ms Haynes, I can't let my teacher see me talking to you. My mother says it's a disgrace that this thing is happening here at our school."

Then, go quickly," I warned. "I don't want you to get yourself into any trouble."

One May day the room 18 teacher was absent. This was rare and conspicuous. Although he was consistently late and rarely signed in, he was generally present. As I entered my home at the end of that school day, the telephone was ringing. I answered and heard one of Grape's dedicated parents excitedly tell me, "Ms. Haynes, I just left the Medical Building on 103rd Street. There was an artistically printed sign that read 'FOOD IS POISON AT GRAPE STREET SCHOOL MS. CARRIE A. HAYNES, PRINCIPAL." I hurried home to call school to see if I could catch Mr. Fukushima to have him go and take the sign down. I didn't get to call until 5:00 o'clock so I thought I should call you at home." She named two other persons who were accompanying her and reported that the three of them had been astonished, bewildered, and dismayed.

I called a person whom I knew who worked in this building, but it was too late, and the office was closed. Later, I located a person who volunteered to go to open the building and check. His return call informed me that no sign was posted. This sign obtained no publicity and has remained a mystery.

That same day I received a community petition that had been sent to the area office and forwarded to me. Since it was an unsolicited derogatory communication, my superintendent requested that I show it to the teacher concerned and offer him an opportunity to review it and to respond in writing to the area office with a carbon copy to me as principal within ten days. One hundred thirty-seven names and addresses were affixed.

Somehow, in spite of all the confusion and the trauma, the school was proceeding with the business of teaching boys and girls in most classrooms. We were making use of the accumulated transferred Title I funds. Substitutes were arriving, and teachers were visiting other classrooms in the school. Some were returning to their classrooms to work cooperatively with the substitute in the afternoons. Sometimes the released teacher visited all day in one or more classrooms. Often the released teachers found some time during the day to work with a consultant or alone in the curriculum room. Released time was used in varied and creative ways.

At 9 o'clock sixth-graders stormed into my office demanding an answer to, "Why are you firing our teacher?"

I sent them back to their room, but all through the morning students were questioning and protesting. After they were dismissed at 12:20 p.m., there was a luncheon in the teachers' room. As I started toward the cafeteria, someone informed me. "Two of your tires are going down. It looks as if there are some pieces of glass under your car."

There were indeed pieces of glass under each of my four tires. By the time I walked onto the parking lot, my car was sitting on four flats. A young White male substitute teacher walked over to say, "I think I could identify two of the boys. I saw them come out of that room upstairs."

"Never mind," I told him. Get checked out, and have a good summer."

In due time the police came and issued a DR number, and a tow truck came and hoisted my disabled car. The room 18 teacher stood alone at the fence and queried, "What happened?"

10

ON OUR WAY

In the fall of 1971 there were thirteen teacher vacancies, including one for room 18. I interviewed, accepted, and assigned seven females to classrooms before summer vacation period began. This was the first time I felt I could be somewhat selective in my choice of teachers. These seven, four Blacks and three Whites, had been chosen from eleven who had applied. All were young. I returned for 1-B time, which is the two-week period for office staffs to prepare for the opening of school, and continued interviewing. I could hardly believe the seeming potential evidenced by each prospect who came. One afternoon as one White female walked through the office door, she was greeted animatedly by another with whom she seemed to be acquainted, "Are you just getting out here? I came out for my interview yesterday and got accepted at Grape. Wow, I can hardly believe it! Man, do I feel lucky. I really did want a chance to teach here."

From inside my office I heard the young lady who had been greeted responded, "Yeah, I'm just arriving. I had problems getting them to send me here. What did they tell you?"

The voices became subdued, but I could still overhear, "You mean that consultant downtown? Yeah, he told me that I didn't want to come to Grape because there were weird things going on out here. But I told him that my mind was made up and I wanted to come out and give it a try. I kept insisting and finally he sent me. I've got my assignment. I'm going to teach a third grade."

"Well, I guess by the time I got there he was wondering aloud why so many teachers were asking to come to Grape. He told me about the weird things going on here, too. He really tried to convince me that I didn't want to come way out here, but I made him understand that I wanted a chance to teach in an open classroom setting. I think several of us left him quite bewildered, but three of us got referrals. I hope there are still openings here."

There were. Two of the first four young women who appeared were accepted. So were the next three. Rooms and classes were assigned. I looked over the school organization chart and saw there was only one vacancy left. It was for room 18. Why hadn't one of the teachers interviewed been placed in that room? What a good question. Then suddenly it dawned upon me. Each of the last five teachers selected were young White females. This had not entered my mind during the interviews. My concern had been quality and qualifications, and in my opinion each of the young women chosen had these and thus had been assigned.

Because the former faculty chairman who had occupied room 18 had been transferred to another city school, a replacement was needed. Somehow, I wanted that person to be a Black teacher. I didn't want to put a White teacher who had any possibility of failing in that room. And even if I placed a Black teacher there, I wanted to be very sure that she or he would be a strong or an outstanding teacher. These thoughts were racing through my mind when late on the last afternoon before school officially opened, I was told that a Ms. Miles had arrived for an interview.

"Have her come in," I instructed.

My head turned, and I saw a smooth ebony face encircled by a medium-length well-rounded natural hair-do and the slim tall body of a young woman who pranced through my office door with the carriage of a young filly. There was direction, confidence, and determination in her voice as she simply said, "Hello."

"Are you interested in teaching here?" I asked.

"Yes, after several interviews I asked to come here because I want to work with minority children and I heard this was an open classroom school." She looked as if she were ready, willing and anxious to make a classroom come alive. We talked some more, and then I told her, "You call the personnel office to let them know. I'll do the same. You will be assigned a sixth grade in room 18."

I summed up Josephine Miles as being just right for Grape Street School as well as just the teacher for room 18. My appraisal was accurate. She and her students developed a model open classroom.

Much orientation was needed for the many new teachers on the staff. Fortunately the majority lived up to their apparent potential. Yugo Fukushima had taken the principal's examination, placed third on the list, and been assigned to Magnolia Elementary School.

Murray Goldberg was assigned to be the new vice-principal at Grape Street School. I divided our responsibilities. Mr. Goldberg delegated much of his responsibilities to the new upper and lower-grade consultants, Adele Wilder and Beverly Washington. He was impressed with the flow of visitors that came to see our program, and designed an adhesive identification tag, with a border of grapes, which we have continued to request visitors to wear. Each morning he checked the roster, assembled the group, and presented background and information about the development of Grape's open classroom program.

We planned staff development sessions.

"We've got some problems that we need to consider," announced Coy Roberson. "Teachers need to review playground rules. Too many children are leaving their assigned areas and causing problems."

"They surely are. Upper-grade students come over into the kindergarten yard every day to disturb our children's program. At first we tried having the older students serve as monitors, but this only seems to draw larger numbers and it gets out of control."

"During the primary recess some of the little children come upstairs to speak to older brothers, sisters, or friends. Some small groups just seem to enjoy walking through the halls. A few of them are noisy and disturb our activities."

"What's wrong with our recess periods? Most of us seem to be pretty well organized in our classrooms. What's the problem?"

"That's a good question. I guess that's what this discussion is all about," Dennis Helper summarized.

"You know what? I have an idea what may be wrong. In our classrooms we are giving our children some choices. When they go out on the yard, we assign them to a certain area. Maybe if there were lots of games and they could make choices out there, it might work better," suggested Elna Cook.

"That's the free play concept. We'd better give that a lot of thought before we get ourselves involved in that. It really will be chaotic it it isn't well organized," remarked Gloria White.

"There are a few schools where such a program works well. I know of one near here. I believe we can make it work, and I'd like to give it a try," volunteered Adele Wilder. She was granted the opportunity. She, Mr. Roberson, and two male education aides went to observe two free play programs. They compiled a shopping list, and table and bench games were purchased.

"We'll be ready to begin operation on the first day of the mid-semester. I need to arrange to talk to each of the classes before we begin," Ms. Wilder informed me.

"Schedule a half-hour period for each grade level to meet with you in the auditorium. Then you can explain the new program and answer questions about it."

She did. Groups assembled in the auditorium for instructions and to review basic procedures. Teachers and students were informed about the many and varied games that would be available to them. Rules for playing each game were distributed to the teachers. Classes were informed that they would leave their rooms, walk out onto the yard, choose a game activity, and stay with it throughout the play period. Teachers and education aides were assigned to man various stations and areas at recess. Education aides and noon duty directors relieved teachers of this responsibility at the noon lunch and play period.

The first day this program went into operation, it was a thing of beauty. Students were escorted out. If the game of their choice was filled, they chose another. Since the carom tables, checker boards, and pool table games were new, they were preferred, but no one pushed or shoved.

I walked around on the yard and spoke with teachers, "My goodness, there is nothing to do" was their reaction. I brought out my camera and took pictures. Our yard was unbelievable. Students were as involved outside as they were inside in almost all their classrooms.

"How do you like this play time?" I asked a boy at a carom table.

"Oh, boy, Ms. Haynes, why haven't we been doing this all the time?"

What a good question. The staff development dialogue and discussion had set the direction. We followed through; and it was working.

Los Angeles City Schools have two student-free days each school year. The first one is scheduled for the day before students arrive in the fall. Each school has the option to hold the second one at the mid-term or on the last day of school. This time is allowed for staff preparation or evaluation. It is also the time that the school superintendent, Dr. William J. Johnston, delivers his annual and mid-term message to the large, widely spread staff. In the fall of 1971, the Grape Street staff sat in the auditorium listening to him speak. Gasps were audible, and our faces revealed our astonishment when we heard Johnston say, "Grape Street School was cited by *Newsweek* magazine as an outstanding example of a non-traditional elementary school." What a pleasant shock it was for us to receive this recognition at the beginning of the new school year.

One midyear student-free day we received an even higher honor. Superintendent Johnston sent buses for the school staff, and we spent the morning sitting in the KHJ—TV studio as he addressed the other 60,000 employees and generously announced, "As you may remember, Grape Street, located in the Watts Community, received national recognition last spring as one of a new breed of schools that has broken away from traditional education restraints. With its dynamic staff, Grape Street symbolizes the revitalized hope for the future of urban education. I have asked faculty and administration of this fine school to join me to honor them for their many fine achievements." This was a shining hour for us indeed.

On March 20, 1972, the Grape Street staff members, their friends, and other interested persons throughout the country turned on their television sets to view the program, "What Did You Learn In School Today?" a PBS Special of the Week produced by the National Programming Division of WNET/13.

This documentary is a revealing study in contrasts between traditional classrooms and the new, freer open classrooms now being implemented successfully in some American public schools and England.

We had been anxious about the fact that Grape Street was the school from Watts. Because I was scheduled to be away from the city the day the filming crew arrived, I answered questions and made comments about our program on a tape. On my return I heard the filming had gone well, but there were also rumors circulating that someone in the crew had been overheard saying, "There just isn't enough deprivation here. Maybe we should go out and find or make some." This was disturbing. It was being discussed and caused apprehension.

When the release time arrived, our eyes were glued to television sets in our various homes and gatherings. Traditional school and classroom scenes were shown first, and Lady Plowden commented extensively and insightfully. Then there it was--the flames that symbolized the 1965 Watts riots, the police cars, the wailing siren, and the Watts Towers spiraling in the background. This brief scene faded as groups of Grape Street students walked proudly through the streets of some of the best-kept areas in the school neighborhood. Then the focus changed to students and their activities in Josephine Miles' room 18. This class had been selected because its organizational structure vividly evidenced superior teaching and learning in the content areas. The filming crew had portrayed well what our school program represented. We had been given a good image. Our fears were allayed, and we were proud!

The film concluded with a roundtable discussion by Charles Silberman, author of *Crisis in the Classroom* and an advocate of the open classroom concept, the Sloane Foundation's Dr. James Koener, a proponent of traditional education, and M. Carl Holman, president of the National Urban Coalition. The crux of the discussion was that American parents (and school children, for that matter) can improve their schools in this time of educational crisis if they will organize and act in concert. Grape Street School had been recognized as a school making an effort to move in this opening direction, and its participation in the documentary served as much needed inspiration.

During the year upper grade students who were having reading difficulties were selected to tutor first and second graders. The older girls and boys took great pride in teaching the younger ones. They accepted their responsibilities seriously, and rarely did one of them loiter or saunter when traveling from one room to another. The younger students enjoyed the individual, special attention the tutors gave, and teachers were pleased with the reliability of the older children.

To give the tutors self-confidence and provide proper instruction, the primary teachers taught simple basic reading skills to them twice a week. They, in turn, transferred their learnings to their students. This effort enhanced the reading program for everyone involved.

As this and other aspects of the school's program were being discussed, the idea of initiating multi-aged classrooms was generated. This would mean grouping more than one grade level together, such as grades one, two and three, in one classroom. Some of the teachers seemed fascinated with the prospect and openly examined the pros and cons. The guidance committee met and deliberated at length. The invisible grapevine picked up the notion, and it became a topic of conversation. By the time the plan was ready to be presented to the faculty, the barometric reading was one-half for and one-half against.

Realizing that something was needed to tilt the scales, I called Dr. Keuscher, one of the Open Classroom Project directors at the International Center of Educational Development. He readily agreed to come to our faculty meeting.

"We'd like to have the guidance committee members present the reasons they are for or against multi-aged grouping. We need to know what we are considering and why," the discussion began.

"If we organize in this manner, each teacher will keep some of the students now in his or her classroom, even though they pass on to the next grade."

"Why is this important, or is it?"

"It is quite important because the children who remain with the same teacher will already be familiar with the room environment and the general procedures and management of the classroom. They, in turn, will be able to assist in orienting the new students."

"Won't it be hard to try to teach two or three grade levels at one time?"

"In this kind of organization teachers only keep grade levels in mind as they individualize instruction to meet the needs of each student at whatever level she or he is."

"It seems to me that record keeping would be overwhelming. I don't know if I'm ready for this or not."

At this moment Dr. Keuscher arrived. He listened to the interaction that was becoming more positive and was asked to speak. He began by telling the assembled teachers that he was prejudiced toward multi-aged grouping and gave several reasons why. As the discussion continued, more and more favorable arguments emerged.

"In this type of organization, our children would not experience failure. Slow second-grade students would be placed in a one, two, three grade. They would pass to the third grade but would be able to work on the first, second or third grade levels as their capabilities allowed in various subject areas.

"Cross-age tutoring, which primary and upper-grade teachers find successful, would be a built-in factor."

"Conversely, a more capable first or second grader would be able to move ahead smoothly in a one, two or one, two, three combination.

Positions for and against were summarized. It was agreed that teachers would think about such a change seriously overnight. The next day I placed a survey sheet in their mail boxes, asking them to indicate the grade or grades that they would choose to teach the following year. They responded promptly, and all, except the kindergarten teachers, chose two or three grade levels. Multi-aged grouping would work well, it was decided.

We presented this new proposal at the next School-Community Advisory Council meeting. The sophistication and receptivity of the parents were truly amazing. Ms. Parks, the mother of one of our identified gifted students, set the tone.

"I guess it's a concidence," she announced, as she held a paperback book in the air, "but I've been reading about the Summerhill School that was developed by A.S. Neil. This is a handbook for parents and teachers. I surely do like a lot of things he has to say. And it surely does give me some background about grouping children of different grades in one classroom. I am all for it."

"Yes, there is much good material in that book," I responded, but I think I should point out that Summerhill is classified as a free school where the students make choices with little or no direction from the teachers. We are using an open education approach where the teacher provides the environment from which the student may make choices. But it remains the responsibility of the teacher to guide and structure each student to become a self-motivated learner. I just want to point out this important difference before we proceed with our discussion."

They understood. One by one the parents convinced each other that a multi-aged organization would be more beneficial to the slow, the average, and the more capable students. The only dissenting voice was one of a visiting school board employee who kept interjecting, "I think you should have some regular classes for parents who choose not to have their children make this change." The Advisory Council gave its unanimous consent to multi-aged grouping, and *Happenings Along the Grapevine* reported the faculty's decision and the Advisory Council's approval.

In the late spring of 1972 the faculty assembled on a staff development day. I had provided each teacher the number of students from each grade level that she or he was to have the following year. Prior discussions had determined that each teacher, except for the kindergarteners, was to keep a number of children who were passing on to the next grade. Each teacher had been given a pack of organization cards and an organization sheet that indicated the overall student distribution.

This was a memorable session. With care, concern, and deliberation, teachers matched children to their own style or the style of others. The library became a beehive of activity with much chattering and interchanging of cards. The cards were handled as if they were really student personalities. Sometimes twins were placed together, sometimes twins were separated, sometimes siblings were placed together, and sometimes siblings were separated. Certain friends or cliques were separated. Children with problems were of special concern. Their placement received high priority. In many instances, more than one teacher selected the same child.

One well-known hyperactive youngster was such a case. Immediately after the meeting, he made himself obvious as he moved in a slow skating motion through the hall announcing, "Three teachers chose me to be in their rooms. Now I can choose the teacher and the room I want to be in." He did, and what a different boy he became.

During this time period I was told that a school official, who had never come to visit our building and consequently had never seen any aspect of our program, had declared authoritatively, "Grape Street School is a disgrace to the world."

11

THE WAY LIFE REALLY IS

Toward the end of the 1972 summer session, several teachers visited Mr. Fukushima who was then serving as principal of Cortez Avenue Elementary School. They were exuberant about its art exhibit and the curriculum development room. On their return, they asked if they might develop a curriculum room at Grape. A survey showed that almost all the materials and equipment needed were on hand. The teachers came in during the two weeks before school began. They met Thomas Stevens, the new vice-principal, and immediately involved him in their project. Altogether they unearthed, located, moved, arranged, classified, and categorized the many things necessary to transform room 22 into a functional curriculum room. Colorful curtains were hung at the windows, professional books filled the turnstile racks, and orange lounge chairs were moved from across the hall. Typewriters, an electric ditto machine, tape recorders, and other equipment were brought in, and audio-visual materials were organized for circulation. Catalogs, bulletins, guides, source books, and many other publications were systematically arranged.

Teachers became enamored with this facility on sight. At once they began using it; in fact, many came early in the morning. They asked for someone to service it, and Mary Baker, an education aide, was chosen. She efficiently performed the many clerical tasks required and cataloged, laminated, and checked out professional and instructional materials.

Tom Stevens, a young White man, had been assigned to Grape from the eligibility list of vice-principals. It was immediately apparent that he had willingly come to work, to learn, and to do whatever was necessary to fulfill his responsibilities. A number of city and area meetings were scheduled, and I knew these would provide some general orientation for him. After the second one it was obvious that he was growing impatient to get into the thick of the work he knew was waiting at school. He kept asking questions in an effort to find out exactly what was expected of him. We discussed philosophy, and I assigned him a few routine responsibilities and gave him a handbook to read. I suggested that he become acquainted with the plant, the office and custodial staff, and the teachers who were early arrivals. He was johnny-on-the-spot whenever requests were made but, nevertheless, he daily inquired of me how I wanted things done. I couldn't tell him. My repeated answer was, "I don't know."

Finally in mild exasperation he confronted me, "I keep asking how you want problems handled and you keep saying to me that you don't know. Is that you way of telling me to just use common sense in handling situations as they arise?"

"You're getting the message," I replied. "There is no way to predict what or how things are going to happen. I've been here three years and have seen no predictable pattern develop. There's no sense trying to prescribe for hypothetical cases. Every day is different--the sequence of any one day would provide enough material for a book. We'll make an effort to get together every morning, but you'll find that most times we'll become involved on arrival, and we may each be going separate ways throughout the day."

On several occasions I commented to Tom that it was good that he consistently wore short-sleeved shirts because there would not have been time to roll them up. From the day school opened officially, incidents started happening; the momentum became diversified, fast, and furious, but he moved with it.

Teachers openly expressed their pleasure--"He doesn't mind working."

"Did you see him supervising the lunch area?"

Parents and students added their comments about "The way Mr. Stevens talks with the children, moves around the yard, and observes in the classrooms." There was no doubt that he was dazzled by the action of the first few weeks but he kept his cool. On the rare moments when we found a chance to communicate, our talk usually ended with him sighing resigned but positively, "Well,...whatever." And that was just what he meant. With a sense of humor we have accepted, "Well,...whatever" as a wholesome administrative philosophy for Grape Street School.

The 1972-1973 school year began on a high note. All the thirteen teachers who had been new the year before had received termination notices in the spring of 1972 because of the school system's financial difficulties. Fortunately funds had been restored, and all returned except two. What a difference it made to begin a school year with almost all of the previous year's personnel still on the job.

Teachers arrived anticipating the new multi-aged grouped organization. A few teachers were apprehensive, and provisions were made to assist them. Some teachers who had taught only one grade were worried about how they would work with younger and older children. Teachers who did not have regular classes supervised while other teachers visited and observed classrooms that were functioning effectively. Working with children within multi-aged settings became the talk of each day. Ideas were discussed during morning, recess, lunch, and afternoon sessions. With this new type of grouping we found it totally unnecessary to undertake the massive reorganizations we had dealt with in prior years. Individual and small groups of students were transferred at the request of teachers, parents, or students or for other valid reasons. The three Miller-Unruh reading specialists pretested the first, second, and third graders, collaborated with their classroom teachers, and taught small groups for one hour each day in spaces provided within each open classroom setting. These adults complemented each other as skills and ideas were transmitted and shared.

On the first student-free staff development day, I presented the plans I had worked out giving each teacher a leadership responsibility during the coming year. "Each staff member has been assigned a topic and date. Look over the schedule. If you wish to make any changes or adjustments, please let me know," I announced.

Pages rustled and turned as each person looked for his or her name. I sensed a satisfaction among the group. A few requested topic changes, partner changes, or date changes. On the whole, every following session was of high professional quality. Participants planned, researched, prepared, and presented offerings in a variety of unique and substantive ways.

Patricia Douglas and Andrea Roberts had both begun as extremely traditional teachers. By now the general positive mood of all the teachers was reflected in the activites of the students. Involvement abounded. Ms. Douglas's husband assisted her in developing an enriched environment by delivering odd pieces of lumber and furniture and working with them until they became functional. Shelves, display cases, filing cases, animal cages, book holders, and many other items made this classroom come alive.

The children wrote creative and exciting stories to accompany the pictures they illustrated. They worked with task cards that contained questions about foods on the menus Ms. Douglas furnished. She acquired Tom and Patty, a pair of white mice, and Patty gave birth to a litter of mice. What conversation! What writing that stimulated! One girl brought in a box of old dress patterns and assisted by some of her friends, wrote tasks asking the size of each pattern, how much material was needed, what kind of material was best, how many pieces were in each pattern, how many styles could be made from each, and many other problem-solving variations.

It was Andrea Roberts's room 17 that had been photographed in *Newsweek*. She and her students were selected by most film-makers and television crews that came because there was order, beauty, substance, variety, a calmness and in-depth involvement in her room. She and her children made good subjects for newsmen because they talked freely and in detail about their classroom and the way the activities within it had changed from a traditional to an open classroom setting.

All the paraprofessionals employed at Grape Street were classifed as Education Aide III, which meant they were to assist teachers by relieving them of routine duties and working directly with children in the classroom. This necessitated, among many other responsibilities, writing words for children. Children in the primary grades are taught a form of lettering we call manuscript writing, and most students are taught to transfer to cursive handwriting in the third grade. Only in rare instances will a new education aide have a mastery of handwriting skills, especially manuscript. Teacher leaders planned several sessions to teach aides basic handwriting skills.

One day as I was visiting teacher mini-workshops, I received a message to, "Come at once to the education aide workshop. Things are getting out of hand."

I walked into a silent room where the women were eyeing each other suspiciously. One of the teachers spoke out, "They want some answers to some questions that we can't give them, so we sent for you. Now, you can ask Ms. Haynes your questions." For a lengthy period no one spoke.

I heard a timid voice say, "She's here now. Somebody ask her."

One of the aides straightened up and said, "We want to vote to change our name to assistant teacher because, after all, we're teaching just like the teachers are." Then I understood why the teachers couldn't answer their question.

"Well," I replied, "let me explain. There is a job category called assistant teacher for which students enrolled in a four-year college may apply. You applied for the position of education aide, which requires a high school education or the equivalent. Some of you came with more than this and some of you are taking college courses for which we commend you, but, until you apply and qualify for another category, there can be no name change. Your position will remain that of an education aide."

"Ms. Haynes, isn't there a rule that teachers shouldn't ask us to do anything that they wouldn't do? someone asked.

"Less than five years ago there were no education aides in classrooms to assist teachers. Everything that was done was performed by the classroom teacher and her or his students. Personally I never had the luxury of having someone paid to assist me during my lifetime in the classroom, so it is difficult for me to see how teachers would request you to do something that they wouldn't do themselves. Now, by the same token, the very fact that you are here means that teachers should assign you some of the more routine duties and they may not work side-by-side with you at every task. Remember, the teacher is the person in charge in the classroom and you are there to assist."

"Well, what about us getting paid when other children come into our classrooms?" another inquired.

"I don't understand," I responded honestly.

"You know, when a teacher is absent and her children are divided up to stay in other classrooms. Don't the teachers get some extra pay for them? You see, we're teaching them too. Don't we get some extra pay?"

"Oh, you mean replacement pay. Yes, when teachers are assigned an absent teacher's children they do receive an apportioned amount for the time they keep and instruct them. This is for teachers. There is no such pay for education aides and no consideration is being given for any."

"Well, I guess we got our answers," one concluded. The air was cleared. At the next in-service session the aides continued working to improve their handwriting skills.

Early in the school year Lester Hooks and three companions had come into my office to request permission to give a surpise party for their teacher. The class had already planned it and brought the party food to school.

"But, Lester," I explained, "if I let your class have a party, then I'll have to let any other class that asks me have one. I'm sure you understand that this could get out of hand." "Yeah, but the food is already here," countered Lester.

"I know, you told me. That's all the more reason I can't give you permission. As soon as you have a party, everyone will want to have one."

"We'll keep it a secret," announced Melvin.

"No way," I exclaimed, "There's no way that you could have a party without other classes knowing about it."

"We won't tell," they promised.

"I'm sorry, it won't work. I have to say no," I concluded.

Reluctantly, they left, mumbling. Once outside, a great disturbance arose. Children banged on the outside doors and called out. "I need to see Ms. Haynes again. It's a matter of important business." Lester's voice was distinctly recognizable.

"They're mad outside. They're yelling and saying bad words. They're mad about the party, Ms. Haynes," he panted.

"Yes, I know, Lester. You know, you could help quiet your friends."

"Aw, I know, but I'm mad too," Lester admitted.

"You said you wanted to have a surprise party for your teacher, didn't you?" I asked.

"Yeah, that's right. I chose her for my teacher 'cause she's a good teacher."

"I'm sure you want to do things to make Ms. Penzella happy, but, do you think she will like the way you are acting up, right now?"

"Naw, but you know something, Ms. Haynes, I don't understand you. If you didn't want us to give a surprise party for our teachers, why didn't you tell us so at the assembly?" Lester implored.

"What a good idea! We'll have an assembly tomorrow morning, and and we'll talk about ways we can show our teachers how much we like them. Let's shake on it, Lester."

Lester hesitantly extended his hand for the shake saying, "I hope you say the right things tomorrow, Ms. Haynes."

"I'll try, Lester," I promised.

He strode briskly out of the office. His class was standing in a huddle formation eagerly awaiting him. He raised his right arm high, moved it forward in a beckoning fashion, and exclaimed, "Come on, let's go. I think she'll take care of the matter."

The next morning was a bright sunny one. When the children gathered outside for assembly, I went to the microphone. "Good morning, boys and girls," I greeted them.

"Good morning, Ms. Haynes," they chorused.

"And a very special good morning to our teachers. You are the reason I called this assembly on this beautiful day. Yesterday a group of students came to me to ask if they could have a surprise party for their teacher. I had to say 'No' to them, and they felt I was being mean. I happen to know that there are other groups waiting to make the same request. It really makes me happy to know that you children like your teachers so much. And I can understand why.

"It is early in the school year, and parties at this time could easily distract from what your teachers are trying to do. There are many other ways you might express your gratiude. You might write a letter, design a card, make a poster, make an award, make a scroll, or make something your teachers can keep forever.

"Now let us make this compromise. If, in the month of January, you want to give your teacher a surprise party, then choose a representative or a committee. Have them contact Ms. Ewell or Ms. Helton. They have agreed to serve as a clearinghouse for you. They will help you plan the details. In the meantime, I know that you will think of many ways, more than those I've mentioned, to show your teachers how much you appreciate them."

"That wasn't too bad, Ms. Haynes," Lester acknowledged, as he passed me on his way to his room.

Thelma Walker had joined the staff during the fourth week and had secured order in an upper-grade class that had become chaotic. After three days she had made obvious progress. During this period she had planned the room arrangement with her class, but the next two days she was absent. When she returned, she found that her classroom environment had been extensively developed. She was puzzled. She came to the office to find out who had been working in her room, but no one could give an answer. We spent the first morning half-hour fruitlessly trying to find out who did it.

When the bell rang, teachers and children went to their rooms. I walked up to room 15 to see if I could help discover who had been working in Ms. Walker's room. As I entered, she met me with a smile.

"Ms. Haynes, I've found out what happened. My education aide and my children followed through on the plans we had made, and they developed this environment. It is so well done that I thought surely one of the consultants had come in and set it up. I'm sorry I caused all that concern this morning, but I am proud of the way the class carried on in my absence."

On a midyear visit to Elois Taylor's first grade, it was evident much purposeful activity was going on. The bulletin boards were laden with motivational ideas, tasks, and displayed children's work. Two students sat weighing items, while a third recorded the outcomes. Two sat counting out play money. Three were practicing a play with finger puppets through the window of a cardboard theater. Two sat dialing a telephone making a call to a trash man whose phone number was posted to report the need for a pick-up. Five were writing and illustrating an experience story with the help of the education aide. Ms. Taylor was directing a reading lesson with four children, and six boys were working with blocks. Robert had just reported to Ms. Taylor that Clarence, the foreman, would not select him for the construction crew. Ms. Taylor had suggested that maybe the other six had been chosen before he could be included.

"That's not the reason," Robert revealed, "It's because the other boys brought cars and toys to pay him off. I didn't have nuthing to pay him off with. That's the real reason."

A lone little fellow sat using a commercial stamp pad. I walked over to him. He had stamped on an "A" and a "Z." He looked a little puzzled. "What are you making?" I inquired. There was no response.

"What is your name? Are you making your name?" I asked.

Still no response. I leaned over wondering what question to pose next, when a bright-eyed youngster slid up to us proudly holding a flash card.

"His name is Anthony, Anthony, see your name, Is that first letter an 'A'?"

"Yes," answered the previously tongue-tied boy.

"Then, is the second letter like this?" he pointed to the name card. Anthony shook his head.

"What is this letter, Anthony?" Joseph insisted.

Anthony pondered and whispered, "N."

"Then find an 'N' like this one," Joseph instructed. Anthony looked carefully and picked up an "N" stamp.

"Start over again, Anthony, and make your name right." Anthony followed directions, and Joseph returned to his research about ships.

There were still other activities going on in this room. One group was cutting out items to make "sets" tell stories, another was planning to build an aquarium from plastic sheets for a fishing game, and another was discovering and pasting on pictures to represent television programs on appropriate channels.

Kristine Johnson, a young White teacher of first, second, and third grades, and Gail Penzella, a young Black teacher of fourth, fifth and sixth grades worked in rooms 2 and 3 across the hall from each other, and they agreed to develop and operate a math lab in room 6. This was over and above their own class responsibilities, which each one performed well.

Whenever I needed samples of children's writing, I walked over to room 2. "Take whatever you need," Ms. Johnson would offer. "We love to write, and we keep writing reams and reams. Help yourself."

Creative writings adorn all the doors and walls of that room. The children write prolifically about themselves, their families, their friends, the TV shows they like, the topic of the day, or whatever. They write and write and write. Ms. Johnson has developed an atmosphere that fits the personalities of the children and herself. It is a joy to observe her working with her children in a lighthearted, airy, low-keyed, sophisticated manner. She works and involves herself with the children so that each one knows she cares. She is pleased with each one and tell them so. Without raising her voice, they respond to her beck and call. Her rich and motivating room contains a travel agency, a puppet stage, plants, animals, books, numerals, scales, measuring cups, key word cards, and creative writing and creative writing and creative writing.

Across the hall, blazoning in large capital letters along the back wall, is room 3's motto: THE ROAD TO SUCCESS IS ALWAYS UNDER CONSTRUCTION. These words have meaning for the class. There are as many learning centers as there are students. Tasks are lined along the tables against the back wall, and throughout the room are groupings of two tables. Carrels divide each of these into two or four sections. Composition books, folders, or projects are housed in various filing boxes, shelves, or other storage places provided. There is an unmistakable emphasis on academics, but Ms. Penzella approaches them in a practical way.

One day a boy brought in two lizards he had caught along the railroad tracks. Immediately a committee began doing research so that they could develop a natural habitat, determine what the lizards would eat, discover their habits, their need for camouflage, where they could be found, their relationship to other reptiles, and so on. Some branched out into research on the forest, domesticated animals, wild animals, and food chains.

These two teachers developed and managed the math lab. They take turns accompanying their own classes to try out the tasks, the games, and the varied instructional aids. The room is developed on the basis of the evaluation and enjoyment of these classes. If they like it, others seem to also.

Their students helped to cut out the large black capital letters placed on the wide bulletin board:

PICK THE ONE YOU WOULD USE TO MEASURE

c	h	*fevers*	d	c
l	o		a	o
o	u	*height*	y	l
t	r		s	d
h	s	*weight*		
		milk	f	b
			l	o
			o	o
lemonade		*vanilla*	o	k
			r	
			s	

Scattered among these labels on the bulletin board were a papercup, a measuring cup, a milk carton, a ruler, a yardstick, a measuring tape, a set of measuring spoons, a clock face, a wall thermometer, a calendar, a nursing thermometer, and a date book page. On a table were balancing scales, a cloth, a diary, weighing scales, and measuring games. Plastic containers holding sets of Cuisenaire rods were placed on a table between a descriptive legend. Another chart proclaimed MATCH EACH COUN—TRY WITH ITS MONEY. World maps, names of countries, and money names were supplied.

Across the room was a bulletin board with an interesting arrangement of triangles, circles, rectangles, and squares in varying large sizes. The caption above them read THE SHAPES OF THINGS ABOUT US. The children cut out items and placed them in the properly matched shape.

On one side of the room was a teller's window between two tables. Money, checks, deposits slips, and withdrawal slips were all in readiness for business.

A few steps away two pushed-together tables were covered with a colorful plastic tablecloth, flowers were in the center, and place settings were at each of the four sides. A menu awaited a waiter and his customers.

Lower and upper-grade classes are scheduled to use the room once every other week. No one mans the math lab. Each teacher accompanies his or her class to work with the materials, and each teachers and class is expected to leave this lab as they found it for the use of the next class. This arrangement is working well.

One morning as I walked down the hall, I saw two eight-year-old boys hopping up and down, peeking through a small window, and futilely twisting at the knob of a door. The door was locked. Generally, Grape's classrooms are kept locked because there were many times in the past when uninvited secondary students or others entered the halls or rooms. This has happened far less often recently, but locking doors has become a habit.

"What's wrong, boys? Why aren't you inside?" I asked.

"We got to school just a little bit late, Ms. Haynes, and Ms. Stock, we don't think she's going to let us in."

"Ms. Haynes, would you please ask our teacher to let us come in. We don't want to miss our time in the math lab."

"If you knock at the door, won't she let you in?" I queried.

"Well, Ms. Haynes, to tell you the truth, we got into a little bit of trouble. We pushed some boys in line, but we didn't really mean to get into trouble. We'll apologize. Ms. Haynes, please ask Ms. Stock to let us come in."

"What would you do if she does let you come in?"

"I know I'm too late to get to those scales. I like putting different things on both side of the scales to see what amounts make the scales balance. Then I put it on paper to tell the story.__ But I know everybody's got those tied up, so I could do some measuring.

"Well, I know what I'll do. I weighed six of my friends, and I know how many pounds each one weighs. I want to get over in the corner and use those special ink colors to make a graph. Please, hurry up and ask her, Ms. Haynes. We haven't got much time left."

I unlocked the door and spoke softy with Jo Ann Stock. "You have two boys outside who asked me to intercede for them. They admit they arrived late and pushed others in line. They say they want to apologize and come in. They seem quite anxious," I explained.

"Surely, if they are willing to apologize to their classmates, they may come in," she agreed. I stepped aside.

"Come on in boys," she invited. They started to lower their heads and scramble in, caught themselves, stood tall and walked into the math lab.

I was delighted the day Jewel Williams, a young Black woman, informed me that she was interested in returning. She had taken a child-care and substitute leave shortly after my arrival. She had been among the few teachers I had originally found who had some definite plans and was implementing a meaningful program.

By this time the total school milieu had changed, so when she returned in the middle of the 1972-1973 school term, she was apprehensive. Grape had been acclaimed and was moving along as an open classroom school. She felt she was quite traditional and needed to make some drastic changes in her teaching style to adapt or phase into the program. I assured and reassured her that she should work with her students using the approach she knew and in whatever manner she felt comfortable, as long as her students were learning.

There was another reason she felt some anxiety. Diane Dozier, a young White woman who was the only teacher I knew who had formerly trained in an open classroom setting, was coming to work in the room whose door opened into hers. Charlotte Keuscher, the wife of Dr. Robert Keuscher and an open classroom consultant, had been her master teacher. Ms. Dozier's personality, training, commitment, and lifestyle were open class-

12

GROWING FROM WITHIN

O n an afternoon in March 1974, I opened the library door and entered an exotic environment representing the South Pacific Islands. Waiting to greet and lead the session was Valcour Williams attired in a full-length pale yellow dress from Manila. Posters of the ports of Tahiti, Fiji, the Phillipines, Hong Kong, and Korea brightened the walls. Children's creative writings and drawings covered the library stacks. The front table was filled with artifacts. Soft island music floated through the air. Teachers arrived and settled themselves in the casual and relaxing setting.

Ms. Williams showed a few slides of the experiences she had had the summer before on the World Campus Afloat, a Pepperdine University seven-week cruise. She played tapes of welcome songs and asked us to join in singing some of them. She explained the artifacts, their uses, and differences in some of the customs. Special attention was given to the creative writing of elementary school children in the South Pacific area. Their beautiful letter formations indicated the extent to which their small muscles were coordinated because of the regular hand exercises in which they engaged while working with various sizes and varieties of shells. Though each was different, their stories were expressive of their sea shore life. Moving pictures of natives of New Guinea, who covered their bodies with mud and isolated themselves within their community of mud huts, were shown. This was more than a presentation--it became a happening.

In almost total contrast on a subsequent Tuesday a recording instructed, "Pick up a questionnaire from the table and take a seat please," as the staff entered the library. Over and over this resounded until everyone was assembled, and the multi-media session began. A heavy melodic rhythmic beat reinforced the psychedelic movements on the screen. A length of clear plastic was maneuvered across an overhead projector. Students had used rainbow colored crayons in a splish-splash manner to create a kaleidoscopic effect for the title of the session, "Educational Futurism," followed by the names of the producers, Gaydelle Brown, Samuel Pecot, and room oriented. She had been assigned to 97th Street School in the fall, where a good and effective program was being implemented, but it wasn't open. When the situation was made known to me, I called the school's principal whom I knew well. She was understanding and graciously allowed Ms. Dozier to transfer to Grape. Ms. Williams and Ms. Dozier soon became good friends and complimented each other.

Wilnora Ewell moved into the library and made it come alive. She took ideas that had been lying dormant, personalized them, and developed a task-oriented library media center. Using colored tagboard and her perfected manuscript lettering, she presented challenging and meaningful tasks and motivated much student involvement. The library theme was Fantasy Land. Children discovered there were no characters with whom they could identify, so Ms. Ewell announced, "We'll have a contest, and write your own books." They were to fantasize on the title, "The Black Prince" or "The Black Princess." Many students became inspired. Some similarities to the classic fairy tales were discernible in many, of course. Other exposed personal anxieties, frustrations, and wishes. Some students related their dreams, while some fantasized upon social issues and concern. The important thing was that our students were motivated to write--and they wrote and wrote. The shortest book submitted was sixteen pages, of which the upper portion of each page contained illustrations. This was the basic format. A few illustrated a whole page and wrote a whole page. The lengthiest book submitted was twenty typed half-pages. Some were in manuscript, and some were in cursive, but all had illustrations. Most of the art work was done by the authors, but a few had separate illustrators and authors. Some had a table of contents, some had an index, some had a glossary, and some just contained a story. There were forty-five entries.

The covers were also interesting. Some students bound their books carefully. Books were covered with colored construction paper, flannel, contact paper over chipboard, colored tagboard, and burlap. Toothpicks, roving, ribbon, cloth, pipe stems, straws, beans, shells, and other small items were employed to spell out the titles on the covers.

The children enjoyed the involvement. Nila Wells, a fifth grade girl who had been quiet and introverted throughout her six school years, expressed herself so vividly in writing and illustrations that she was awarded the first blue ribbon prize. Nine other ribbon prizes were given, and each of the other participants received a certificate of recognition. The original books remained on display for a month.

"All the other stories ended with 'and they lived happily ever afterward,'" Nila explained. "Mine didn't end that way. My story said 'and the Black princess kept looking and kept looking and trying to find some happiness.' That's the way life really is. I put some make-believe all in between. I guess that's why I won the first prize."

Donald Walker. The musical mood sobered and the sound lowered as Mr. Pecot began the video-taped interviews. All three teachers had projected themselves into the future of 1985 and discussed their educational concerns, some of which were: (1) Will schools disappear? (2) Will family size be predetermined? (3) Will man be biomedical? (4) Will the laser beam be used as an instructional aid? (5) Will chemical gases be released through ventilating systems to keep students and teachers alert? (6) Will parents give their children learning enzymes?

The participants gave credits chiefly to Alvin Toffler's *Future Shock* and other relevant research sources used in their deliberation. This was truly a different, insightful, and thought-provoking session.

Esther Zack, Ethel Taylor, and Mary Fischer planned a SWAP MEET. Teachers became ecstatically involved in an interchange of materials and ideas for the total period.

The eleventh session of the 1973-1974 year was led by Ramona Selby and Yvonne Almeida, who had chosen "Involving Parents on the School Team" as their topic. A questionnaire they developed had been disseminated among the faculty prior to the meeting. When the concerns of the teachers were determined, they were categorized and relayed to the administrative consultant of the Staff Development Branch of the Los Angeles Unified School District. This session's co-leaders had invited the consultant to be guest workshop leader. Immediately Thomasina Pleasant involved us in group process activities, and the hour passed before we could complete all the planned program.

For the past three years Grape Street had been given permission to dismiss early each Wednesday so staff development sessions could be held to improve the school's innovative program. At the beginning of the fourth year we were informed that we should discontinue early dismissals and use only the ten shortened days allowed all Los Angeles City schools. For the first ten Thursdays the upper grades were dismissed at 2:20 p.m. and the faculty became involved in staff development until 3:45 p.m. Then came the time for decision. There was a consensus that staff development sessions should continue because they had been the motivating force in Grape's efforts to make significant improvements. Without lengthy consideration it was decided to hold a teachers' meeting for administrative matters on one Tuesday of each school month and continue the staff development sessions on the other three. The quality of these sessions continued on a highly professional level.

During the 1972-1973 school year everyone was involved in the staff development act. Because there was time, the sessions were diversified and had a variety of formats. Toward the end of the school year Ms. Gilbert and the rest of the office staff role played the responsibilities, duties, and needs for promptness and accuracy in the performance of clerical functions. The humor of office interruptions--the ringing phone, parent inquiries, teacher demands, student requests, and examples of other activities that prevent any day from being a dull one in the school office--were dramatized. Many of the faculty commented, "They should have been scheduled earlier in the year. We didn't know their work was so involved and how much it affects each one of us." This presentation motivated the secretarial staff to meet each Tuesday for its own staff development sessions.

Mal Neely, the pupil services and attendance counselor, is a young alert Black male who had come in the fall of 1973. He quickly became acquainted and involved and soon led a session at which he briefly outlined his job description and told how he was working with children, teachers, and parents. He counsels students as individuals and in groups, and much of his work involves home visitations. Teachers had already expressed their appreciation for the insights he gained and shared after making home contacts. During his session he portrayed some of the different approaches he uses as he travels through the housing project. Donning an oversized jazzy cap and slanting it to the side of his head, he gave a one-legged dip with short measured steps on his two-inch heel oxfords, hunching up one shoulder of his tall slim body as he imitated the walk that conveyed, "Hi ya, soul brother," and gave him entrance into sections of the Imperial Courts. He outlined his plans to reorganize the Block Parents.

His organization of the Grape Street All Star Basketball Team has been phenomenally successful. The team was initially formed from the group of boys he counseled. They played other teams within the uppergrade cluster group, and they played the male teachers. Mr. Neely then made arrangements for them to play against other schools in the area. What excitement and what motivation this engendered!

All games are played after school, and all players must be in good standing with their teachers in their classrooms. There is continuing collaboration. As Mr. Neely walks through the halls, he becomes the Pied Piper, as one can hear him amiably inform the jack-in-the-box boys surrounding him, "I'm on my way to check with your teachers. If you're holding up in class, you'll play today." Almost no players are denied. Since the first game, there has been little need to call for security guard protection for the more than two hundred students, teenagers, and community spectators who ring the basketball court and cheer for the teams.

Betty Heintz, the White nurse, showed a film depicting some of the responsibilities of the school nurse, and the impact of her presentation was unquestionable. Grape has one problem with her--she is scheduled for only three days a week, and everyone wants her here for five days. She has established rapport with everyone, and there are times when her office resembles Grand Central Station.

I can get a barometer reading of anxieties, frustrations, boredom, restlessness, or tenseness from the number of referrals she receives from certain classrooms at certain times of certain days. When yard activities are not challenging to some, it is reflected in her office. When the menu of the free lunch program fails to please the appetites of a few, they come. The slightest scratch or injury is brought in for major attention. The children like the nurse, and they use any excuse to come for a moment of solace. Ms. Heintz is frequently invited to make presentations and answer questions on various aspects of health in classrooms.

Lydia Daniels has been a constant stalwart. She was serving as a counselor on a limited basis when I arrived, and when the Title I program was instituted, we chose to involve her on a full-time basis. In her staff development session, she reviewed her procedure for qualifying children for placement in the educable mentally retarded (EMR) program, the educationally handicapped (EH) program, and the gifted program. Lists of characteristics to look for and information to be included on the referral forms filled out by teachers were outlined.

From throughout the school referrals were submitted. Evaluations resulted in the identification of over twenty gifted students. A specified amount of state funds is allocated so that these students may receive a minimum of 200 minutes of enrichment instruction each week. Mayme Sweeney provided this and more.

No child is given a test, and no special placement is made without the consent of a parent or guardian. Ways of working with students with certain identifiable problems and a special EMRT program were explained. There was a fund designated for students who had spent time in an EMR class, had scored out, and were now making the transition to regular classrooms. About eleven children in the EMR classrooms were definitely slow learners who had scored just over the recently lowered 72 I.Q. border and were returned to regular classrooms. Each school was allowed to use the fund to plan a special program to help these students to adapt to regular classroom and school life. Special teachers taught reading one hour each day to each of these children.

It takes a great deal of cooperative and consistent effort to identify and qualify a student for EH placement. There is no EH class at Grape Street, so when all the work-up is completed, the candidate's name is generally placed on a waiting list. One day when a call came through for a boy who had been excessively disturbed to be placed, he had become adjusted to the point where he, his mother, and his teacher wanted him to remain in a regular class. He did so with considerable success.

There were times when teachers were quite openly disgruntled. I remember Dennis Hepler, a young White teacher who taught the upper EMR class, remarking to me, "You know, Ms. Haynes, you tell us when we've done things well. And you also let us know if we aren't cutting it. I'm quite satisfied with the way you let me know about my work, but, there are a lot of teachers here who don't think you praise them enough. They say you don't appreciate what they're doing. They just seem to be hungry for recognition."

How right he was. One day after most of the classrooms were opening up quite well, Joan Dunning, who was now teaching a fourth, fifth, and sixth-grade cluster, greeted me with, "Ms. Haynes, if you don't come in to visit room 14 soon, I'll have to introduce you to my children." I caught my breath. The last time I had been in her room, I had been accompanied by a visitor from London. We were awed at the peace and tranquility with which her students involved themselves in their abundantly enriched orderly, and well-organized classroom. Ms. Dunning had spent the previous summer in South America, and we contended that she must have brought some of everything she saw back with her, for she had created an environment second to being there for her class. The items were not just for show--the children used and interacted with them. At the close of the school year when she packed to leave, she reported that not one item was missing.

During this particular visit, the London educator and I moved around the room slowly, observing the students' performances. As we turned to leave, Vincent Lemos emerged from the United Nations area and walked over to our guest.

"Here's a flag of your country for a souvenir," he said, as he offered a 5x7-inch replicated flag of the United Kingdom to her. "I made it for you while you visited in our room. I hope you like it, and we hope you like our school."

Lavatryce Rice had come to Grape Street with some experience in an open classroom setting, and she fitted into our milieu with ease. Her first and second-grade classroom is bright and cheerful and contains a variety of meaningful offerings. For a period whenever I opened her door, some children would exclaim, "There she is...There she is. Ask her...ask her. Ask her when we're going to get a trip."

Ms. Rice's eyes would sparkle as she explained, "They've asked me so much about a trip that I suggested that they ask you when you come to visit."

"Why don't you plan a walking trip until a bus trip can be arranged?" I suggested. "There are many interesting places in our neighborhood. Ms. Sweeney has a list of places some of the other classes have enjoyed. Check with her."

"I'll do just that," she replied.

"In the meantime, we'll try to get you a bus trip as soon as possible," I promised.

Some time later Ms. Rice came to the office to report that she had five children whose readiness for reading seemed delayed. In discussing her concern with other primary teachers, she had learned that Annie Hill had three such students and she wanted to know if I would approve of her using the Initial Teaching Alphabet with them. She had her plans with her.

I perused them quickly and reminded her that, "We have agreed that teachers may use any acceptable approach they feel will be beneficial to their students. So if you believe this approach to be the best one for these children, go right ahead."

She was pleased. Thus, a small group of students at Grape Street are learning to read with the I.T.A. approach.

When I received a letter from the principal of Miguelito Elementary School in Lompoc, California, a city about one hundred miles north of Watts, inviting a class from Grape Street to come and spend three days and two nights attending its school and staying in their students' homes, room 14 was chosen. Immediately Ms. Dunning and Dorothy Wagner, the Lompoc teacher, began communicating, and the students in both schools began getting acquainted through pen-pal letters. It was an enriching interracial and intercultural relationship. Mayme Sweeney and her enrichment class also benefited from the trip and the associations.

After one noon recess period, Josephine Miles came bounding into and through the office. Every part of her body was in movement as she demanded, "Where's Robert? Where's my boy? I heard a primary teacher report that my boy hit her with a bottle. Did she see it?"

"No, she didn't see Robert hit her," I answered. "She isn't sure he was the one that threw whatever was thrown. And whatever hit her made such a small scratch that it would take a magnifying glass to see it. We think the sound frightened her more than anything else. Here's Robert. You may take him back to the room with you."

"Thank you, Ms. Haynes," she sighed. "I'm glad it worked out this way because I sure was going to be angry with anyone accusing one of my boys of anything, if she didn't know what she was talking about." And she meant just that. Ms. Miles has a demonstrative concern for her students. They reciprocate.

It has taken long and arduous effort to eradicate the notion that the principal's office is synonomous with swats.To help change this idea, Yvonne Almeida and Susan Friedhof bring their pre-kindergarten children in to become acquainted with the personnel in all the administrative offices. We are all introduced as friends. The kindergarteners in Jocelyne Lew's room cut out their body figures from brown construction paper. Each arranged the appropriate colors and length of yarn for his or her hair style and cut clothing from yardage remnants to dress themselves. Each child wrote and posted his or her name on the figure. These are displayed in a row along my north wall. Whenever one of these children come or bring their parents or friends to my office, a finger points and the announcement is made, "There's me." All teachers are encouraged to send children to the office to share projects or good completed work. Each time a child or a group presents an achievement, I write a personal commendation that may be shared in class or at home. More and more the office is being recognized as a place where concerns may be aired and resolved amicably. It is also becoming a place where achievement is recognized.

When I entered Shirley Helton's second, third, and fourth-grade cluster class with a visitor from India who was dressed in her native attire, several of the children stopped their activities and gravitated over to inspect her.

"Is that a ruby on your forehead?" asked Patricia Moffett.

"Why are you wearing that jewel on your head?" inquired Monica Sweeney.

"Doesn't that hurt you? Is a pin holding that stone up there? It must hurt. I stuck my finger with a pin and it bled," interjected Rodney Jackson.

"That long dress--do you wear it every day?" queried Tiffany Wells.

The questions flowed as interest mounted. The visitor explained, "I wear this because it is the costume of my country. We call the round dot on my forehead a kumdum. It is worn as a mark of beauty. My dress is called a sari. Wealthy women wear saris made of silk with borders of gold thread. A sari is a straight piece of cloth draped over and around the body. Women in Northern India wear full trousers with a long blouse and a veil. Indian women usually wear earrings and bracelets, as I am doing."

"My mother wears earrings and sometimes she wears a bracelet. But she doesn't wear that kumdum," remarked Monica.

"I guess not, because she doesn't live in India," explained Rodney.

"Where is your country?" Oscar Real inquired.

Before she could respond, Douglas Adams opened the cupboard and pulled out a map. "Here's a map. Let's find where she lives on here," he proposed.

"Man, we can't find where she lives on that United States map. She's no Indian-and cowboy-Indian. We need a globe to find her country," Rodney clarified.

Oscar went for the globe.

"Let's locate where we live first," I suggested.

Quickly Rodney pointed to Los Angeles on the West Coast of the United States.

"Now, where's your India?" he inquired.

The visitor pointed to her country on the globe.

"Wow, man, look at that! She lives on the other side of the world."

Douglas faced our visitor, released a heavy satisfying but questioning sigh, and asked, "Do you mean to tell me that you came all the way from the other side of the world just to see us?"

At the 1972-1973 midyear staff development session led by the administrators, a self-evaluation survey had been developed. In the past, almost any type of personal survey induced immediate negative reactions. Teachers were suspicious that anything they wrote down would be held over their heads or used in a retaliatory manner against them in some way.

The Grape Street faculty had come a long way. Teachers no longer hesitated to contribute orally, and interchanges were free, alive, and meaningful; acquiescing was negligible. I knew it would be invaluable to all concerned if the teachers really felt free enough to put their honest evaluations in writing, but I wasn't quite sure they were ready for this. Tom Stevens and I discussed the possibility at length, and we concluded that if we wished teachers to use the self-fulfilling prophecy we were advocating with their students, then we should demonstrate the same faith in our dealings with them. The evaluative survey designed was administered.

When I distributed the five-page stapled legal sheets to the teachers, there were gasps as I instructed, "Fill in each area as honestly as you can. The evaluations will be used to chart our direction for future programming

"My goodness, this is like college work," remarked Elna Cook.

"How do you expect us to complete this in a little more than an hour's time?" asked Josephine Miles.

"Do as much as you can in the time you have allotted. If it becomes necessary, we can complete it later. But whatever you do, give it thought, and respond in the way you feel our program is affecting you and your students."

They did. At 3:30 p.m., many were still writing. Only a few were succinct and gave one word or short answers. Ninety percent of the group wrote and wrote and wrote. Near the close of the sessions, I overheard one teacher say, "I wonder if all this effort is going to do any good. No one is going to read all of this detail that we're writing down. I do believe this is a waste of our time."

The next day, in different ways, each teacher learned that his or her comments had been read. Mr. Stevens and I were able to clarify several misconceptions immediately and make some valid and necessary adjustments. Throughout comments indicated that teachers dislike the Miller-Unruh reading specialists teaching small groups within their classrooms. The reading specialists themselves were opposed to moving from place to place, so arrangements were made for Mamie Hamilton to develop her own reading lab in room 4, while Virginia Snyder developed half of room 37 and Alma Lurry developed the other half.

"We should be getting college credits for all this professional reading, study, and work that we're doing," commented Harriet Nunley at a staff development session in late February.

"Do you think there's any possibility that we could get a master's program at our school? queried Gloria Pellebon.

"That was one of the suggestions I made on that evaluation survey," added Marilyn Arrington.

"Well, you know I like to take the attitude that nothing is impossible," I responded. "If enough of you are interested, why don't you put it in writing to me?"

The very next day I received a petition with thirty-six signatures requesting that I contact Pepperdine University and endeavor to secure a master's degree program for Grape Street School. I did willingly.

Progress was slow. Early in April, when my new Area B Superintendent, John Leon, came to visit, we discussed this concern; he gave his support. I called Dr. Arthur Adams in the Education Department of Pepperdine University, and wheels began to turn. It was impossible to forget efforts to negotiate for this program. Every day one teacher or another would inquire, "Are we getting the master's program?"

School closed in June 1973 with me confidently predicting, "I feel sure we will have a master's program here this fall." I met with Dr. Adams and several other principals a week later at which time he presented a packaged program. It seemed that all signs were "Go." I learned that the program was being offered to all schools throughout the city. This was good, but Grape could only begin in the fall if two other schools were ready to initiate a program at the same time. Early the next week, I received a call informing me that 75th Street Elementary and Washington High Schools had agreed to participate. I immediately wrote to each teacher who had indicated an intention to enroll.

They responded quickly. Everyone still in town confirmed her or his commitment. The enthusiasm for this program was so great that I received enough requests from former teachers, friends of teachers,, and parents who wanted to enroll to overflow to another class. Grape's own school staff provided our quota.

In the fall of the 1973-1974 school year, thirty teachers enrolled in the Master of Arts for Urban School Teacher, the MUST Program, at Grape Street with Mayme Sweeney and me as school leaders. Excerpts from the Pepperdine University proposal which affected us stated:

This master's degree program will focus on and be primarily located on public school sites for school staffs committed to a school-wide innovative program.

The basic program is designed to provide a core of 15 units, including social, psychological, and philosophical foundations of education, educational research and curriculum, and teaching/learning methods. The basic program will be scheduled for three weekends each trimester (nine per year). These weekends will be conducted by Pepperdine staff and resource consultants.

The second part of the program will be designed mutually by the university and the local school to provide the skills and knowledge to enable school staffs to research and plan the implementation and evaluation of the school-side educational program. (Grape's program emphasis was the open classroom.) This part of the program will be scheduled on a weekly basis under the leadership of selected and trained school members (principal and a staff member) with the guidance and monitoring provided by Pepperdine staff. The program will be divided into three trimesters emphasizing 1) educational planning, 2) implementing educational changes, and 3) evaluation and assessment of educational programs.

The third part of the program will draw from the experience of the Pepperdine current full-time and part-time staff and outstanding authorities and experienced school personnel in specialized fields. This personnel will be utilized in the leadership training, for each of the core courses and for supervising, coordinating and monitoring the individual and group research.

Concurrently throughout the year one afternoon a week will be devoted to the application of field work and action research. These meetings will be jointly planned and conducted by the local school leadership and the Pepperdine staff utilizing specialists. The cost of this program is $82 a unit (with the teacher deduction $61.50 a unit) totally $1,845.

This was an unusual and an ambitious endeavor. The meetings for the applied program were held in the school library each Monday and Thursday afternoon for two hours. At the first session Grape Street teachers made a commitment to give up holidays and weekends to work, study, and learn ways to improve students' achievement. Dr. C.K. Currey, the instructor of Education 689, "Educational Research," came to meet with us during the third session to prepare the group for the first weekend session. He outlined his expectations for the course. The next morning teachers came alone, in pairs, and in groups of threes to see me. Their concerns were similar.

"Ms. Haynes, I don't think I'm going to make it in this master's program."

"We've discussed it, and we want to get out of this program."

"I just don't see how I can do all this work for you and do all of those assignments Dr. Currey says he's going to give us."

"Some of us haven't read a professional book or taken a college course during the eight or ten years we've been teaching here."

"And just think. We've got two more instructors we haven't even seen yet. I just got my bachelor's a year ago. I can't keep going under this heavy pressure."

"My husband says this is just too much for me to undertake right now."

A few shed tears, nearly half the group was distraught. I tried to allay their anxieties to some extent by asking them to defer any drastic retractions until after the first weekend. I conveyed their concerns to Dr. Currey. He did not rescind any of his outlined assignments, but he did assure them of his availability for assistance throughout this endeavor to learn to apply research methods to the solution of educational problems. On Friday evening it became obvious that some of the tensions were being relaxed. We met at the Pepperdine Library on Saturday. The librarian explained the use of the facility. Dr. Currey assigned tasks involving the use of library resources. Teachers began wandering through the stacks, pulling publications from shelves, and recording their findings. Lines formed seeking assistance from Dr. Currey as he reclined in one of the leather chairs ready, willing, and able to give guidance. Others came to the opposite side of the room to get some direction from me.

I only regret that this scene wasn't photographed. Teachers were at tables, on rugs, in chairs, moving to and from the shelves, working alone, in pairs, calling out to one another, and doing whatever was necessary to complete the research assignments. Each was involved. Sighs and signs of satisfaction became evident. The scene was, in essence, and adult replica of some of the well organized classrooms at Grape. The thirty participants were well on their way to earning the five units that emphasized action research methodology.

The other core courses were "Foundations of Urban Education" (social, psychological, historical and philosophical), and "Curriculum and Teaching/Learning Methods," 5 units. The applied program included: "Educational Planning Program," "Implementing Educational Innovation" and "Educational Evaluation and Accountability."

Each participant's field work resulted in a thesis that was submitted at the close of the third trimester.

On August 2, 1974, twenty-nine of the thirty teachers who had enrolled at Grape donned caps and gowns and marched at the Pepperdine University exercises with over five hundred other graduates to receive their master of arts degree in urban school teaching. They witnessed the conferring of an Honorary Doctor of Law Degree to Mayor Thomas Bradley, who delivered remarks for the commencement. It was a day of pride and accomplishment for each of the participants. I stood, shook hands, and congratulated each one as did Dr. Currey, who had attended as a final tribute to Grape's graduates. Then he put his feelings into words.

"You know, they are really a good group. I surely did enjoy working with them. And you know what? I'd like to go on record as stating that these teachers will never be the same."

I smiled in agreement and silently thought to myself, "How right you are! They never will be the same and neither will the children they teach nor the parents who have become our partners nor the immediate community who continue to take a growing pride in Grape Street School. Oh my! How we have grown and what changes we have made for the better! We now are really making a difference in the lives of children. It is true.... The news on Grape Street is good."

13

THE BICENTENNIAL TOUR

Early in 1976 Good News On Grape Street: The Transformation of a Ghetto School rolled off the Citation Press in New York, N.Y. Books were shipped and arrived in time to be autographed and sold at the Hollywood Palladium on Sunset Boulevard in Los Angeles, California on Friday evening, March 26, 1976.

It was a bold and daring risk on the part of the staff, parents and friends of that inner city school who engaged that spacious entertainment hall to hold an activity. Each night was one of agony for me as I wondered "Who will come?" Our avenues of publicity were limited. But a dedicated, committed and determined group moved ahead brazenly. As if by the providence of God on Monday, March 22, 1976, as I entered a meeting room on "The Hill" (Board of Education) a colleague complimented, "Congratulations! That was some review you got this morning, and of all the book critics, yours was written by the "Chief" himself." What a blessing! I was so glad that she had a copy of the paper with her because before I could finish reading the review myself radio stations had caught up with me for telephone reviews. Those and two television appearances served to give the very needed publicity for the tribute.

Revivifying a Ghetto School

Los Angeles Times
THE BOOK REPORT

Mon. Mar. 22, 1976

Revivifying a Ghetto School

BY ROBERT KIRSCH

Times Book Critic

Paperchase:

"Good News on Grape Street: The Transformation of a Ghetto School" (Citation Press: $4.95) by Carrie Ayers Haynes is a moving story about the metamorphosis of Grape Street School in Watts from an institution under siege, target of vandals and thieves, with a dispirited student body and lackluster teachers just hanging in, to a model school of which students, teachers and the community are proud, one in which some daring programs in new educational techniques have been pioneered.

Ms. Haynes, principal of Grape Street School, blends professional competence with humane understanding, leadership with a willingness to listen, common sense with inspiration. The added bonus in this spirited, vivid and candid account is that it may help to transform education in general. It cannot be read condescendingly or sentimentally.

There are no panaceas offered here. The ideas in innovative learning, open-classrooms, cross-age groupings, special programs, staff in-service training were tested and some were rejected. But in themselves they offered no miracles. "One can't 'make' human beings implement any program. The basic need at Grape Street School at that time was to develop a positive attitude toward students and a desire in more teachers to want to facilitate learning."

112

Easier Said Than Done

This was easier said than done. Ms. Haynes had been in the Los Angeles school system for nearly 18 years when she was assigned to her first principalship at Grape Street. Before that, she taught at Buffalo, N.Y. Her experience covered every elementary grade, involved demonstration teaching and teacher-training. In the fall of 1968 she passed a competitive examination to become No. 1 on the eligibility list.

Grape Street School was considered no prize for a beginning principal. The buildings were continually broken into, equipment stolen, classrooms wrecked. The teachers --39 Blacks and five Whites --mostly resisted anything that would shake the status quo. Tenure made them resentful of innovation.

"There were times when teachers were quite openly disgruntled. I remember Dennis Hepler, a young White teacher who taught the upper EMR (educable mentally retarded) class, remarking to me. 'You know, Ms. Haynes, you tell us when we've done things well. And you let us know if we aren't cutting it...But, there are a lot of teachers here who don't think you praise them enough. They say you don't appreciate what they're doing.' "Ms. Haynes notes, "How right he was." The feedback had its effect.

Walking Principal

Ms. Haynes did not tiptoe around; the teachers and the students called her "the walking principal," at first resentfully. It became a compliment. And her criticism of the teachers was matched by a criticism of the media."..I was conditioned to listening to reports of vandalism at Grape Street. The assessed monetary amounts of the damage were usually ballooned out of proportion by at least one additional digit."

Ms. Haynes worked with teachers, encouraged the nucleus of dedicated and involved teachers, went after the negligent and slovenly, engaged parents and the community, encouraged the special programs funded by the federal government, began to encourage a warmer learning environment, smaller groups, more contact with teachers, student self-evaluation and increased responsibility. Grape Street became a school where students wanted to be and where teachers enjoyed the challenge of teaching. And, indeed, of learning, for on Aug. 2, 1974, 29 Grape Street teachers won their master of arts degrees in urban school teaching through an in-service program organized with Pepperdine University.

Grape Street is no educational utopia but a place where accomplishment is made an adventure and recognized where the community, the students, the teachers are part of the same enterprise. That is what education is all about for Ms. Haynes. "We now are really making a difference in the lives of children. It is true...We will never be the same."

And so on Friday evening, March 26, 1976 the marque over the Hollywood Palladium blazoned:

A TRIBUTE TO AN AUTHOR

CARRIE AYERS HAYNES

Led by our own city's Mayor Tom Bradley, State Senator Diane Watson, Assemblywoman Teresa Hughes, Assemblywoman Maxine Waters, Councilman David Cunningham, friends and supporters, to include each of those persons who had previously informed me that they could not be there, filed in to fill the heart of this huge entertainment hall to capacity. This was the highlight of the 1975-76 school year effort by parents and teachers in planning for their children and/or students an 8-day and 7 night Bicentennial Tour to our nation's capitol, Washington, D.C. The response in paid attendance, books sold and gifts donated netted our previously, struggling effort over twenty thousand dollars. Our Bicentennial Tour was assured.

Students were selected based on sponsorship of parents or teachers. Early in the morning of June 4, 1976, 44 students and 10 adults boarded an American Airlines DC-10. One student did not arrive. The airline assured us that they would send him on the next plane if he did not get there before the take-off. As our entourage marched on board and proceeded to be seated, one of the hostesses remarked, "Oh, my God! I should have stayed in bed this morning." By the time we were airborne securely and on our way she came back to say to me.

"I was sure in for a surprise this morning. This is the most well behaved large group of youngsters I've had come on the plane at any time." I thanked her as I swelled out my chest. The students had helped to plan their activities and behavior for this tour. For most of them this was the first time on a plane. Preparation by their teachers and parents had been thorough. Each had a three ring folder with a list of what to look for and questions to ask. They conversed with each other, and with the adults to which each of four was assigned. Several asked to speak with the pilot or co-pilot. The pilot came out for a period. He spoke with the group and with individuals. Throughout the flight he gave out the kind of information the students were weeking. What made the plan fly? How high up were we? How many hours did he fly? Over what state, point of interest were we flying? At what rate of speed? Where did he get his training? Weather conditions? Emergency procedures? Comparison - Contrasts and on and on. Each of the work books contained a desk map so that each student could trace the trip across country in red and the return trip in blue.

Our airplane arrived with all travelers aboard in tact in the early afternoon at Dulles Airport. Then came the experience of riding the hydrobus into the airport. We filed through the Dulles Airport, received the message that our late arrival was on board the next plane and was on the way to join us. The Continental Trailways Bus was waiting. Josephine Miles who had a friend to meet her agreed to wait for Wendell Shirley. We boarded the comfortable vehicle and were driven to the Girl Scouts Camp in Bethesda, Maryland. Our room and board cost $10 a day per person. Our home for the week was one large room with double bunks all over. Title IX was in full effect because there were no provisions for separation of boys and girls. We set up schedules for travel, free time, showers, meals and sleep. At midnight when all the lights had been turned off from a master control, our late traveler arrived. We had just coaxed all of the group to go to sleep when this disruption developed into one verbal tremor after another, most interspersed with waves of laughter. A flashlight provide enough light until we were all tucked in again.

Each morning the Continental Trailways Bus arrived to pick us up for the days' journey. During the following days, we visited Philadelphia, PA; Jamestown, VA; The White House, The Capitol Building, a session of the Assembly; Ambassadors Row; Washington, D.C. the Frederick Douglas Home; the Mary McLeod Bethune Statue; George Washington's Home in Vermont; Arlington Cemetery; the Smithsonian Institute and rode a boat down the Potomac River.

Everyone of the 45 students, 4 parents, 4 teachers, 1 nurse and I became involved in an experience that will be imprinted indelibly upon us for our lifetimes. Some memorable highlights were being met by the then Congresswoman Yvonne Braithwaite Burke and escorted to ring seats around the Assembly and watching the then Congresswoman Barbara Jordan speak in her own eloquent inimitable style.

On the following day Congressman Augustus Hawkins met with our total group in a scheduled room in the Rayburn Building. He talked with us and answered the 'insightful and intelligent questions posed' by the students. That summer when the Democratic Convention was in session my telephone began ringing repeatedly when students who had returned from the Washington, D.C. trip saw Congresswoman Barbara Jordan on television delivering the opening keynote address. These students of ours were able to relate to their own people in power as their friends or at least as people they knew personally.

When the test scores were released at the end of this school year of 1975-76 almost all of the students were on grade level. Before the school year ended I, as other principals throughout the LAUSD, had been informed that our staffs must be racially balanced with a 60/40 ratio. This directive was agonizing for me. It meant that at least eleven of my well staff-developed, competent, highly dedicated and committed Black teachers would have to be transferred and replaced by White teachers. I cried inside and went about the business of trying to help get them placement where those who wished might be helped to aspire for promotions. Word was passed around throughout the staff that, "Mrs Haynes is getting rid of her best Black teachers replacing them with White teachers." Everywhere there was an assembly of principals I went to try to effect an equitable trade-off in the transfer of teachers. It didn't work. The fall of 1976-77 was an exercise in starting all over again. The system works against attaining or maintaining success for students in inner city schools. At Grape Street Elementary School in the heart of Watts, we had worked against all odds and proven that by involving staff, students, parents and the total community in learning how to create a positive climate in which each person is respected as an individual with potential and dignity, our children and the adults were motivated to learn how to learn. As soon as we reached a respectable degree of success, our staff was dismantled and the approach which we used has not been replicated in any known public school since that time, to my knowledge.

This was the year that schools in all of the other nine areas were being configured to provide parents an opportunity to select a school with special offerings away from their neighborhood to send their children. Dr. John Lingel, an Assistant Superintendent heading this task force drove out to my school one morning and informed me, "Carrie, you know members of our task force have been travelling all over the country trying to find and study an open classroom school. While touring the St. Paul's Open School in Minneapolis, Minnesota the staff there told us the best open classroom school in our country is in your own city school system. Go back to your own inner city Grape Street School." That's where they had come and studied how to administer and implement their open classroom school. He asked if I would write a configuration so that they might consider listing Grape as a School of Choice.

During this time the 100 member Community Advisory Committee on School Integration (CACSI) on which I was the principal representative from Area 2 was meeting evenings on a regular basis. Many of these meetings lasted until early the next morning. I remember the night that Grape Street School was being proposed and discussed as a potential Magnet School. At this propitious time Dr. Julian Nava, then president of Los Angeles Board of Education came to the podium accompanied by Dr. William Johnston, Los Angeles City School Superintendent. Dr. Nava spoke to the group. It was at two-ten that next morning that I struggled to find the freeway, drove through a pea soup fog, drove off the wrong ramp and almost became frantic as I concentrated on finding my way home. From that time on I heard no further consideration being given by that group to making Grape Street a Magnet School, a school where White parents would have been given a choice of sending their children into an inner city school. The next month the CACSI group was dismantled. I wrote the configuration for the Schools of Choice task force. But to this day to my knowledge there has been no attempt to replicate the affective approach used in the Grape Street experience. Members of the task force who came to visit the school told me that our philosophical open classroom was an enigma to them. They could not understand the two basic prevalent principles which were:

1. Organizing a school to match students' learning style to the teacher's personalities, and

2. Supporting teachers in using any positive teaching approaches and techniques with which they are comfortable as long as each student knows and understands what he/she is learning and why.

It can work. It did work at Grape Street Elementary School, a public school located in the inner city.

14

THE GRAPE STREET MODEL REVIVED

On June 30, 1977 I left the cab and walked through the masses of humanity in the John F. Kennedy Airport in New York. I had just completed my last "Success in the Inner-City School" Workshop in Rochester, N.Y. Beginning in the fall of 1971 I had been a member of the Educational Consulting Associates, Inglewood, Colorado team traveling on scheduled tours to ten cities throughout our country each year making presentations. It was getting dark and I was on my way home for the first day at my new position as Administrative Coordinator, Integration Office in Administrative Area B. Dr. Sidney Brickman, Area B Superintendent, had said to me, "Carrie, this is not going to be easy for you. It's going to be like becoming an assistant principal again. And we all know how you thrive on being in control and totally autonomous." These words were going through my mind as I stood second in line waiting to board the American Airlines flight when all the lights in New York blacked out. We sat through the night on the lighted plane with all of the world around us in darkness. As the dawn broke the plane lifted and brought me home.

Upon landing I called the Area B Office to say I needed to go by my home and freshen up before coming in an hour late. I walked into applause, laughter and teasing, "Carrie, some people come up with some far-fetched excuses for being late." That I survived. The administrative responsibilities of the office were divided four ways. I was accorded all of the privileges of each of the other three. The Area Superintendent Sidney Thompson monitored the secondary schools. The elementary schools were divided between Fred Martel and me. I was given the privilege of choosing the schools in which I would evaluate the principals. It was amusing when teachers from some of the schools would call to tell me that her principal wanted them to help get the school together because Carrie Haynes would be visiting to observe what was going on in the classrooms. My chief responsibility was that of Integration in a totally racially isolated area. I had a good staff because I brought in teachers who were or had been successful ones at Grape Street, namely Josephine Miles, Kristine Johnson, Eloise Blanton and later Andrea Roberts. Clayton Moore was assigned. We set our goals and made plans for holding staff development workshops.

On the first Monday in October 1977, I went for a physical and came home with a clean bill of health. That Friday, just as a routine, because I remembered a program Ida McKay had presented in one of our National Association of University Women's meetings, I self-tested my breasts and felt a very small lump in the left one. That Saturday I returned to my doctor. I went through a series of tests. One was scheduled for a Saturday on which I was to speak to a Delta Kappa Gamma Society, Intl. group. I appealed to my doctor. I told him that I had made this commitment a year ago and felt I needed to be there. His simple and direct instructions to me were "Cancel it." I did. The following Thursday I left work, my husband drove me to the hospital and the next morning I had a mastectomy. During my days of recuperation I held two staff meetings in my hospital bedroom and then one each week at home before I returned to work after a month's absence. Two months later I chose to take chemotherapy treatments. I remember going on the third Wednesday of each month, being released and arriving on time to assume my responsibilities as the president of the Council of Black Administrators.

It was at this point that my adopted "little sister" Lorene Davis appointed herself to drive me and assist me in my travelling and perform various other duties related to my public service activities. She has been so delightfully dutiful that I have grown to expect it from her with much gratitude.

I had come in the fall of 1977 to serve as Administrative Consultant in the Integration Office of Administrative Area B. This was the only one of ten areas in the LAUSD that was totally 'racially isolated.' We received the minimum of monies with which to operate. Dr. Raymond Terrell, Dean of School of Education, California State - Los Angeles wrote creative proposals which provided some very badly needed funding. For three years my staff and I provided training services for administrators, teachers and parents in the area. Classes and groups of students were paired with those of other ethnicities for Student-to-Student Interaction activities. Because my new area superintendent began to attempt to thwart the training activities my staff and I were administering with much obvious success, I retired in June, 1980.

In May, 1981 Mrs. Nettie Manning, then National President of the National Association of University Women delegated me to accept an invitation to attend the National Convention Planners courtesy trip to Miami, Florida. It was there that I was introduced to the National Assault on Illiteracy Program. I learned that a group of Black fledging publishers associated with Black Media, Inc. in New York, N.Y. had come to the realization that one of the reasons that Black people were not buying their papers was because nearly half of the Black population (47%) could not read well enough to become gainfully employed and were therefore classified as "functionlly illiterate."

This report was made at the National Convention of the National Association of University Women held in Chicago, Illinois, August, 1982 when I served as the national Convention Chairman. A resolution was passed by the Convention to adopt the National Assault On Illiteracy Program. This phenomenal concept conceived by Dr. Benjamin Wright, serving as National Senior Volunteer of AOIP, was the beginning of a networking of 90 Black led national organizations committed to work to- . gether toward the common cause of eradicating the root causes of the abounding illiteracy so prevalent among our Black populations.

Immediately after my return from the Convention Planners Meeting in Miami, Florida, I was asked to serve as National Chairperson of the Curriculum Planning and Evaluation Committee of AOIP. I accepted. My responsibility became that of developing instructional materials into a newspaper format to be used in all AOIP tutorial programs. Dr. Edgar Easley, now deceased, along with Deborah Wright Igiehon for a short period, and I developed the initial narrative format of The Family and Community Reading Newspaper, simply known as The ADVANCER. The art work is done by Brandon Brunswick, a noted syndicated cartoonist and other persons from Black Resources, Inc. New York, N.Y. where Ms. Jeanne Jason is the executive editor of The National BLACK MONITOR. Dr. Betty Mansfield is the project coordinator of the ADVANCER and the Who Am I Guide To Learning, out of that New York office.

The ADVANCER places a heavy emphasis upon integrating the affective approach with that of the cognitive domain. Each article is written in such a manner so that a person with limited reading skills may relate to each in a very personal way. The approach used in The ADVANCER is based on the success experienced with its use at the Grape Street Elementary School in inner city Los Angeles, California. After a year of publishing and circulating The ADVANCER, the AOIP Executive Board adopted it as its official ego-strengthing tool.

In 1983 I was asked to take the position of chairperson of the National Interorganizational Liaison Committee. With enthusiasm and commitment I travelled over the country, with my expenses being paid by the Black Media, Inc. publishers, making presentations, leading workshops and organizing AOIP State Divisions and Local Units. As I travelled I learned that persons interested in tutoring found The ADVANCER an invaluable teaching tool but too difficult and frustrating for the total non-reader. So I began writing the "Who Am I?" Guide to Learning, which uses the Language-Experience Approach to teach reading, with a focus on SELF and a design to build self-esteem. Both of these teaching tools are described at the end of this chapter.

All during this time Dr. Calvin W. Rolark, chairman of the BMI Cooperative was providing guidance, finances and support as he continuously lead the joining interorganizational groups to believe and take action by having us repeat after him "Nobody can save us from us, but us.

If it is to be. It is up to me." On March 5, 1984 the National Assault on Illiteracy Program/United States Department of Education held its first historic workshop in Washington, D.C.

"Never in our fondest dreams did we think this ever would have materialized. But, the workshop did materialize and some wonderful and unexpected things have begun to happen."

These were the words of Dr. Gary Jones, Undersecretary of Education, on March 5, 1984. The observation was made at the conclusion of an unprecedented, at first resisted and extremely hard won, two-day exploration at the United States Department of Education (USEd). The participants were 85 of the top-level policy makers and professionals within US-Ed and an equal number of the distinguished national Black-led organizational leaders within the Assault On Illiteracy Program (AOIP).

The reasons for this resistance to the Black/White educational exploration might be better understood if we bring to mind two facts. These are:

1. There are a good many persons in seemingly well-entrenched high positions of authority for decision making who are never eager to have their long-held notions challenged in open discussion or debate...and, this resistance is particularly so when the outcome might be the need to share that decision making responsibility with others. And

2. Basic educational policies--with few exceptions--were never made with the unique support, of affective, needs of our nation's Black population in mind. Little or no consideration ever has been given to the most serious deterrent to learning among many Black Americans, i.e., an image of self and of community so negative and deep that many Black Americans still do not feel good enough about themselves and their environs to want to learn. This is an ego diminution among Black Americans brought on by deliberately-imposed policies and practices of the past--and which continue today in largely unredressed form.

Among the "wonderful and unexpected things" that began to happen as a result of that historic workshop were:

1. USEd's deeper awareness or recognition that learning truly is both an affective and cognitive process-that the severely damaged egos uniquely among so many within the Black population must be addressed as a prelude to teaching that is both effective and lasting.

2. A recognition by all parties that the image predicament is so comprehensive that a joint and continuing high-level AOIP/USEd Task Force on AOIP concerns needed to be--and was--established so that all AOIP uplifting programs could be supported fully. And

3. A deeper awareness by USEd and AOIP that an interorganizational, long term and overall community-building and/or "uplifting" focus within Black America to save the young and redeem the older would have to be considered as crucial. The success of any optimally-effective literacy enhancement efforts, which would remove this embarrassing and long-ago imposed burden from America as a whole, would depend greatly on large-scale environmental and/or support changes with Black America.

Illiteracy remediation is to every American's benefit and is every American's responsibility . In this process, there are certain unique roles that only Black Americans can play..but they require and deserve the help of all others. This manual is designed to provide new and much needed guidelines developed by a wide cross section of all of AOIP's leadership. By following this route, Black Americans can begin working far more earnestly and productively together in new community-building ways for the uplifting of our people...our communities..and our nation as a whole. In that way, "wonderful things and unexpected things" will continue to happen for us all.

UNITED STATES
DEPARTMENT OF EDUCATION

FOR RELEASE
Friday, June 22, 1984

Secretary T.H. Bell announced today that the Department of Education has established a continuing working relationship with the Assault On Illiteracy Program (AOIP) in a concerted effort to carry out the National Adult Literacy Initiative announced by President Reagan last September.

AOIP is a framework which allows national Black organizations to work together to encourage Black Americans to improve their literacy skills. They have united to focus their considerable strength and expertise on youth and adult literacy.

In a recent workshop, members of the AOIP, who represent national Black organizations, and senior Department officials met to discuss strategies for solving problems of illiteracy in the Black community. AOIP has called the workshop an historic example of cooperation between the Federal government and Black Americans.

The Secretary this week is sending to all 50 State governors letters emphasizing that one of the goals of AOIP is to work with literacy groups at the State and local levels and to organize State and local AOIP chapters.

In the letter, the Secretary said, "Attention must be given to the unique aspects of the problem of illiteracy among Black Americans for whom the rate of functional illiteracy has been estimated at approximately three times that among White Americans."

As the Department's Regional Offices coordinate plans for involving Federal employees in literacy programs, they will call upon the resources of AOIP. The Secretary also informed the governors that the Department's regional staff will be available, upon request, to assist the States in working with organizations on literacy efforts.

AOIP receives invitations to participate in meetings and conferences that address the National literacy efforts and meet with members of Congress about the level of funding for Black Americans in the Adult Education Act.

Secretary Bell said, "The Department will continue its cooperative efforts with AOIP as they begin their community building approach toward literacy promotion. Literacy affects too many of our citizens for one group to tackle it alone. These organizations represent a valuable source of volunteers for literacy."

Subsequently Regional AOIP/USDED Workshops were held 12/26/84 Washington, D.C.; 12/27/84 Atlanta, GA; 12/28/84 Chicago, IL; 12/29/84 Los Angeles, CA. During the spring I initiated, did the initial writing and contributed largely to the much needed *UPLIFTING——OUR PEOPLE——OUR COMMUNITIES and——OUR NATION——A Manual For Local AOIP Unit Formation.* A "Why and How To" Organizing and Programmatic Manual for Local Units Within the Assault On Illiteracy Program (AOIP).

In July, 1985 at a follow-up AOIP/USDED Workshop held at the Shoreham Hotel Washington, D.C. Ozell Sutton, National Chairperson presented me a gold braclet inscribed "Mother of AOIP - Carrie Haynes." It was the National Assault On Illiteracy Program's highest honor.

Early in May, 1982 over 160 representatives from 60 major Black-led national organizations were called together in Miami, Florida. They were brought to the realization that the unconscionably high rate of "functionally illiteracy" among Black youth at age 18--nearly 50% now--and the predicament facing us because of this are both a burden and a shame. It was there that they all agreed and made a commitment to become involved in an interorganizational approach to work together to eradicate the prevalent negative self-images and strive in a community building way to help each individual feel good enough about himself to want to learn those skills needed for him to survive in this society.

The Family and Community Newspaper, simply known as The AD—VANCER is an 8-page tabloid designed to use as a supplementary teaching tool in Chapter I type classrooms and as a teaching tool in all Assault On Illiteracy Program projects. It is being written by Black educators chiefly from the National Sorority of Phi Delta Kappa, Inc. Any person with limited skills in reading has been turned off from books already. Saying "Let's read to find out about the news," gives dignity. It is an adult-looking newspaper with its name symbolizing the focus. A sequential arrangement of blocks with each letter showing its own individuality serves as a foundation for building the sophisticated city whose skyline is the background. Each front page features a vocation to which a person with limited reading skills may relate and aspire. Cartoons and comic strips may be read for meaning before the narrative text is attempted. The Blackboard page features Black Role Models, heroes or African Fables, Folktales or Legends designed to help members of the Black family understand and appreciate their heritage. Geography, nutrition, "We Are Somebody" Corner, Crossword Puzzle, Science and Citizenship articles help the reader build self-pride and self-esteem. A Tutor's Guide is upside down on each page six. The uniqueness of this newspaper insert is that it is written so that each individual student may relate to the content in a very personal way.

The Who Am I Guide to Learning are lessons designed to be used by teachers or tutors in teaching total non-readers and those with limited reading skills. The lessons are presented in a developmental sequential pattern which moves from SELF, to FAMILY, to the NEIGHBORHOOD, to the LARGER COMMUNITY, and an exploration into the WORLD OF WORK. By beginning with each person's SELF, confidence is accrued as a foundation upon which to build. Reading is an individual matter and must be dealt with as such. The way each person feels about him/herself is basic to the inner motivation necessary for any student to want to learn to read. The seven steps included in each lesson in detail are: (1) Teacher Preparation, (2) Introductory Motivational Activities, (3) Directed Lesson, (4) Skill Lesson, (5) Closure, (6) Independent Activities, (7) Reinforcement. A compilation of 52 lessons and 26 phonetic analysis exercises plus information on How to Use The Advancer are available in the Why & How to Use AOIP's "Affective-Oriented" Material Manual.

National
Assault On Illiteracy Program

A nationwide community-building program of Community Motivators, Inc.
William Waters, President

410 Central Park West (PH—C) New York, NY 10025 (212) 967-4000

The Importance of Community-Building Role Models in Eradicating Illiteracy

Two Essential Learning Aspects: Learning has two aspects. One is what is known among educators as the "cognitive" (or tutorial) aspect. The other is known as the "affective" (i.e., ego-consideration or environmental) aspect. It is widely accepted that students who do not feel good about themselves or their environments (i.e., their communities), often have no will or desire to learn. Many excellent "cognitive" materials-and approaches-are readily available for easy *group* use...and these are used every day by almost all teachers. On the other hand, and for a variety of reasons, few teachers deal with the "affective" aspect of learning which, for them, often involves *individualized* evaluation and remediation planning. "Affective" learning is based primarily on strengthening and building a submerged ego and sense of hope. Learning then can proceed at a good pace.

Why "Affective" Aspects Are Omitted: Obviously, the "affective" aspect initially, at least, takes far more time and effort. Moreover, many teachers understandably (even if not correctly or rightly) feel that the matter of negative family and community-induced predicaments, which are far more prevalent among Black and other disadvantaged minorities, should not be their responsibility. Consequently, teachers tend to neglect this aspect of learning. Thus, more and more of our "disadvantaged" youth seldom are taught within the school setting in a manner that motivates them to want to learn.

The crux of the matter is that our Black children and others are suffering to an unconscionable degree in terms of literacy enhancement because of the awesome state of Black family life and the general condition of the Black community.

Black Community-Building Essential: This means that those of us who are concerned, able and willing must do the "affective" kinds of things we can most readily do for each of us and our organizations to become effective role models. Among the things we can do are the following:

1. *Focusing* our attention on enabling our community-*building* organizations to do a far better job of the uplifting things for which they were organized. Thus, one of AOIP's primary concerns is strengthening our organizations' present programs.

2. *Informing* all persons in and/or around our so-called "disadvantaged" communities about how lack of concern about-and support for-the housing conditions, the businesses, the churches, the schools and other entities therein, impacts far more in a negative way on literacy enhancement. This is done best initially by an interchange of ideas within a workshop setting wherein all types of issues should be explored continuously.

3. *Getting* commitments from all of our community-*building* organizational leaders to encourage their members and all others living in or near our largely Black communities-to strive for indigenous ownership and control of the homes, businesses, schools, churches, professional offices, media, etc. *And,*

4. *Assisting,* as best as possible, with the establishment of a working relationship between our schools and AOIP. By this means, the schools can see that they have many new and never-before-possible resources in the form of direct aid from our volunteers as well as access to AOIP's care-

fully prepared supplementary reading-motivational and comprehension-enhancement tools which include *The Advancer and The Who Am I Guide to Learning.*

Organizing Is Primary: Again, our illiteracy predicament is of crisis proportions due to long-term neglect of many of our "affective" needs. AOIP surely needs many to become tutors, who integrate the two learning aspects. However, joining AOIP and dealing with the "affective," or community-*building,* aspects of learning not only is the most urgent of all needs...but also it is an aspect for which the help of everyone is needed and everyone can participate. It also is one aspect from which our organizations and everyone benefit enormously. But, if we are to effectively complement the fine work that can be done by our schools, proper initial organization is the key to community-wide success!

Immediately following this occasion I joined Winnie Palmer, the newly elected Supreme Basileus of The National Sorority of Phi Delta Kappa, Inc. as co-chairperson of the National Professional Education. Together our committee composed of Ida Bell, Gwendolyn Deas, Linda Linton, Dr. Betty Mansfield and Emille Smith planned and implemented the first Tutorial Training Workshop held at the University of the District of Columbia in Washington, D.C. on Friday, September 20, 1985 for over 90 participants.

On the windy and rainy morning of Thursday, September 27, 1985 when our nation's Capitol was experiencing the side swiping of Gloria, the tornado, a select group of AOIP members gathered at the U.S. Department of Education to meet with the new U.S. Secretary of Education,

Dr. William J. Bennett and U.S. Under Secretary, Dr. Gary Bauer. Dr. Ozell Sutton, our National AOIP Chairperson made the following remarks:

Dr. Bennett, your new distinguished associates in the U.S. Department of Education, our long and respected friend---Gary Buaer---and other concerned persons in the Department, we come to you this morning as a group far more seriously damaged in terms of literacy than any other body of citizens in this nation of such great potential.

We represent well over 25% of America's entire so-called "illiterate" or "uneducated", population. Thus, we would have to come to you this morning *both disappointed* by what this Department and others have allowed to occur *and apprehensive* because we have seen little evidence of reasonable remediative concern about our people's awesome plight even today.

Our "functional illiteracy" rate according to your Department's own statistics, is three times as high among adult Black Americans as it is among adult White Americans. Statistics also show that adult Blacks of West Indian-type background have a literacy attainment level, on the average, which is slightly higher than that of the average for adult White Americans.

From this, we would have concluded that the illiteracy predicament we face has absolutely nothing to do with either inherent or intrinsic learning disabilities due to our being Black or of African descent.

Thus, we have had to conclude also that the "root causes" of this phenomenon must have been due to some extremely - powerful things- or a set of emotionally - devastating conditions - imposed on, and/or experienced by, Blacks of African descent here in America. Our Black educators and others have assessed the vast array of exogenous factors - i.e., those not relating solely to the classroom or cognitive aspect of learning - and concluded that the major culprit is a deliberately imposed negative image of self (and environs) so deep that many Black American do not feel good enough about themselves even to want to learn.

Our concerned educators went on to tell us that the phenomenon was of such proportions *in some cases* that so-called "integrated" educational environments, as they are constituted today, are not helpful to those desperately in need of a postive identity. Effective and long-term remediation, these educators pointed out, would rely to a great degree on the actions of Black Americans, *ourselves*. Our focus would have to be on becoming far more positive personal role models and re-building *our own* communities into secure and hope-filled environments wherein our young and others would be motived to become literate.

Accordingly, Dr . Bennett, we have come to you this morning neither for a "hand out" nor to put the entire blame on your Department or the educational system as a whole. Rather, we have come to you as a group of so deeply concerned Black Americans that we have clearly broken the widely perceived mold, or notion, that Blacks won't do for themselves. Within the Assault On Illiteracy Program (AOIP), which began to take shape just over 5½ years ago, we have done what no other group has done, we are told. When we came to the government for help, we did not ask for a single penny for salaries or wages in our urgently - needed uplifting" cause...and we were told by those in The White House, that they had never been presented with such a proposal. As a result, President Reagan not only invited us in but also praised our then-fledgling cause and promised us help. However, we were stopped almost dead cold by some in well established positions right here in this Department. Few persons, we have found -- welcome change even if it is necessary.

Mr. Secretary, it was only at the near close of the past administration that rays of hope for reasonable cooperation became evident. And, so we come to you today to ask for your cooperation...not as an extension of the past, but instead based on the convictions of a thinker and doer who -- in the relatively short time he has been at the helm -- has dared to disconnect himself from the traditional mold of doing...and make his own decisions based on a welcome kind of pragmatic decision-making not possible by bureaucratic idol worshipers. Yesterday's events were typical of what we have seen.

Thus, Mr. Secretary, we come to you with far more hope than one might have imagined. We bring a serious challenge to you and your Department based on some greatly unmet needs that cannot be remediated by you alone by any means.

We have come also to bring you unusual support...not only from us in a massive and unprecendented way..but also to assist you and your department in becoming unshackled from the enormous burdens induced by others, but which have been laid at the doorsteps of education alone. Every department in government needs to be involved in remediating the "affective" things which have impacted so negatively on the learning process. We ask for nothing to put into our pockets..and we ask for no radical change even if justified because of resistance we know will come. Instead, we ask only for some initial facilitating assistance that we alone should not have to bear. Our request has been shared with you."

A question and answer period followed. Our group is committed to follow through. It has been reported by The National Commission On Excellence in Education that we are A Nation At Risk. In our public schools here in Los Angeles, throughout the state of California and the nation there is an inverted dimension that affects the quality of education which we dispense. It is that most of us plan and implement teaching subject matters to students with an intent designed to help them pass the required tests. If ever and wherever teachers are planning so as to teach *children* in an effective manner subject matter which is meaningful to them they will become able to pass any test required of them. At Grape Street we proved that we could stay within the public school system and accomplish the task.

That being the case, it must be clearly understood that we as Black people must be about the business of the Assault On Illiteracy Program and work at it with a fierce determination and a steadfast commitment until the acronym AOIP can begin standing for ADVANCING OUR INHERENT POTENTIAL.

At a press briefing held by AOIP at the U.S. Department of Education on May 12, 1986 Ben Wright addressed Secretary Bennett with, "We are not here asking for government grants or hand-outs. What we want is a promise from you that we can become a part of what the department is doing on the policy making level with respect to eliminating illiteracy in America. We feel we represent Black America, thus, we are desirious of a closer alliance with you, (the Department) as we become a respected partner to provide the Black American point of view."

Secretary Bennett commended the leaders of AOIP and said "fair enough" with regard to establishing the requested partnership. After openly communicating with Undersecretary Gary Bauer, he added, "Yes, I give an unqualified Yes."

15

A Challenge To School Administrators, Especially Black

L ogically, this is where my book should end. But this is December 21, 1985, my 68th birthday and I feel a compulsion to put aside modesty and constraints to say a few words before I close these covers. Administrators, principals, teachers, too many of our Black children are dying in our classrooms right before our very eyes. The tests show, on a continuing basis, that schools scoring lowest in academics are those with the highest percentage of Black students enrolled. Three weeks ago I sat with the Black Leadership Coalition on Education and listened to Dr. Ann Reynolds, Chancellor, California State University System, Dr. Herbert Carter, Vice-Chancellor, and Dr. James Rosser, President, California State University, Los Angeles tell us that on the whole minority students are enrolled into their schools by special permission because they are lacking in preparation. Each of them agreed that the universities are in a remedial business. Fifty to sixty percent of the students enrolled will have to have remediation in the foreseeable future. It seems to me that this is a sad commentary on the schools that prepared these students to get to this point. And may I call your attention to the fact that these are the cream of the crop. At least they got through the doors into the halls of higher education.

Many who get through high school stop their education at this point. These are among the more fortunate. A late statistic reveals that 50% of the Black students who get to the tenth grade drop-out before graduating. The masses of students who drop-out of school at any level without the acquisition of the basic academic life-coping skills have necessitated the need for the national Assault On Illiteracy Program. Research, studies and reports proliferate about our nation at risk. If you will take note you will find that most of the remedies prescribed are for bolstering education in the secondary schools. Class periods, class time, class subjects are added on to the school program. Requirements have been increased with minimal or no support for implementation. Too few have been the times when I have heard the statement which was uttered by Dr. Winston Doby,

Vice-Chancellor, UCLA, who in a small group session proposed that "The focus of support must be at the elementary level, the junior and senior high levels can only apply band-aids. Research documents that at ages 9, 10, 11 the peer group becomes the referenced group for establshing self-esteem for Black males. Adult influence is needed to serve the surrogate parental role when one is not there. More Black male role models are needed to counteract that negative peer influence." At last my conviction was confirmed and verbalized by an educator, and a distinguished one from the ranks of higher education at that - which is, that our focus must be on the elementary schools where students should be given a basic foundation upon which to build.

The reason that I have extended this edition of Good News on Grape Street is to continue to show that the staff, parents and community were able to work together and prove that, given the opportunity all of our children can learn. It is a tragedy that the same low scoring schools that were included in that first 39 Title I Target Schools remain the same 39 Chapter I Schools with many joining this list since 1966. Actually the first list was extended to a Target 55. Many of us questioned why there was such a prolonged delay before we were advised that our programs could begin. We heard that the list was stretched to embrace a school where a personal friend of the, then, President Richard Nixon, was the principal.

It is true that there is a multiplicity of variables that serve as barriers to the education of our Black children. To name a few - poorly prepared teachers, demoralized staff, unruly students, monumental amounts of paperwork, excessive numbers of meetings, unrealistic guidelines, inadequate support personnel, apathetic parents, consistent vandalism. And then for many of us, particulary Black women there is the United Teachers of Los Angeles. Any or all of these mentioned and more were encountered in this initially hostile environment. Anyone of us can bring about a positive change for our Black students if only we choose to do so. If this writing can just impress upon principals one thing it would be that there is no magic formula to getting it done. There is no research, no professional literature, no publication, no administrative guide or any one else's proven-to-be successful program that can provide a foolproof formula for another principal's success. Each principal must determine in his or her own imaginative and creative leadership style how to involve everyone productively in achieving success.

Late in the fall I was sitting as a member of a small circle at a retreat of the West Regional, National Sorority of Phi Delta Kappa Training Workshop. Each one of us was sharing and telling about some person who had most influenced our lives. Most of us had referred to the influence our parents or grandparents had had on our lives. I had just finished sharing. Then we all sat listening as Mary Jane McCoy related, "My parents had a great influence on my life but the person who most influenced my professional career and life-style is sitting right here in this circle. It was over ten years ago that I had read this article about a Black woman principal who had turned her school around. So one day I called Carrie Haynes from San Bernardino, CA and asked if I could bring a bus load of students to come and visit her school all day. She welcomed us. The arrangements were made. A busload of us visited in the classrooms and interacted with the students and teachers all day. Mrs. Haynes gave me some personal quality time. I asked a lot of questions. She responded to each. The message she left with was - ''Go ahead, observe, take notes, get all the ideas you want from here and elsewhere - but the thing that matters most is what you and your staff do with them after you get back to your local school. What matters most is that you and your staff meet together on a regular basis to decide how to overcome obstacles, set goals, make plans, do the work necessary, monitor each other in the process, learn how to celebrate results and move on to the next task.'' I heard and understood her. So we returned to San Bernardino and began working on this type of implementation. I find that it can work, if you are willing to work at it and I plan to continue doing so.''

That testimony gave me an unexpected morale bolster. So few administrators seem to understand that if what you are doing continues to produce students who are scoring at the bottom of the list, year after year after year then some revolutionary change should be given serious consideration. As Black administrators, particularly, we can not continue to wait to find models that are working to give us direction, we must, each one of us, decide that we will each find our own way to develop a model within each of our schools which will result in raising the academic level of learning for each of our students.

There has never been a more propitious time and a more exigent demand that we as Black administrators look introspectively and honestly at ourselves, plan together to bring about a change and then go into each of our schools and work together to produce visible positive results. The timing is right because among many other things we, in Los Angeles, California, recognized highly as an educational trend setter, have in place the Honorable Congressman Augustus G. Hawkins, Chairman of the powerful House, Education and Labor Committee whose commitment, dedication and concern for the maintenance of functional EFFECTIVE SCHOOLS is unequivocal.

Our own California State Assemblywoman Teresa Hughes, co-author of Senate Bill 813, who presently chairs the State Education Committee seeks diligently to develop legislation that will provide opportunities for our schools to implement programs that work for our children. Although she would be among the first to admit that SB 813 is a major step it does not address the education of poor students. It places a focus on increased standards and does not deal with content. In the fall of the 1985-86 school year the Los Angeles Board of Education elected, for the first time ever, its first Black President. Rita Walters, the only Black, among the seven who received national publicity previous to this when she introduced what has become a Board Rule relative to students maintaining a "C" average without receiving an "F" grade in order to be eligible to participate in extra-curricula activities. This, we understand, is the most rigid rule in the country. And although the challenge is necessary it would be far more beneficial especially to our students if it carried a support system along with it.

These three leaders in the three highest positions affecting education in our nation, our state and our city, who each evidences a commitment to providing legislation and funding to make it possible for administrators and teachers to function effectively in our schools, must be disappointed, disturbed and even embarrassed at the low academic scoring records which the schools populated preponderantly by Black students continue to maintain.

There should be little need to remind us that the urgent need to begin revolutionizing our educational focus is already past. Our continuing plateau of low academic scores of Black students are published annually. Statistics that reveal the many negative-type spin-offs from this basic fact proliferate from the national to the local level. The increasing drop-out rate, the growing rate, almost 50%, of Black adults who are "functional illiterates," the constant flow in and through the juvenile justice systems, the bulging overcrowding of incarcerated Blacks in jails, the statistic stating that about half of the Black babies are being born to un-wed young Black mothers (children having children), the excessive use of heavy drugs and alcohol, the accelerated growth in suicides, killings, robberies, rapes and many other anti-social behaviors all dramatize the ills pervading our society today. Within this climate, which we are aiding in creating, we live in a semblance of fear. We have placed bars on our windows. We pay for patrol protection. Businesses are building structures without windows. Hired protection of some type is a must everywhere. It is my firm conviction that we can do much to bring about a change on a preventive level for the students still in our charge and on a remedial level for many of the students who have dropped out.

There are some things that did work for me at Grape and I believe some could be adapted to bring about a positive change within any inner city school that would give them enough serious consideration to work out ways of making them happen. Some of these ideas may take some new or adaptive legislation or Board Rules. But if you, as administrators, become convinced enough that it can work for you in making things better for teaching students, there is no doubt in my mind that those in power would be most receptive to doing what needs to be done in order to help make it happen.

The first premise proposed is that every identified target school bring in teachers at least five days for staff development, planning and preparation before the students arrive. All authorities agree that classroom discipline is predicated among teacher planning and preparation. The way it is now in L.A.U.S.D. the teachers return one day before the students arrive. The morning is spent in a Teachers' Orientation Meeting. During the day, the total staff is addressed by the School Superintendent. There is little time allowed for teachers to get supplies and select books. There is no time left for teachers to set up room environment and make plans to meet the students on the following morning. At Grape Street School, our highest priority in planning our Title I Budget each year was that of setting aside professional expert funds to pay teachers to come in as many days near five as we could afford. I would recommend wholeheartedly that at least five days be provided for the teaching staff to be involved in specific participatory meaningful staff development, planning and preparation so that each teacher will be ready to receive and involve the students upon their arrival on the first day of school.

The focus on upgrading the success of implementing the instructional program must be on the teacher. The teacher must be given time to be involved in meaningful on-site participatory interaction, planning, preparation and time to teach in the classroom. Too many teachers are becoming frustrated because of the many interruptions during the teaching hours. The intercom was used at Grape Street during the school day only for emergency measures, which generally averaged twice a year. Students and other teacher messages were restricted to an absolute minimum. Approved classroom visitations were made with the understanding that the teacher was not to be disturbed. My visitations were expected on a regular basis. Teachers knew that when I entered the classroom my mission was to talk with students to find out what they were learning, why they were learning it and of what benefit it would be to them.

The pre-school staff development was the beginning of what continued throughout the year on a weekly basis. For three years we were permitted to dismiss school one hour early on Wednesday. This gave us an hour and a half block of time for work. At the first meeting we arranged a calendar of topics and leaders to cover each staff development session. Some of my peers criticized this effort saying that, 'We were like the blind leading the blind.' For us it worked. It was a demonstration of high expectations of the teachers. They lived up to them, honed their skills and developed their leadership styles. Most administrators feel that staff development should be planned and provided for new teachers only. We found that involving all teachers gave a commonality of purpose and a better understanding among us about the direction we were taking as it related to our students. The experienced teachers assessed their value as that of contributing, among other things, stability and experiential background.

The newer teachers assessed their worth as that of bringing enthusiasm and creativity. Those in between brought many other necessary attributes. The balance that this mixture assimilated served to develop a highly professional and productive series of staff development sessions from which each of us and the students in particular benefitted. Only twice in three years were outside persons invited to participate in the leadership. Teachers researched and planned outstanding presentations which involved the others in such a manner that each person left with some new concept, new material or different processes which could be adapted in some manner for use in their classrooms. There was a cooperative competitive climate generated. Each group tried to excel the ones who had presented before them. Enthusiasm, anticipation and excitement prevailed. These staff development sessions were the key to our staff building the quality of confidence in itself as individuals and as a group that led to the success we had in building the self-esteem in our students which ultimately led to their academic achievement. It may be that this kind of time for on-site participatory staff development needs to be legislated. It is my conviction that if enough administrators can become convinced that there is such a a need, a way will be found to provide it.

This type of staff development is entirely different from the type that brings in specialists to speak to a staff, inspire them and leave. We've done this throughout the years and go back to our classroom to the same old routine. The same thing applies to our conference attendance. Those attended get involved, get inspiration, take notes, buy tapes and go back to school to get into the same old rut. This type of on-site participatory involvment places and keeps the focus on the students and ways of getting them involved in their learning as an on-going process.

Another major concern is that of the norming date in the Los Angeles Unified School District. Classroom norm ration is 27:1 in the Chapter I Schools, as one outcome of the Crawford Case which related to desegregation of our schools. So as students enroll in school each is placed in the appropriate class and room. On Friday of the fourth week of school teachers fill in the names of students enrolled in their legal register as required by California State to report the Average Daily Attendance which determine the amount of state funding our city schools will receive. Immediately after this date classes are normed. If a teacher has more than 27, these students are transferred to another room. If a teacher has less than 27, students are moved into this room until the number 27 is reached. In some cases norming date can be very disruptive. As students are shifted to increase or decrease numbers there are times that classes are closed out; there are times that new classes are formed; there are times when classes are shifted so that some teachers may have an entirely new group of students. I saw this happen to a new young Black male who had gotten his fourth grade class organized and under control. After the norming date he was confronted with a class full of undisciplined fifth graders. By the time I, as another teacher at that time, walked into his room, I could only witness him disintegrate before my eyes. Those fifth graders took over his class and forced him literally to walk out of the room and away from the field of education permanently. For many teachers the first four weeks are a loss of time. There are those who do not wish to get too organized or too attached to students whom they may lose after a brief time period. For most teachers its a time to begin all over again. At Grape we minimized this disruption by organizing in multi-graded groupings. This made it easy to keep our classes balanced and caused a minimum of, if any, disruptions when the classes are normed. Something must be done to prevent losing the first four weeks of teaching time that is lost for too many of our students.

It's amazing what happens to the attendance of teachers and students when everyone is involved in creating a warm and inviting climate. Everyone wants to come to work. Teachers teach and students learn. It was quite pleasing to me to realize that the NEWSWEEK correspondent captured the spirit of our effort in this title of the articles *DOES SCHOOL + JOY =* learning which appeared May 2, 1971. We were able to respond to this inquiry in the affirmative. Getting teachers, who are people, to work together isn't always easy. But if you place the emphasis on teaching students it can be done. It takes work. You must be determined, positive and persistent. You must model the involvement of teachers in their own teaching/learning process as you wish them to replicate in their approach with their students in the classroom.

There can be no dispute that the EFFECTIVE SCHOOLS legislation being introduced by Congressman Augustus Hawkins is a good bill which lists five factors identified by effective school research as distinguishing effective from ineffective school as follows:

1. strong and effective administrative and instructional leadership that creates concensus on instructional goals and organizational capacity for instructional problem solving

2. emphasis on the acquisition of basic order and higher order skills

3. a safe and orderly school environment that allows teachers and pupils to focus their energies on academic achievement

4. a climate of expectations that virtually all children can learn under appropriate conditions, and

5. continuous assessment of students and programs to evaluate the effects of instruction.

There is no argument to refute the necessity of each of these correlates being implemented in any school that is an effective one. Yet, I would hasten to add a sixth factor without which there would have been a void in the effectiveness of the program at Grape Street. That number six is parental involvement. Helping parents to clarify their own roles and guiding them to learn ways to support the education of their children was a most essential factor in building self-esteem and promoting academic achievement for our children.

Now having the legislation in place is important and necessary. But it must go further than that. It must be implemented in the schools and in the classrooms by people. This is a people business and good things will not happen for our Black children until Black people are moved to positive action. If we want the principals and teachers in our schools to implement these correlates that will make them effective, *TIME* must be provided for them to meet, to set goals, to develop a plan of action, to get the necessary work done in order to be ready to accept, respect, expect, teach and get positive results from each student assigned in each classroom. It can be done. It takes work. It takes dedication, commitment and determination. And it takes *TIME*. Time must be given prior to the opening of school and on a regular basis throughout the year. The principal and the teachers should be held accountable for the use of this time in the form of reasonable expectations and results. Class size should be lowered to 25 with only certificated specialized personnel out of the classroom. Every school should have at least one pupil service and attendance counselor, school psychologist and a nurse assigned full time as an administrative staff team member. Until *TIME* is provided for school staff to work and interact on a continuing on-going basis focusing on the best way to make education meaningful for their students, it will remain very difficult to implement the correlates with a commonality of purpose which will move people into action and get positive results.

Arrangements should be made for school administrators to meet on a regular basis in leaderless groups, rotating the facilitating responsibility and discussing ways of working with each respective staff in order to develop an *EFFECTIVE SCHOOL* model process in each. We do not have time to wait for one or two schools to develop models for others to replicate. We need to begin now to motivate and support each other so that each principal becomes inspired, motivated and determined to involve his/her staff, parents and community in the development of a model effective school where success is the result of the teaching/learning process. The time to begin is overdue.

EPILOGUE

Friday, June 27, 1986 I sat beside my Soror, Harriet Williams at a luncheon session during our Far West Regional Conference of Delta Sigma Theta Sorority, Inc. where Soror, Gwendolyn Bishop is Regional Director. Almost 600 of us listened intently to the profound address being delivered by our Immediate Past National President, Mrs. Mona Bailey. Among the notes I took were two sentences that I used later in the afternoon at a workshop where I was a presenter on Summit II. These lines were *"Minds of Black children are being wasted because they are not being taught."* and *"I Can is just as important as I.Q. for our Black children."*

Summit II refers to the Black Minority Women's Single Parent/ Homemaker Project which is being sponsored by Delta Chapter singly and cooperatively in networking patterns throughout Deltadom. This workshop was convened most ably by Anne-Cade Wilson, Century City Alumnae with Homoiselle Davis, San Francisco presenting Black College Convocations, Carrie Haynes, Los Angeles South Bay Alumnae, Summit, et al. Hortense Canady, National President, Resource and Lori Blakeney, Kappa Chapter, Recorder.

Because my National President, *Mrs Hortense Canady has commended me uniquely for keeping Delta Sigma Theta Sorority, Inc. out in the forefront of the Assault on Illiteracy Program it affords us the opportunity to promote the use of the AOIP Affective-Oriented materials in all of our Delta sponsored projects. Her support and promotion of our efforts are motivating the much needed proliferation of the Assault On Illiteracy Program focus wherever Deltas are located and wherever the need exists.*

In my own local Los Angeles South Bay Alumnae Chapter we have written a proposal and secured funding from the Carl D. Perkins Vocational Education Division of the State Department of Education. Our Immediate Past President Julia Williams and I serve as Project Directors. Our National President Canady informs us that these are funds for which the Deltas lobbied and they are available in every state.

Our first local AOIP Tutorial Training session chaired by Jacquelyn Snead, Los Angeles Alumni Chapter was a huge success. The 75 members in attendance were largely our own Deltas; Kappa Alpha Psi Fraternity and Silhouettes being chaired by Anne Butler, Los Angeles South Bay Alumnae Chapter President; teen-agers brought by Yvonne Payne, the

Director of the Westminister Neighborhood House in Watts LACER, a networking group organized by Jackie Goldberg, a LAUSD school board member.

Many branches in the National Association of University Women have begun an Assault On Illiteracy Program effort to include New Orleans, LA: Beaumont, TX; Brooklyn, NY; Crowley, LA; Elizabeth City, NC; Long Island, NY; Los Angeles, CA; New York, NY; Philadelphia, PA; Raleigh, NC; Shreveport, LA; St. Landry, LA; South Bay, CA; Southern University, LA; Winston-Salem, NC and Tallahasee, FL as reported by Lillian E. Ross, our National 2nd Vice President who is Program Development Committee Chair. Next year we expect every NAUW Branch to have an AOIP Project.

We invite all other organizations, churches, and other institutions to join in this Assault On Illiteracy Program effort, so that the *GOOD NEWS ON GRAPE STREET* WILL SPREAD TO *GOOD NEWS THROUGHOUT OUR LAND.*

APPENDIX A

Three S Management Strategy for Student Success Incorporates Carrie Haynes' Philosophy and Principles

Carrie Haynes and I began working together in the Fall of 1979. Carrie had sponsored the Three S Management staff and organizational development training project in the Fall of 1979 for her staff and 30 Area B principals in the Los Angeles Unified School District. She was a participant in the training process and at the conclusion of it decided to retire and join with me in the effort to encourage schools to use this process of leadership and management. The Three S Management concepts, processes and strategies were in alignment with her philosophy and methods that she used successfully at Grape Street School.

Since 1980 Carrie and I have been working deligently to build the Three S strategy into training modules that can be used by administrators, teachers, parents and students.

One of the reasons Carrie first became interested in the Three S Management strategy was that it paralleled the way she brought about the transformation at Grape Street School. **The first S** of the Three S strategy is Self-Management. This Three S strategy begins first with the individual, with his own leadership and management. The Three S strategy establishes that it is the individual who is unique and special with all kinds of talents and abilities who is the key to the productivity and success of any enterprise. As you read through this book, note how Carrie learns about each person and works with each individual to encourage him to take initiative and responsibility for his own leadership, management and success.

The second S of the Three S strategy is System Management. System means the total enterprise and can be viewed and understood in the following ways:

System Direction: the purposes, beliefs, principles and goals which guide the school's day to day, and year to year operation.

System Structure: the organization's design, plan, policy and order by which the school's leadership and management are to operate; the pattern of relationship of authority and responsibilities that governs the leadership and management of the people in the school.

System Process: the involvement of the staff individually and collectively in problem-solving, goal setting, planning and leadership processes and strategies to be used to fulfill the purposes and achieve the goals of the school.

System Results: the measure of productivity and accountability of a school in terms of its purposes, beliefs and goals.

As you read this book, keep in mind system management as it relates to Carrie's leadership in bringing about unity of purpose and action and in developing the system structure and processes to obtain the desired academic results at Grape Street School.

The third S in the Three S strategy is Synergistic Management. Synergistic Management means that when individuals work together cooperatively to achieve common goals the results will be far greater and the school will be a productive and wholesome place to be. Synergistic Management is how individuals relate to each other and how they work together cooperatively to achieve common goals and meet the overall purposes of the school. It is the care and concern the individuals within a school have for one another. It is how authority and power is used effectively and appropriately within a school to produce outstanding results. These results are produced through the individual and cooperative actions of the people who make up the school. Note throughout this book how Carrie uses her authority and power to bring about synergy within the staff that ultimately leads to the student academic success desired at Grape Street School.

Carrie used all Three S's to gain the success she desired so much for the students at Grape Street School.

Why the Public Schools are Failing and What You Can Do About It- A Message and Plan of Action for Parents, Teachers and Administrators

Carrie and I are now writing a book and a training module for individuals such as teachers, parents or administrators who want to put the Three S strategy and process into practice now. It is entitled, **Why The Public Schools Are Failing And What You Can Do About It - A Message and Plan of Action for Parents, Teachers and Administrators.** This book reveals the root cause and real solutions to the educational delimma in the U.S. (The Three S Management Training Institute is already available for group use by administrators, teachers, parents and students in schools).

This book and training module will enable you as an individual to start where you are to begin to influence the course of events in a positive and productive way in your school. It is planned to be published and available in the early part of 1987.

Ben Gieringer

EVERY PERSON CAN LEARN TO READ

Every person can learn to read. Phonics is the key that opens the door to the most important tool that any student needs in order to acquire the skills necessary to learn how to read. As we already know reading is the basic skill which everyone needs to master in order to be successful in school, in the world of work and in our society. Every student, in America, young or old, should learn how to speak, read, write and spell in Standard English. For this reason, we have developed a sequential developmental program of phonetic analysis skills which may be used in teaching reading with The ADVANCER.

The English Language is constructed from the 26 letters in the English Alphabet. Students should be taught to say, recognize and read the alphabet in its proper sequential order. They should understand why they need to acquire this knowledge. One of the basic reasons is to acquire the left to right tendency of movement in reading. Our words, our sentences, our paragraphs are written and read from left to right. An alphabetic sentence is read from left to right. Later, the knowledge of the sequence of the alphabet is necessary for finding words in the dictionary, names in the phone books and finding basic types of information.

Phonics is the science of sound. There are 44 sounds in the English language to master. Teaching phonics to students helps them to read, write and spell words by the way they sound. as soon as they have learned the sounds of letters alone, in combinations, and how to blend these sounds to form words, they become independent readers. It is important that phonics not be taught in isolation.

Children begin to acquire a speaking vocabulary as they hear the family and those around them converse. Teachers should listen to determine the extent of each child's speaking vocabulary. As the sounds of the alphabet are taught, the teacher should show the student how each of the sounds and the principles taught apply to words that are meaningful to the student. For instance, how does your name begin? What other words begin as your name does? What principles apply to the sounds of the vowels in your name? Helping the student to relate letter sounds to words that are known and meaningful will facilitate the learning of the sounds and the principles that govern them.

As students learn to analyze words phonetically they will be better able to exercise word attack skills. That is, they will be better able to sound out words that are totally new to them. Until a person can pronounce a word, it does not become a part of his vocabulary. As a person gains in each level of success, the more confident that person will become. Reading is a skill that is developed best by reading, writing and spelling. The more anyone reads the more competent one becomes in the skill of reading. Reading should be done for a purpose. You read to get some information you want or need or you read for enjoyment or pleasure.

Every person can learn to read. Learning letter sounds and the rules that govern them in words provide the key to unlocking the door to student achievement. The guide should be used discriminately by the teacher to teach and reinforce the skills of phonetic analysis. By relating these skills and build upon success. When family members or any other significant persons take an interest in the learning of the student (whatever the age) and become involved in supporting and learning along with them, then the rewards of success are bountiful.

APPENDIX B

The Grape Street "How To" Manual

INNOVATIVE STAFF DEVELOPMENT

THAT PROVED

TO BE SUCCESSFUL

IN AN

INNER—CITY SCHOOL

GRAPE STREET SCHOOL

'Staff Development Workshops or Seminars 1972-73
Every Wednesday, 2:00 - 3:30P.M.

September 13. . . . . . . Implementing the Stull Act in the Open Classroom
Goals and Objectives at Grape Street

Ms. Carrie Haynes	Mr. Tom Stevens
Principal	Assistant Principal

September 20. . . . . Developing Terminal Objectives for Vertically
Grouped Open Classroom

Ms. Carrie Haynes	Mr. Tom Stevens
Principal	Assistant Principal

September 27. . . . . . . Developing Instructional Classroom Environments

Ms. Mayme Sweeney	Ms. Andrea Roberts
Curriculum Coordinator	Curriculum Consultant

October 4. . . . . Constructing Performance Objectives For Teaching
Reading in Multi-Age Groupings

Ms. Carol Reiss	Ms. Veronica Morris
Grades 1-2	Grades 4-5-6

October 11. . . . . Teaching Spelling in the Informal Classroom

Ms. Eloise Taylor	Ms. Esther Zack
Grades 1-2	Grades 3-4-5

October 18. . . . . Personalizing Performance Objectives in Math

Ms. Joy Zimnavoda	Ms. Bennie Wyatt
Grades 1-2	Grades 4-5-6

October 25. . . . . Humanizing Written Expression in the Open Classroom

Ms. Ruby Helire	Ms. Kristine Johnson
Grades 1-2	Grades 1-2-3

November 1. Teaching Discipline Through Art

Ms. Joan Dunning	Ms. Joycelyne Lew
Grades 4-5-6	Kindergarten

November 8 . . . . Personalizing Performance Objectives in Science

Ms. Ann Matthews   Mr. Coy Roberson
Grades 1-2-3   Science/Resource

November 15 . . . . Teaching Pupils Sportsmanship in Play

Ms. Gloria White   Mr. Dennis Hepler
Grades 1-2-3   Upper EMR

November 22 . . . . Providing for Effective Use of School Equipment

Mr. Tom Stevens, Assistant Principal

November 29 . . . . Teaching Reading Skills in the Open Classroom

Ms. Virginia Synder   Ms. Alma Lurry
Reading Specialist   Reading Specialist

December 6 . . . . Guiding Creative Expression Through Art

Ms. Mildren Stock   Ms. Mayme Sweeney
Grades 1-2-3   Curriculum Coordinator

December 13 . . . . Facilitating Learning through Rhythmic Activities

Mr. Donald Walker   Ms. Ethel Taylor
Int. EMR   Grades 3-4-5

January 3 . . . . Facilitating Learning through Dramatic Activities

Ms. Mamie Hamilton   Mr. Kevin Alberts
Primary Reading Specialist   Grades 4-5-6

January 10 . . . . Suggested Ways of Developing Learning Centers

Ms. Elna Cook   Ms. Wilnora Ewell
Grades 3-4-5   Teacher-Librarian

January 17 . . . . Use of the Library as a Resource Center

Ms. Wilnora Ewell, Teacher-Librarian

January 24 . . . . Translating Obsolete Items to Instructional Materials

Ms. Nada Fuller   Ms. Lavatryce Rice
Primary EMR   Grades 1-2

January 31 . . . . Integrating Music throughout the Curriculum
Ms. Shirley Helton, Music-Reading Teacher

February 7 . . . . Facilitating Learning through Rhythmic Activities
Ms. Ethel Taylor Grades 3-4-5
Mr. Donald Walker Int. EMR
Ms. Susan Friedhof Pre-Kindergarten

February 14. . . . Program Evaluation as stated in Goals and Objectives
Ms. Carrie Haynes   Mr. Tom Stevens
Principal   Assistant Principal

February 21. Expanding Intercultural Relationships in the Open Classroom
Ms. Gloria Pellebon   Ms. Joan Dunning
Kindergarten   Grades 4-5-6
Ms. Susan Friedhof
  Pre-Kindergarten

February 28 . . . . . . What You've Always Wanted to Know About School
Resources and Have Been Afraid to Ask
Ms. Delores Allen   Ms. Mary Fischer
Grades 2-3-4   Grades 3-4-5

March 7 . . . . Conducting Pupil and Parent Conferences as Related to
Performance Objectives
Mr. Mal Neely, Pupil Services and Attendance Counselor

March 14. . Maintaining Good Health Habits as Related to Performance
Objectives
Ms. Betty Heintz, School Nurse

March 21. . . . Creating Relevant and Exciting Learning Centers Based on
Pupils' Interests and Needs
Ms. Yvonne Almeida   Ms. Patricia Douglas
Pre-Kindergarten   Grades 4-5-6
Ms. Ramona Baham   Ms. Joe Ann McMillon
Kindergarten   Grades 4-5-6

March 28. . . Counseling and Guidance as Related to Terminal Objectives
Mrs. Lydia Daniels
School Psychologist

April 4. . . . . Expanding the Horizon in the Vertically Grouped Open
Classroom
Ms. Valcour Williams   Ms. Gail Penzella
Grades 1-2-3   Grades 4-5-6

April 11. . . . . Learning to Live in Today's World
Ms. Harriet Nunley   Ms. Josephine Miles
Kindergarten   Grades 4-5-6

April 25. . . . . Facilitating the Learning of Communication Skills
Ms. Jewel Williams - Grades 1-2-3

May 2. . . . . Review of Scheduling for Open Classroom Activities
Ms. Annie Honeysucker   Ms. Diana Dozier
Grades 1-2-3   Grades 1-2-3
Ms. Elna Cook
  Grades 3-4-5

May 9. . . . . Multisensory Approach to Learning
Ms. Marilyn Arrington   Ms. Mary Yzuel
Kindergarten   Grades 1-2-3
Mr. Michael Walters
  Grades 4-5-6

May 16. . . . . Personalizing Office Management
Ms. Naomi Gilbert   Ms. Pauline Bryant
Office Manager   Intermediate Clerk Typist
Ms. Glorious Cole   Ms. Gloria Brooks
Intermediate Clerk Typist   School Clerk Typist
  Ms. Cira Rivera
School Clerk Typist

May 23. . . . . 1973-74 Multi-Age School Organization
Ms. Carrie Haynes and Faculty

May 30. . . . . Teacher and Education Aide Relationships
Education Aide III Staff
Ms. Mary Baker   Ms. Luella Burton
Curriculum Aide   Education Aide

June 6. . . . . Projecting Staff Development Plans for 1973-74

Ms. Carrie Haynes   Mr. Tom Stevens
Principal   Assistant Principal

GRAPE STREET SCHOOL

Staff Development Workshops or Seminars 1972-73
2:00 - 3:00 P.M.

Education Aides

November 8. . . . . Use of Curriculum Lab as a Resource Center
Ms. Mary Baker   Ms. Mayme Sweeney

December 6. . . . . Facilitating Learning through Reading Games
Ms. Alecia Jackson   Ms. Thelmarie Gray
Ms. Shirley Helton

January 10. . . . . . Creating Relevant and Exciting Math Games Based on
Pupils' Needs and Interests from the Math Lab
Ms. Luella Burton   Ms. Gail Penzella

February 14. . . . . Suggested Ways of Developing Science Centers
Ms. Inez Henderson   Ms. Rose McClellan
Mr. Coy Roberson

February 21. . . . . Guiding Creative Expression through Art
Ms. Annette Adams   Ms. Mollie Ashton
Ms. Doris Efferson   Ms. Yolanda Villareal
Ms. Joycelyne Lew

March. . . . . Use of the Library As a Resource Center
Ms. Charles Ella Davis   Ms. Mattie Stubblefield
Ms. Wilnora Ewell

April 11. . . . . Suggested Ways of Using Obsolete Materials for
Language Arts Centers
Ms. Alberta Shorter   Ms. Geanetta Thomas

April 25. . . . What You've Always Wanted to Know About Audio Visual
Equipment and Materials

Mr. Calvin Davis, Jr.   Mr. Theopolis Schrock
                    Mr. Tom Stevens
        Mrs. Mayme Sweeney, Curriculum Coordinator

Initially our education aides accompanied their teachers to staff
development sessions. Then because feelings were expressed that they had
some special needs the following agenda was developed with the aides
supplying their own leadership under supervision provided by the certificated persons, whose names are underlined.

GRAPE STREET SCHOOL

Teacher - Diana Dozier

Staff Development

Self-Evaluation Survey

1. How do you feel about your pupils?

I love them!!!I am continually inspired and delighted with their creativity, ingenuity, antics, stories, ideas, thoughts, emotional outbursts and recoveries. My enthusiasm drown my inevitable frustration, as do the helpful people at Grape Street.

2. Have you become acquainted?

Yes. Initially I had a 10 minute conference with each child, surveyed their interest, home situation, brothers and sisters, chores at home, pets, dislikes, etc.

3. Do you know their areas of strengths?

Yes I do, and get them working in needed areas. Yes, I hope I can work out a schedule with my partner so I can have an aide part of the A.M. Now I'm alone in the morning and have help only in the P.M. My mornings suffer.

4. Do you know about significant personal problems?

Being new here I feel I need more time. I have two cases in particular where I know there are home problems. I spot behavior and immaturity problems in the classroom. I don't know all the backgrounds of the children yet and hope to get to know the parents soon!

5. Do you know their interests?

Yes, and our centers and the children's projects show this greatly.

6. Do you have faith in their ability to achieve?

Yes--definitely. I am deeply, emotionally, and intellectually committed to open structure--a *child centered room*, and I feel my faith in children stimulates this commitment.

7. Can you accept each child as he is?

Yes, I take a child from where she or he is at and dismiss prejudices or labels of "slow" or "handicapped." Children unfold and blossom most fullest if allowed to do so at their own pace.

8. How do you maintain control?

Initially I quiet the children down and have them sit on rugs. Then we discuss what each child is going to do for that period and I individually dismiss each child to do his project. To change activities I recall them to the rugs and individually get them involved in the new activity. I separate conflicting children.* I deprive children who break the room standards, which we initially established, of special privileges.

*Notes go home to parents if the child's behavior continually breaks the room standards. We have discussions on areas of concern to children and myself. EX: *How to keep materials in the room.*

9. How would you interpret your pupils' feelings about their classroom?

They love it. The children want to come inside the room before school starts. Many want to stay in at recess. Many come to the room during lunch to see if I'm there to let them in. A few 1st and 2nd graders have notes to stay until 3:00 on those days. They put up their work, are proud of it, enjoy reading to each other, establish little cubby holes of their own feel generally relaxed and free, I think.

10. Do they maintain regular attendance?

I would say so. I only have pupils out when they have a valid excuse, sickness, doctor's appointment, or rain.

11. Do they arrive on time regularly?

Everyone except two boys and I think there are home conflicts which cause this. I accept their tardiness because after talking to them I feel its's unavoidable.

12. Do they return promptly after each recess?

Yes, and before it if I'll let them in.

13. How would you describe the pupils' attitudes in your room?

The children are accustomed to freedom now and resent most teacher imposed assignments. They are very creative in their thinking and enjoy doing reading, writing, math, art, science, geography, etc., as long as it's in an area they're interested in. The students enjoy helping each other and try to influence other children to do their best and follow room standards.

14. How do you feel about the program you are implementing?

I believe in it deeply, am overjoyed to be practicing it and feel it has much growth and learning potential.

15. Room Organization

Basic centers with manipulative objects: Math, Science, Reading, Writing and Art.

16. Room Environment

Very stimulating. Children's work shown. It's their room and they help arrange it.

17. Learning Centers

Project area for children's individual group project: store, space ship, etc. Scheduling of activities

Each child gets his academics within the area he's interested in. Projects, math, and chart stories in the A.M. P.M. reading with reading teacher, key words, and project finishing. Generally 20 minute periods per activity.

18. Diagnosing Needs

Informal and formal.
Determing interests

Surveys, conferences.

19. Record Keeping

Done in reading and math; indicates where each child is.

Development of and Maintenance of Profiles

This comes in time as the children and I become better acquainted. I'm aware of and note individual progression of students via their work samples and growth in the depth and quality of work done.

20. Pupil Achievement

My children are proud of their work and respond greatly to verbal praise, putting work up, taking it home, etc. The children are happy, learning and developing.

21. Group Conferences

Yes

22. Pupil Relationships

Needs work--immaturity causes many conflicts as well as bickering.

23. Pupil Recognition

I try to stimulate sharing something a child did with whole class, having a child read a story or tell about his project.

24. Classroom Management

I try to get the students to assume as much responsibility for this as possible whenever they show the ability and desire to assume it. Much verbal praise given for taking responsibility.

25. How do you feel about our Staff Development Program?

I've only been to three so far. They're better than what I was used to, but I feel there should be more time for sharing and exchanging ideas and bringing in things children did to share. This is an alternative to listening to and watching a pre-structured show where you learn and do another's ideas without discussing it or adding to it and expanding it.

26. Organization

Could we have a ''Show and Tell'' type meeting where we volunteer ideas or even break into small groups according to interests? People who need or have science ideas go to Room___; people for math in Room___; people for art in Room_____;, people for sewing to Room_____, etc.

27. What people have been helpful to you?

The people at Grape have been most helpful to me. I feel welcome, accepted, loved, cared about, and general good feeling about the whole staff here. The chances to meet and talk with the people here I greatly appreciate.

28. How can it become more helpful to you?

I feel the staff development should become more individualized. For instance, some teachers already had nutrition knowledge and were bored and felt their time wasted at the Dairy-Nutrition Program. The last idea of a signup for music, rhythms, etc., was much better. Maybe our choices could be expanded and more teachers could lead in the groups so more teachers' needs and interests could be met.

29. How do you feel about assistance being provided by supportive personnel. Indicate what has been helpful and what could be more helpful.
Education Aides

Working out very well. Mrs. McClellen has adjusted to the new room environment very well and is great in bringing out creative work with the children. She's very helpful.

Miller-Unruh Reading Specialists

Miss Hamilton is doing an excellent job with my first graders. Language experience is used and I follow it up.

Remedial Reading Teacher

Don't know her.

Librarian

Not acquainted with her yet. I have tried to get certain books for interested students--such as on nurses and doctors--and there were none there.

Music

Haven't met the teacher yet. I play records for dancing with the children as well as record stories. We need a set of head phones that work!

Resource Teacher

Mrs. Sweeney is a fantastic person and I feel lucky to have her help. She's given me many ideas and was a life saver during a cooking session.

Enrichment Teacher
Don't know her.

Nurse
She seems very concerned with individual student's needs and seems to give very attentive care.

Pupil Service and Attendance

Attendance seems well managed and amazingly efficient with all the various problems.

Counselor

I'm not very well acquainted with him yet.

Custodial Staff

Seem very very warm, concerned, helpful, tolerant, understanding, and patient. I admire their very good dispositions.

Clerical Staff

Very friendly and helpful people. I appreciate the extra time they spend with me on questions I have as a new teacher here.

Vice-Principal

I appreciate his offers to help in any way he can and his patience in explaining things to me.

Principal

I'm inspired to find a principal who is so down to earth, approachable and understanding and fair with us. I feel very comfortable around Mrs. Haynes and also that she supports us greatly and tries her best!!

GRAPE STREET SCHOOL

TO: All Teaching Staff

FROM: Carrie Haynes, Principal

PERSONALIZED STARTER SUGGESTIONS - No. 1

1. *Initial Consonants, Consonant Digraphs and Counting*

Count the *boys* in our room. Cut out things that begin as *boy*.
How many *girls* are in our room? Cut out things that begin as *girl*.
How many *children* are in our room? Cut out things that begin as *children*.
Cut out things you like to eat.

Which two italicized words begin with one consonant?
Which two italizcized words begin with consonant digraphs?

Which two *italicized* words begin with one consonant?
Which two *italicized* words begin with consonant digraphs?

Variations: This task card may be shortened or varied. Directions may be
read to non-readers.

2. *People* - Counting - Visual perception and discrimination

Make the people in your family. Name them.
Make some of your friends at school. Name them.
Make some of the big people at school. Name them.

3. *Maps* - Directionality

Draw the four streets around our school. Name the directions.
Make a map of the buildings on our school ground. Show the directions.
Draw the street on which you live. Put in all the houses on your side of
the block. Put house numbers on each one.

4. *String* - Color Identification, Comparisons, Creating

Place several (4) pieces of different colors and different length of roving
(string) in a learning center. A task card might read:

What colors do you see? Which color is the longest? Which color is the
shortest? What can you make with string? Draw, color, and name each
thing you can make?

5. *Observation* - Visual Perception

Take a walk around the school yard to observe and/or look around the room to observe:

What are some tall things? What are some small things? What are some hard things? What are some soft things?

6. *Lunch Book* - Record Keeping

Make a Lunch Book. Record what you eat for lunch each day.

Monday	Tuesday	Wednesday	Thursday	Friday

Use the Dictionary to check your spelling.

7. *Population* - Counting, Comparisons

What is the population of our class?

Boys	Girls	Adults

What is the population of the room next door?

Boys	Girls	Adults

What is the population of the other third grades?

Boys	Girls	Adults

Comparisons may be made.

8. *Parts of Speech* - Nouns and Adjectives

Name some things you see on the way to school.

1.	5.
2.	6.
3.	7.
4.	8.

Put a descriptive word before each one.

Variations: Other locations may be used such as, on the school trip, in the classroom, on the school yard, in your house, in the auditorium, at the assembly, at the school play, on a television program, etc.

9. *Fruits* - Categorizing, Spelling, Research

1. Name some fruits you have eaten.
2. Name some fruits you have seen in the market.
3. Name some fruits you can find in the sales paper.
4. Use the dictionary to check the spelling of each fruit.
5. Find out where some of these fruits were grown.
6. Tell how your favorite one got to you.

10. *Description* - Oral, Illustration, or Written

1. Describe a girl classmate. Have some friends guess who.
2. Describe a boy classmate. Have some friends guess who.
3. Describe something in your room. Have some friends guess what it is.

11. *Time Zone* - Geography

When school begins in Los Angeles, what time is it in:

Chicago, Illinois   Washington, D.C.   Houston, Texas

Name two other large cities. What time is it there?

Variations: Places where pupils' relatives, friends live or where relevant news has occurred may be named. Other times may be used.

12. *Telephone Area Codes* - Locating Geographical Areas

What are the telephone area codes of:

Los Angeles, California   Chicago, Illinois   Washington, D.C.
Houston, Texas   New York, New York   Denver, Colorado

Variations: The list may be extended. Pupils may name places that have an importance to them.

PERSONALIZED STARTER SUGGESTIONS - No. 2

1. *Class Book* - Letter Identification

Teacher or pupil manuscript or write the first name at the top of the left page and the last name at the top of the right page of each class member. Pupils cut out items or draw pictures of items that begin as each name.

Variations: First name only may be used for readiness.

Other Variations: May extend to a variety of skills.
Classification: Appropriate dress may be selected for each pupil, foods liked, or biographical sketches presented in creative or unique ways.

2. *Picture Grammar* -Parts of Speech

Have pupils select a picture interesting to them. Cut it out and mount it. Pupils' tasks would involve identifying and recording the persons or things (nouns), the action being taken (verbs), and/or descriptive phrases about the picture. Each task might involve one part of speech or it may be extended so that a creative story may result.

3. *Clothing Coordinates* - Multiplication Facts

Develop task card which will direct pupil to make himself or herself. Have pupil cut out or make a certain number of blouses and skirts (girl) - shirts and trousers (boy). Direct pupil to determine how many different outfits he can make from each combinations, such as 3 blouses and 2 skirts, 4 shirts and 4 trousers, and on and on.

4. *Lunch Table Record* - Counting, Recording

Make a graph to show the number of children who ate at your table by using different colors.

Sunday - purple	Monday - red	Tuesday - yellow
Wednesday - blue	Thursday - orange	Friday - green
Saturday - brown		

Comparisons and conclusions may be drawn at the end of each week as long as the interest holds.

5. *Class Attendance* - Counting, Tallying, Drawing Conclusions

Tally the number of pupils present. Keep a record for a specified period - week, month, or longer, Determine whether or not any identifiable pattern develops.

6. *Sales Catalog* - Math Computation

Cut out items that have been overstocked or have not sold. Announce a $1.00 Off Sale - or Two items for .01¢ more Sale, - or ⅓ Off Sale - or ½ Off Sale, or other.

Make a Sale Catalog showing the items, the regular price and the reduced price.

7. *Travel Log* - Geography

Miss Messing flew back from Vancouver, Canada with a new name and husband. She is now Mrs. Phillip Douglas. What were some of the points of interest that she could view out of her plane window on her return flight?

Mrs. Haynes boarded a United Airlines plane on a beautiful sunny day. What were some of the points of interest that she saw on her way to Baltimore, Maryland? At 5:00 p.m. there she called Grape Street School. What time was it here?

Mrs. Haynes took a non-stop airplane flight to New York City on the morning of March 18, 1972. List some points of interest that she should have seen on the flight.

8. *Car Book* - Identification - Visual Discrimination

Make a book of cars. Try to find models for two or three years. Tell how each has changed. Vary assignment on basis of interest.

9. *Football Geography* - Determining Locations

Identifying football helmets. Cut out and place each one in the geographical locales from which the team comes. (The place mats with the helmets are from one of the International Pancake Houses).

10. *Class Geography* - Map Study

Survey class and teacher:
(a) Determine where each was born. Place name on map.
(b) Determine places pupils and teacher have been. Use different colors to place names on map.

11. *Global Geography* - Map Study

Survey staff members. Determine places they have been in the world. Place name on map at points visited. Use other variations.

PERSONALIZED STARTER IDEAS No. 3

1. *Tic-Tac-Toe - Letter Identification and Discrimination*

Use *b* and *d*　　　　Use *m* and *n*　　　　Use *a* and *o*　　　　Use *o* and *i*

Any two letters may be assigned or chosen. Give close attention to correct letter formation.

Initial Consonants and Blends

Use words that begin with any two consonants. Words may remain the same as spelling practice or they may vary to reinforce other skills. Example:

Use *run* and *jump*　　　　　　　　　Use *play* and *please*
Use *car* and *bus*　　　　　　　　　　Use *stop* and *fly*

Use a different word each time beginning with *h*.
Use a different word each time beginning with *g*.
Check your spelling in the dictionary before declaring a winner.

Initial, Medial, Ending Digraphs

Use *wheel* and *white*　　　　　　　Use *chair* and *church*
Use *mother* and *father*　　　　　　Use *watch* and *with*

Variations: Infinite words skills may be developed or reinforced using this frame. Pupils may draw this frame. They may be placed under acetate or used in any appropriate manner.

Numeral formation may be practiced in the tic-tac-toe frame.

2. *Telephone Posts* - Directionality and Counting

Take a walk.

Count the telephone posts on the *North* of our school.
Count the telephone posts on the *East* of our school.
Count the telephone posts on the *South* of our school.
Count the telephone posts on the *West* of our school.

Report your findings: (1) in a tally. (2) in a graph. (3) in story form.

Variations and/or Extensions:

Include the street name in the report.
Find what type of tree is used for telephone poles.
Locate where they are grown.
Find out how they get here.

3. *Grape Street School Community Safety Maps*

a. Trace the most direct route to school.
b. Use a different color to show each safety sign or light around our school block.
c. Use a different color to show each safety sign or light you see going to and from school. Make a legend.
d. Use a different color to show each safety sign or light you see in our school community. Make a light.

4. *Grape Street School Map* - Map Study and Following Directions

Make a boundary in red around the upstairs rooms.
Circle the room numbers.
Trace a direct route from your room to the Nurse's office.
Make a boundary around your room in green.
Boundary all of the other rooms on your grade level in green.
Draw a direct route from your room to the cafeteria.
Write N for North, S for South, E for East, W for West.

Variations: Use this school map in many and varied ways. Directions may be given orally or task cards may be developed.

PERSONALIZED STARTER SUGGESTIONS - No. 4

1. *Image Building* - Comparisons - Consonants - Vowels

Draw *you* with your family. Write the name under each one. Who is tallest, shortest, oldest, youngest, others. How does each name begin? End? What are the consonants in each name. Circle. What vowels are in each name. Box.

Variations: Older, younger, taller, shorter, others. Initial consonants. Name other persons whose name begins as each family name. Find a gift in a catalog for each family member. Purchase an outfit for each family member. Compute cost.

2. *Consonants* - Vowels

Make a consonant sheet or book. Items for the consonant being studied may be drawn or cut out. When completed, pages may be arranged alphabetically.

Make a vowel sheet or book.
Find things that begin with a, e, i, o , u.
Use picture dictionary, magazine, comics, salespaper.

3. *Kernel Sentences*

1. Have pupils write about things that are relevant to them.

I_____	My school_____
My class_____	My family_____
My teacher_____	My friend_____

Suggestions for fill-ins: talk, laugh, cried, ran, saw, studies, words, eats, sings.

2. Tell in two or three words different things that happen in your room. Use one noun and one verb.

The clock runs. The teacher talks. Children study. Children read.

3. Tell in short sentences about things that happen at our school. Use a noun and a verb.

Children get in line. Some children go up. Pupils get lunch.
Children play games. Teachers meet their classes.

4. *Paragraphs*

1. Have pupils write a short paragraph about members of the school personnel. Give names for starter.

2. Why is the name of our school Grape Street School? Write a paragraph. Name other schools in our area. Were they named in a similar manner?

5. *Individualized Math* -Visual Discrimination

1. Draw 2 boys and 2 girls in our room. Make their clothes the right color. Have someone guess who they are. Write the correct name under each.

This can be extended to various one-place and two-place sums.

6. *Plurals*

1. Add s and make or find pictures to show what happens.

boy	girl	house	tree
boys	girls	houses	trees

7. *Irregular Plurals*

1. Make or find a picture of each word:

children   mice   women   people   men   feet

How is each word alike? Make the singular for each word.

child   mouse   woman   person   man   foot

Find other words that have irregular plurals.

2. When do you form a plural by adding *ies*?

baby	lady	candy	daddy
babies	ladies	candies	daddies

Pupil may draw or find pictures to show meaning and the distinction between singular and plural nouns. Pupil may find nouns whose plurals are formed by changing the *y* to *i* and adding *es*. Use stories, papers, magazines, comics, etc.

3. When do you form a plural by adding *es*?

glass	watch	dish	patch
glasses	watches	dishes	patches

Pupil should be provided opportunity to find enough nouns to determine word endings to which *es* is added to form the plural.

8. *Social Studies*

1. Look through the Los Angeles Times. List 6 cities and states where news is happening. Find the longitude and latitude of each. List 6 foreign places where news is happening. Find the longitude and latitude of each.

Variations: A sentence or a short paragraph may be written about the news items. Geographical study may be extended to the hemisphere, relationship to the Equator, sea level, directional relationships, etc.

9. *Geography*

Make a survey of your class to find out where each has been in our city? - country? Write the names of the places of the pupils or both in a manner so as to associate them with each location on the city's map. - country's map.

Make a survey of a group of the faculty to determine places they have traveled in the country? in the world? Map the location. Include geographical studies.

10. *Globe and Map Study*

1. Which ocean is near where you live?
2. What other oceans can you find on the globe?
3. In which hemisphere is each ocean?
4. Make a survey to find out if any pupils or teachers have taken an ocean voyage.
5. Map an imaginery ocean voyage to a place you have read or heard about in the news, in a story, seen on television.

11. *Classification*

Read the Theater Guide in a newspaper.
Make a list of the movies which are recommended for you to attend with your family.
List the name of the theater and its location.
Use the rating scale.

PERSONALIZED STARTER SUGGESTIONS - No. 5

Make a master list of the pupils in your room.

Phonetic Analysis Skills

Make a list of names:

1. That begin with a single consonant that has one sound.
2. That begins with a single consonant that can have more than one sound.
3. That ends with a single consonant.

4. That have a medial single consonant.
5. That begins with a vowel.
6. That has a long vowel.
7. That has a short vowel.
8. That has an initial consonant blend.
9. That has an ending consonant blend.
10. That has a medial consonant blend.
11. That has an initial consonant digraph.
12. That has an ending consonant digraph.
13. That has a medial consonant digraph.
14. That has a vowel digraph.
15. That has a vowel diphthong.
16. Whose vowel sounds are affected by *r* or *l*.
17. That have the long double *oo* sound.
19. That have consonant variant sounds.
20. That have vowel varient or irregular sounds.

PERSONALIZED STARTER SUGGESTIONS - No. 6

1. *Identification of Shapes* - Clarifying Concepts

Cut out things that are round.
Cut out things that are square.
Cut out things with a rectangle shape.
Cout out things with a triangle shape.

These should be used one at a time. A picture may be used as a guide. Directions should be given orally or written based on the level of the group. Vary in any way practical.

2. *Identification of Shapes* - Vocabulary Building
Cut out things you like that are round. Write the name under each one. Write a sentence to tell why you like each one.

Square, rectangle, triangle may be used.

Cut out things you want that are round. Write the name under each one. Write a sentence to tell why you want each one.

Square, rectangle, triangle may be used.

This may be simplified or extended.

Classifying - Vocabulary Building

Cut out things you like to eat. Write the name under each one. Write a sentence to tell why you like each one.

Cut out things you like. Write the name under each one. Write a sentence to tell why you like each one.

Cut out things you want. Write the name under each one. Write a sentence to tell why you like each one.

Magazines, catalogs, papers, or something which contains the appropriate pictures should be provided along with paper, scissors and paste. This idea is adaptable to many variations.

Phonetic and Structural Analysis

If your class writes and posts a weekly newspaper, a center might be developed within sight.

Read our newspaper.
Write words that begin with b, d, f, h.
Write words that begin with vowels a, e, i, o, u
Write the compound words you can find.
Write words that begin with consonant blends br, fl.
Write words that begin with consonant digraphs sh, ch.

This should be simplified, modified, or extended based on the level of your group.

Comic strips, comic books, charts or stories which hold high interest may be used.

Location Skills-Using the T.V. Guide

List your favorite program for each day.
Write the number of the channel.
Write the call letters for the station.
List the leading characters.
Tell why you like each.

This may be simplified, modified, or extended.

City Government -Research for Specific Information

Whom would you call if:

Your street lights were out.
The corner traffic signal stopped working.
A dog was struck by a hit-and-run driver.
Your garbage cans weren't emptied.
Someone at home became seriously ill.
You were sure a house was on fire.
Someone was robbed.
Your street was littered with debri.

Surveying - Recording - Graphing - Comparing

Make a list of pupils.
Find out the age of each.
Find out the size clothing each wears.
Make line graphs using two different colors.

The groupings may be boys, girls, grades or classes.

Letter Writing - Format and Creative Expression

(Post simple or complete letter format geared to level.)
Write your teacher a letter.
Tell what you like about our room.
Tell what you do not like about our room.
Make some suggestions for improving our room
Tell what you like about your friends.
Tell about classmates who bother you.
Tell about something you enjoyed.
Tell about something you disliked.
Tell anything you want to share.
Tell what happened when I was away.

If more than one choice is listed, pupil should choose one from among any of these:
Write the principal a letter.
Tell what you like about our school.
Tell what you do not like about our school.
Make some suggestions for improving our school.
Tell about coming to and from school.
Tell about somebody who bothers you.
Tell about the people who visit your class.

Write the vice-principal a letter.
Tell what you like about the playground.
Tell what you like about the lunch period.
Tell what you do not like about the playground.
Tell what you do not like about the lunch period.
Tell how you feel about assembly.
Tell how you feel about fire drills.
Make some suggestions.

Allow pupils to choose an adult on the staff to whom they wish to address a letter stating their own concern.

PERSONALIZED STARTER SUGGESTIONS - No. 7

1. *Categorizing, Math Computations*

Make a home floor plan. Include Living Room, Bedroom, Kitchen, Bathroom, Dining Room, Den, more or less.

Place furniture in each room
Label each piece of furniture.
List furniture under proper heading.
Make a furniture bill.
Write a furniture contract.
    Itemize the furniture.
    Find the sum.
    Add the tax.
    Subtract the down payment.
    Determine the monthly payment.
Write a check for the down payment.

2. *Classifying, Identifying, Designing*

Make a furniture catalog. Cut out furniture for a:
    Living Room, Bedroom, Kitchen, Dining Room, Bathroom.
    Label and price each item.
    Design an attractive cover.

3. *Recording, Adding, Comparing*

Copy the number from_____license plates.
>   Find the sum of each.
>   Which is the largest?
>   Which is the smallest?
>   Are there any the same?
>   Write your story.

4. *Location and Map Skills*

Where did the news happen?
>   Locate the places in the state.
>   Locate the places in the country.
>   Locate the places in the world.

5. *Selecting, Math Computations*

Order a balanced meal from the menu.
>   Write the food check.
>   Add the tax.
>   Add the tip.

List the food groups from the menu.
>   Milk Group - Meat Group - Vegetable - Fruit Group - Bread/Cereal

6. *Researching, Reading*

Choose a country you like.
>   Read about the people.
>   Find pictures of how the people dress.
>   Make people and dress them from plastic bottles.
>   Make labels that tell who they are.

7. *Categorizing, Counting, Recording*

Place pop bottle caps of different flavors in a container.
>   Separate like flavors.
>   Place in egg cartons or divided trays.
>   Count the number in each one.
>   Record your story.

8. *Classifying, Location Skills*

Use the Yellow Pages of the Telephone Directory to locate the names of two companies and their phone numbers in our general vicinity.

Bicycles

_____

_____

Carpets

_____

_____

Furniture

_____

_____

Jewelers

_____

_____

Motorcycles

_____

_____

Photographers

_____

_____

Restaurants

_____

_____

Television

_____

_____

Make a list of Emergency Phone Numbers:

    Fire
    Police
    Ambulance
    F.B.I.
    Highway Patrol
    Secret Service

9. *Visual Discrimination, Categorizing*

Develop or have pupils develop a group of pictures. Provide container with categorizing indexes. Suggestion: Animal, People, Plants, Places, Emotions, Time, History, Topography, Points of Interest, etc.

10. *Locating Information*

Use the Area Code Map in the telephone directory. What state would you live in if your area code was?

1. 702   (Nevada)
2. 501   (Arkansas)
3. 612   (Minnesota)
4. 406   (Montana)
5. 912   (Georgia)
6. 212   (New York)
7. 303   (Colorado)
8. 517   (Michigan)
9. 919   (North Carolina)
10. 918   (Oklahoma)

PERSONALIZED STARTER SUGGESTIONS - No. 8

1. *Multiplication Drill*

If you drove up to a gas pump today and the prices posted were:

Regular 96.9¢   No-Lead 99.9¢   Premium $1.99

How much would it cost to buy:

    1 gallon to get the lawnmower started.
    2 gallons for the car that ran out of gas.
    3 gallons because that's all the money you have.
    4 gallons to get you across town and back.
    5 gallons because that's a good round figure.
    6 gallons to get you up in the mountains.
    7 gallons to take a short weekend trip.
    8 gallons to go from the coast to the valley and back.
    9 gallons because that is all the tank will hold.
    10 gallons because it's an easy amount to figure.
    11 gallons to go to work and back all week.
    12 gallons because that will fill the tank.

Remember the gas prices before the energy crisis? List them. How much were you paying for the same amounts then?

What difference are you paying for each? (Prices might need to be rounded off for some students. Those who are able should work with the tenths as they are actually priced. The wording may be changed as fitting.)

2. *Cumulative Sum Drill*

Provide two die. They may be made from cubes. If two play, one may throw and the other may record. One person may play alone and do both.

The object is to:

Throw the die and record each sum. How many throws must you make before you reach the total 20, 21, 100 or whatever number you choose? If the cumulative sum exceeds the designated number, the thrower may lose. The task card should specify the rules. Several learning centers may be developed with variations at each.

3. *Subtraction Exercises*

Secure salespapers that list the original prices and the sales prices of furniture, clothing, toys, or food. If you choose more than one, separate learning centers or task areas should be developed.

Develop a task card for each or the one that asks what is the difference or what is the saving on specific items you or the pupils select to be listed.

4. *Division Exercises*
Find out the number of students in your school.
1. Divide them by 2 so that they may go to separate outdoor assemblies.
2. Divide them by 3 so that they may go to separate auditorium assemblies.
3. Divide them by 4 so that they may rotate for chorus.
5. Divide them by 6 so that they may take turns going to the library.
6. Divide them by 7 so that they may work on Student Council committiees.
7. Divide them by 8 so that service club assignments may be made.
8. Divide them by 9 so that they may organize baseball teams and
   cheerleaders.
10. Divide them by 11 so that they may form May Day circles.
11. Divide them by 12 so that they may organize for drill team formation.

You may vary or list other reasons more befitting for your group.

Open-Ended Task Cards

1. Find the total weight of all the students in the clasroom. How many pounds is this? Find the average weight. Are you below or above the average?

2. How many calories does your lunch contain?

3. Use a mirror to look at your ear. Draw a picture of your ear the same size as it looks to you. Measure the length of your ear. Measure the width of your ear. Is your ear the same size as you drew it?

4. Measure the distance across the room with your feet. Have several other students do the same. Did you all get the same answer? What was the average?

5. Line several students up according to their height. Construct a chart showing the results.

6. Find as many things as you can that weigh the same as your reading book.

7. Make a set of all the circular objects in the room. Triangular, Square, Rectangular.

8. How many steps does it take to go from your desk to the office door? How long does it take to go from your desk to the office door?

9. How many pounds and ounces does the average car tire have?

10. Find the amount of water necessary to fill the class sink?

11. Measure the length of the classroom with some parts of your body (i.e., arm, leg, whole body).

12. How much distance can you cover in one minute of running, walking and skipping?

13. Find out if the area of your school grounds is greater or less than an acre.

14. Find out how sizes of objects are described. (i.e., nails, suits, gloves, shoes, hats, cans of fruit, cartons of milk, etc.)

15. Find the ratio between the height of a bounced ball to the number of bounces.

16. Construct a chart which will show hand sizes for everyone in the room.

GRAPE STREET

Ed. Aides

Ashton, M.
Baker, M.
Burton, L.
Davis, C.E.
Davis, Jr., C.
Efferson, D.
Gray, T.
Henderson, I.
Holmes, T.
Howard, D.
Hughes, M.
Jackson, A.
McClellan, R.
Powell, W.
Shorter, A.
Stubblefield, M.
Thomas, G.
Villareal, Y.
Williams, E.

Custodial Staff

Beasley, D.
Berry, L.
Childs, J.
Ford, B.
Weber, E.

| Hill 26 1-2 | V. Williams 27 1-2-3 | Dozier 28 1-2-3 | Lavatories |
| Reiss 23 1-2 | E.B. Taylor 24 1-2 | J. Williams 25 1-2-3 | Custodial Office |

| Matthews 34 1-2-3 | Stock 36 1-2-3 | Ratliff 38 EMR | Brown 40 2-3-4 |

| Rice 33 1-2 | Reamer 35 4-5-6 | Lurry, Snyder 37 | D. Walker 39 EMR |

| Nunley K-3 Pellebon | Selby K-4 |

| Yzuel 30 1-2-3 | White 32 1-2-3 |

| Arrington 29 K-1 | Helire 31 1-2 |

| Almeida K-1 Friedhof | Lew K-2 |

Grape Street

B-31

Second Floor

Curriculum Room 22	Roberts 20 Reading	Miles 18 4-5-6	E.W. Taylor 16 3-4-5	Pecot 14 4-5-6	Albert 12 4-5-6	Hepler 10 EMR
Helton Fac. Lounge Reading	McMillon 19 4-5-6	T. Walker 17 4-5-6	Lensch 15 4-5-6	Cook 13 3-4-5	Zack 11 3-4-5	Wyatt 9 4-5-6

First Floor

Science Lab 8 Roberson	Math Lab 6	Hamilton 4	Johnson 2 1-2-3	Ewell Library		Bookroom		Custodial Supplies
					V. Prin Stevens	Teachers Workroom	Lav	
Custodial Supply	Sweeney Enrichment 5	Penzella 3 4-5-6	Fischer 1 3-4-5	Neely PSA Counselor	Prin Haynes	Main Office Bryant Wilkerson		Heintz Nurse
				Brooks	Conf	Gilbert Cole		Daniels Counselor

111th Street

Parking

Lunch Pavilion

| □ □ □ | Central Kitchen |
□ □ □	
Aud.	Faculty Dining

42 Creativity Room

RECOGNITION

It is with a sense of great pride that I express my appreciation to Ray Terrell for writing the Introduction, to Ben Gieringer, my business partner for writing the Commentary, to Ben Wright for allowing me to use the AOIP speeches and narratives he wrote, editing my writing and writing the narrative for the back cover, and to Glorious Cole, Intermediate Clerk Typist at Grape Street School for supplying calendar information I needed for dates.

I would be remiss if I did not recognize my professional proteges of whom I am very proud distinctly, namely, 'my little sister,' Doshia Monroe Brown and my four 'children' Eva Holmes, Josephine Miles, Andrea Roberts and Eloise Blanton, each of whom is now serving as an elementary principal in the Los Angeles Unified School District.

To those of you who came to my house almost every Saturday morning from 1959 to 1968 to study to pass the teacher's examination, many of whom are now principals, I take pride in your success. And to all of the students, the teachers, the parents and others who keep me 'honest' by telling me that I served as your role model, Thanks.

To the organizations and individuals who have allowed me to serve and give meaning to my life:

The National Assault On Illiteracy Program where I served as National Chairperson of the Curriculum Development and Evaluation Committee, 1982-84 National Chairperson of the Interorganizational Liaison Committee, 1984-86; and now National Co-Chairperson of the Professional Education Committee along with Winnie Palmer.

To the United Black Fund of America, Inc., Calvin W. Rolark, President who has agreed to accept 100% of the profits from the sale of this book to be allocated categorically to the Professional Education Committee, AOIP for curriculum development, tutorial training and any other of its developmental and maintenance needs.

The Council of Black Administrators as Management Consultant where I serve as Co-Coordinator with John Smith, Assistant to Congressman Augustus Hawkins planning a National Symposium on *Educating The Black Child: A Blueprint for Action* at a Conference Center near Washington, D.C., September 5,6,7, 1986.

The National Association of University Women where as the only candidate for National President, I expect to be elected and installed into that office at the National Convention being held in Los Angeles, California August 1-6, 1986. Based on a unanimous vote to become affiliated with AOIP in 1980 we plan to begin and/or continue a full AOIP programmatic thrust.

✓ Delta Sigma Theta Sorority, Inc., who with the full endorsement of our National President, Mrs. Hortense Canady, has made the Assault On Illiteracy Program one of its National Initiatives; for allowing me to serve as a member of the National Program Planning and Development Committee; as Director along with Soror Julia Williams of the Los Angeles South Bay Alumni Chapter's Black Minority Women's Single Parent/Homemaker Project, being funded by Carl P. Perkins Vocational Education Act (PL 98-524) through the Vocational Education Division of the State Department of Education and, pledging support of the sale of this book for the dissemination of information and use of the profits in the AOIP programmatic development and maintenance.

✓ The National Sorority of Phi Delta Kappa, Inc., where Delta Kappa Chapter made me an Honorary Member and where Deborah Callahan and Lorayne Douglas are coordinating the writing of the ADVANCER, the AOIP Family and Community Reading Newspaper.

✓ All Peoples Nursery-Kindergarten where Dan Genung and Joe Ide Robert Kodama and Lenora Vickland, gave me my first job when I left Buffalo, New York and came to Los Angeles.

✓ All Peoples Christian Church where I was the first woman elected in the Disciples of Christ to serve as a Chairman of the Board.

✓ The Black Leadership Coalition on Education where John Mack, President, Los Angeles Urban League; Dr. Mark Ridley-Thomas, Executive Director, Los Angeles Southern Leadership Conference and Attorney Raymond Johnson, President, Los Angeles NAACP serve as Tri-Chairs.

✓ The United States Department of Education/Assault On Illiteracy Program Joint Workshop partnership relationship announced by Secretary T.H. Bell on June 22, 1984. Later the request to Secretary William Bennett for a continuing relationship on September 7, 1985 which climaxed with his reaffirmation to an AOIP partnership relationship at a press briefing at the U.S. Department of Education on May 12, 1986.

✓ The California Alliance for Literacy, co-convenenrs, Don McCune, Director, Adult and Continuing Education and Gary Strong, California State Librarian who included the Assault On Illiteracy Program as a networking member.

✓ The Advisory Council on Black Affairs to California State Superintendent Bill Honig approved unanimously, a second time, to accept, adopt and plan for the implementation of the Assault On Illiteracy Program with Superintendent Honig's consent. At this same meeting on May 19, 1986 ACOBA had previously approved unanimously the adoption of the

Young Black Scholars program being sponsored by the 100 Black Men and being joined by other prestigious groups. Conversation with Dr. Warren Valdry and Dr. Winston Doby promises to lend itself to developing a relationship between the 16% included in the Young Black Scholars and the 84% remaining to the Assault On Illiteracy Program. The intent would be to develop and maintain a community-service orientation for the small selected group which would circumvent their becoming elitist.

✓ Jonathan Kozol who gave credence in his book *Illiterate America* to the existence of the Assault On Illiteracy Program whom he stated has been so totally ignored by the White press that he had learned about AOIP only as his book was going to press.

✓ KCET—American Ticket has included the Assault On Illiteracy Program as a service provider.

✓ To Diane Vines, formerly with the U.S. Department of Education, now with Adult Education, California State University, Long Beach for referring Anderson Clark, Deputy Consultant, ABC, to Ben Wright and me relative to AOIP. Clark has followed through by making contacts and talking with each of us, reading our materials and questioning sincerely and repeatedly, "What can I do? What can I do to help your cause?"

IN LOVING MEMORY
OF
WINNIE PEARL PALMER

Supreme Basileus - The National Sorority of Phi Delta Kappa, Inc.
Co-Chairperson - Professional Education Committee, AOIP
who died
Friday, June 20, 1986   *Las Vegas, Nevada*

HER WORK WILL LIVE ON FOREVER

E. Lucille Minor, who succeeds her in both positions has pledged that we will work together in a commitment to carrying out the Assault On Illiteracy Program as begun during the term of Rubye Couche to its fullest implementation and even beyond.